New York City

A Short History

George J. Lankevich

NEW YORK UNIVERSITY PRESS
New York and London

Once again, for Jo

NEW YORK UNIVERSITY PRESS
New York and London
© 1998, 2002 by The History of New York City Project, Inc.

Dr. Gary Hermalyn, Project Editor

Library of Congress Cataloging-in-Publication Data
Lankevich, George J., 1939–
New York City : a short history / George J.
Lankevich.
p.   cm.
Includes bibliographical references and index.
ISBN 0-8147-5185-7 (clothbound : alk. paper). — ISBN
0-8147-5186-5 (pbk. : alk. paper)
1. New York (N.Y.)—History.   I. Title.
F128.3.L355   1998
974.7'1—dc21   98-11251
                  CIP

This book was previously published as *American Metropolis: A History of New York City* in 1998.

The author and publisher wish to thank Jeffrey Scheuer and the Menemsha Fund for making the publication of this book possible.

New York University Press books are printed on acid-free paper, and their binding materials are chosen for strength and durability.

Manufactured in the United States of America

10 9 8 7 6 5 4

Contents

All illustrations appear as an insert following page 116.

New Preface

On September 11, 2001, a bright sunny Tuesday morning, suicidal terrorists hijacked two 767 airliners and flew them directly into the Twin Towers of the World Trade Center in lower Manhattan; at least 2,893 persons died in the horrific disaster. Within two hours, the tallest buildings in New York City, icons of the world's leading metropolis and symbols of America's global economic power, imploded into six stories of fiery rubble. In retrospect, it seemed perfectly natural that attackers of the United States would target its greatest city, the vital center of the capitalist system they detested and the heterogeneity they feared. No urban center represents the diversity, the wealth, and the ingenuity of America more completely than does the "Big Apple," New York, New York. If the preeminent urban center of the world's premier power could be humbled and brought to its knees, the goals of terrorism would be achieved. But the attackers totally underestimated the indomitable character, strength, and vitality of a city that for over two centuries has epitomized both the promise and the spirit of America. A deeper knowledge of history might have convinced them that even a successful assault on New York would bring only temporary dividends.

Since their dedication on April 4, 1973, the Twin Towers, erected by the Port Authority of New York and New Jersey, had been the dominant structures in the world's most famous skyline. In typically New York fashion, they were often derided. Insiders called them "David" and "Nelson" in honor of the Rockefeller Brothers whose vision had led to their construction; architects lamented their boxy and banal exterior; and tour guides asserted that the best thing about the view from their observation deck was that you could no longer see the World Trade Center. Yet after a quarter century—virtually an eternity in a city famous for destroying landmarks and chewing up its past—the buildings had become an integral element of New York's image of itself. They were by nature centers of business activity, but like the Statue of Liberty and the Empire State Building, they had become psychic anchors for the people of the city. The nation beyond the Hudson River shared that perception. The shock of their destruction, the devastating loss of innocent life, and the "hole" in the urban landscape, were blows not merely against the city but against all Americans. After the initial rage and tears, a wave of sympathy and support flowed toward the stricken metropolis even from inveterate New York haters; millions believed that for the first time in two centuries arrogant New York had been crushed. Instead, another chapter would be added to the already long chronicle of city achievements.

At the onset of the Cold War, the essayist E. B. White, writing in *Here Is New York* (1949), warned that a single bomb could "quickly end this island fantasy, burn the town, crumble the bridges, turn the underground passages into lethal chambers, cremate the millions." But New Yorkers never really believed that prophecy. After September 11, attacked in unprecedented fashion by airplanes transformed into missiles, the city rallied behind Mayor Rudolph Giuliani and demonstrated once again the resiliency that had characterized its entire history. The human loss was incalculable, "more than any of us can bear," but the physical tasks of reconstruction proved easier to address. By January 2002, over a million tons of debris had been removed and redevelopment plans had progressed far enough to occasion public controversy. The famous, or infamous, New York propensity to challenge every kind of authority was again on display as the city recovered. Faced with monetary losses beyond $105 billion, the loss of over 100,000 jobs, and lacking 25 million square feet of office space, business in the metropolis nevertheless regained its usual fervid pace; the Stock Exchange resumed its functions after only a four-day suspension. Even as the globe lauded the leadership and courage of a term-limited Giuliani, the city hosted a World Series and its electorate calmly selected another mayor. Victimized by the worst terror attack in world history, New York regained its place as a commercial leader within months. Even in tragedy, its singularity was again demonstrated.

New York has always been too worldly, too self-assured, too dense and too ethnic to appeal to the average American. Created as a money-making enterprise in the seventeenth century, New York is an old city whose polyglot population has often alienated visitors and perplexed historians; in 2000 it once again was 40 percent foreign born. Although not physically attacked since the Revolutionary War, every day of its existence featured an unending battle for advantage among its aggressive citizenry. Hard dealing and acquisitiveness have always been the rule on its mean streets, those arenas of constant challenge, fabled congestion, vicious competition and ephemeral triumph. The city was an environment that attracted dreamers and sharpies; it willingly accepted continuing flows of ambitious people drawn to the challenge of competition in freedom. It remains a city which scoffs at people of limited vision or pessimists fearful of the future. As it grew with the nation and outpaced all rivals, it came to dominate the nation's banking, commercial, manufacturing, entertainment and intellectual life. For 200 years it has reigned as the largest and wealthiest American urban center. James Fenimore Cooper grasped its power when he described the city as "essentially national in interest, position, pursuits. No one thinks of the place as belonging to a particular state but to the United States." Mistrusted, misunderstood, and not a little feared, New York won a position both as looming threat and a shimmering model for other Americans. It was for most "a place to visit, but I wouldn't want to live there." And yet its power, its mystique, and the indelible images it contributed to the national mentality made it an unrecognized second home to the rest of the nation.

No city has contributed more to the collective consciousness of the American people. Ellis Island evokes our immigrant origins. Wall Street means finance just as certainly as Seventh Avenue defines fashion. Madison Avenue is synonymous with the advertising industry and Fifth Avenue means elegant shopping. Simply to mention Harlem creates images of the Jazz Age, a cultural "Renaissance," and slum tenements just as "The Village" connotes a Bohemian lifestyle. Broadway conveys wonderful images of musical theater and soul-searing drama, while Tammany Hall is shorthand for the duplicities and graft of machine politics. The Statue of Liberty in the harbor and New Year's Eve in Times Square belong to the Other Coast, the Midwestern farmer, and the Southerner as certainly as they do to residents of New York City's four "outer boroughs." Tragically, it took the events of 9/11 to bring that realization home to a bereaved nation. On behalf of a stricken metropolis the nation willingly went to war.

More books have been written about New York than any other city, its literary heritage surpasses even that of London. But because of its complexity and the abundance of material, no short and accessible general history of Greater New York existed as the city prepared to celebrate its centennial in 1998. This volume was designed to fill that gap, to serve as a foundation for the many courses in city history, and to help general readers gain perspective on America's greatest metropolis. Those goals appear to have been met, and this new edition brings the story of New York up to 2002. In the wake of 9/11, the spirit of the city was challenged but its response to terror was extraordinary. Six months later, muscle and sinew were being restored so rapidly that both nation and world marveled. But resoluteness and ingenuity have always dominated city history; they are qualities also present in a populace always striving forward. To honor that spirit, this volume is respectfully dedicated to the people of New York City.

Preface

"New York is an ugly city, a dirty city. Its climate is a scandal. Its politics are used to frighten children. Its traffic is madness. Its competition is murderous. But there is one thing about it—once you have lived in New York and it is your home, no other place is good enough." John Steinbeck's reluctant accolade to the United States' most fascinating city seems a fitting introduction to yet another volume about New York by one of its admiring residents.

Every American is aware of New York, the "Big Apple" that rose from a trading post to become a national capital and then a world metropolis. One-third of all the people and goods that ever entered the United States came through the mile wide Narrows, now spanned by the Verrazano Bridge. Nonetheless, despite the millions of words and thousands of monographs dealing with its past, no short, popular history of the city is available. Writing such a history is a difficult and daunting task, as the editors of the magnificent *Encyclopedia of New York City* discovered in 1995. Their thirteen years of work managed to compress the city's history into 1,289 pages of triple-columned text, but even so, nearly every review of the encyclopedia lamented the absence of essential facts. Accordingly, this book, too, was written in the full knowledge that it also has undoubtedly failed to do full justice to the story of, for some of us, the world's greatest city.

No other city has been so closely identified with personal freedom and economic opportunity. To generations of our citizens, New York has symbolized the possibilities as well as the dangers of urban life. Its history has always appeared desperate and excessive, elegant yet demeaning, as alluring as some exotic flower yet potentially poisonous as well. Offering the greatest stage for the talented, the city also accepts the misery of millions of others who fail to flourish. No other venue is so public yet so isolating.

New York City presents the sweep of New York's history from its origins as a Dutch settlement to its current standing as one of the world's greatest cities. The history is chronological and necessarily limited, its goal being to offer some perspective on the growth, economic strength, and many peoples of New York. Ever renewed by influxes of population, New York is continuously transformed. If this history has an overarching theme, it is simply that the interaction of politics, economics, and changing communities has given the city a resilience and power beyond its statistics.

New York has been an essential actor at every stage of the United States' national history. It was always a convenient entrepôt for European goods and peoples but never merely a western outpost of continental culture. Manhattan was always something different, a uniquely American creation that represented the character of the New World experience far better than its myriad of critics were ever willing to admit. One visitor said that the city was an "experiment to see if all the world could live in one place," and a modern mayor called it not only the national melting pot but also "the casserole, the chafing dish, and the charcoal grill." Can such a multitude of peoples find common ground; how will they be governed; how can they thrive? New York's answer has invariably been "quite well." Tolerance is too refined a sensibility ever to be acknowledged, but it has been essential to the city's success. Multilingual, polyglot, and capitalist, filled with millions of caring citizens and more than a few cads, the city remains *sui generis*.

1

New Amsterdam Becomes New York

The prime characteristic of New York City, from its origin as a small Dutch town to the dominant urban complex of modern times, has been continuous and rapid change. For more than 350 years the city at the mouth of the Hudson River has been an important center of American life, a funnel through which European peoples and culture entered the United States. Because the city has always been a template of American society, by examining its history we may be able to understand better what America was, is, and might become. Whether a primitive trading post or a financially troubled megalopolis, New York has always had enormous influence. No one is neutral about America's biggest city; it is either loved or detested, but it is essential to the story of the United States.

Like most colonial settlements in America, New York did not emerge as the result of deliberate and rational government planning. Rather, it originated in the economic and religious turmoil that dominated European life in the wake of Columbus's voyages. The Dutch interest in the New York area began as a business initiative that slowly spread to imperial dimensions. The small trading post became a platform across which Europe's civilization and its peoples could be transferred from Europe to America. The first of many formative influences was Dutch, but New York has always been a "crucible of culture," a meeting place of the old and the new, a catalytic agent necessary to transform a new world into America.

Early in the sixteenth century, Europeans lacked a firm conception of the size or geography of the Western Hemisphere's landmass. Christopher Columbus had not reached North America; John Cabot had only briefly entered the frozen northern regions where Norsemen once sailed; and only Ferdinand Magellan had discovered a difficult passageway around the southern continent. Spanish explorers were already exploiting the Caribbean area, but there were still vast areas of unknown land, perhaps including a sea passageway to China. Such hopeful dreams must have stimulated the mind of King Francis I of France when he hired an Italian sailor-explorer, allowed him to borrow a one-hundred-ton ship from the French navy, and sent him out on the historic trip that gave France an early claim to much of North America.

On April 17, 1524, Francis I's Florentine captain, Giovanni da Verrazano (1485–1528), a brilliant navigator who was also a part-time pirate, blundered into what today we call the Narrows at the entrance of New York Harbor. Verrazano anchored his ship, the *Dauphine*, sent long boats into the bay, and noted the "very agreeable location situated within two prominent hills." The sailors rowing into the bay must have seen Manhattan Island because they caught a glimpse of a "great river" before sudden squalls forced them and the *Dauphine* to withdraw. In retrospect, Verrazano seems amazingly lacking in curiosity, for he then sailed away and so forfeited his chance to be the first European to set foot in New York. After naming the upper bay after Santa Margarita, he cruised northward to Block Island and the Maine coast. In July, when he returned to France, he told Francis that an uncrossable continent stood between Europe and China. In 1964, Verrazano's name was selected to designate what was then the world's longest suspension bridge, spanning the mile wide Narrows. During the 1500s the tale of a vast "Sea of Verrazano," told by the twin brother of the explorer, drew other adventurous captains to New York. In January 1526, a Portuguese explorer in the service of Spain, Esteban Gómez, also sighted the "great river" and named it after San Antonio, but he, too, then sailed on.

In 1609, this rumored sea—perhaps the fabled passageway to the Indies— also brought the English navigator Henry Hudson to the great harbor. Like his Italian and Portuguese predecessors, Hudson (d. 1611) was part of Europe's quest for an all-water route to the Far East. A professional seaman, he sold his exploratory expertise to the highest bidder. In the service of the Muscovy Company, he had failed to find a northwest passage (across the North American continent), but the Dutch East India Company hired him to try again. So on March 25, 1609, he sailed his eighty-ton galleon *Half-Moon* out of Amsterdam and into the unknown. By September Hudson arrived off New York Bay and, pushing on through the Narrows, sailed into the harbor. The vast "Sea of Verrazano" was spread out before him, a huge, landlocked harbor south of Barcelona's latitude that would never ice over. Hudson carefully tacked the *Half-Moon* toward what was later called Manhattan. The "land surrounded by hills," the "place of the whirlpool," and the "land of mountains" all have been offered as translations of "Manna-hatin," but no one today knows what the term meant to the Indians then living there.

Despite his bravery and daring, Hudson probably did deserve to be taken to court by his corporate employers, for he had clearly been ordered to sail east from Europe. Yet here he was in the future New York Bay, unmistakably west and desperate to prove that his gamble could pay large dividends. In trade with the Indians, Hudson's eighteen-man crew obtained some fine animal furs, despite some unpleasantness in which boatswain's mate John Coleman was killed. Coleman thus gained the rather dubious honor of being the first white man murdered in New York. On September 11, the *Half-Moon* slowly proceeded up the "western" river until sudden squalls also forced it to stop and seek shelter in Spuyten Duyvil Creek separating Manhattan from the future borough of the Bronx. Subsequently, the vessel advanced as far north as the present site of Albany. Small boats went farther but the water had turned fresh, and the river they hoped would be their route to China turned out to be only a gigantic estuary where the waters from the mountains met the encroaching Atlantic. The hope of finding a passage to the Far East had once again been crushed, and so after a bit of trading, Hudson sailed down and out of the river that was later to bear his name.

Hudson returned to Europe with little to show for his efforts except some beaver furs, a well-written log kept largely by his mate, and historic immortality. His Dutch employers never saw him again, however, for when he put in at Dartmouth Harbor, the British authorities arrested him for serving under a foreign flag and confiscated his ship, log, and furs. It is one of the strange ironies of history that both Hudson and Verrazano were convinced that their missions had failed. Even more ironic was the fact that both returned to the New World to die, Verrazano as dinner for the Carib Indians and Hudson abandoned by a mutinous crew in the frozen reaches of Hudson Bay.

Among the European states, the Dutch Republic was the first to recognize the commercial possibilities of the New World: by the summer of 1610, its vessels had established fur trade stations from Maine to New Jersey. By 1614, a rude fort had been constructed in the Albany area by Captain Hendrik Christiaensen, and during the winter of 1613/14, a group of Dutch sailors led by Adriaen Block (d. 1624) actually wintered on Manhattan Island after a fire destroyed their vessel. In the spring of 1614, in a makeshift craft named the *Restless*, Captain Block discovered Hellegat, where the East River merges with Long Island Sound, and subsequently the Housatonic and Connecticut

Rivers. The *Restless* sailed on to chart Block Island, naming it after the Dutch captain and not for its original discoverer, Verrazano. Block's voyage proved that Manhattan and Long Island were separate entities, a fact soon confirmed by Captain Cornelius May. As a result of these explorations, all the territory between the Delaware and the Connecticut Rivers was claimed by the Dutch and called New Netherland; the land remained theirs as long as they could hold it.

Early in 1614, the States General in the Hague granted a three-year trade monopoly to thirteen Dutch merchants, who formed the New Netherland Company. Although the merchants considered colonization as essential to their undertaking, they completely failed in that regard. After their charter expired in 1618, the Dutch government again sought merchants who would attempt the difficult but potentially lucrative task of establishing a colony in the heart of rich, fur-trading lands in an unmapped continent. A more permanent settlement than a trading post was needed, since both Britain and France were known to have ambitions in the New World.

On June 3, 1621, a twenty-four-year charter was awarded to the Dutch West India Company, a corporation modeled on its great East India predecessor. These two Dutch companies were the world's largest corporations, possessing at least ten times the capital of Britain's Virginia Company. The primary purpose of the new enterprise was to expand trade for the Netherlands throughout the vast area between West Africa and Newfoundland. The company decided that a permanent settlement in the area visited by Hudson would help achieve that goal. Rules for the new colony, an Artikelbrief, were drawn up in March 1623, and a group of Walloon families led by Cornelius May was sent out in 1624 on the *Nieu Nederlandt*. The settlers were given strict instructions not to trade with foreigners and were scattered from Fort Orange (Albany), to Fort Nassau (Gloucester, New Jersey), to Nut Island in New York Bay. More settlers arrived in August 1624, and soon huts were located at Wallabout Bay on the Brooklyn shore and on the fringes of Manhattan. From these varied sites, furs valued at 27,000 guilders were exported to Holland in that year. By April 22, 1625, a settlement known as New Amsterdam had been established on the southern tip of Manhattan Island. Dutch New York was being created.

Although it was not the first settlement created by the Dutch, New Amsterdam rapidly became the focus of Holland's presence in the New World. Cattle, farm equipment, and additional settlers came from across the ocean, and the company also dispatched a rather inept leader named William Verhulst, who, initiating a grand tradition, diverted fur revenues to his private account. Kryn Fredericks, an engineer dispatched from Amsterdam in 1625, designed a fort with star-shaped bastions and also selected the site for the State Street windmill, the town's most distinctive early structure. Land for farms and roadways was surveyed, and both the governor's house and the company office were placed inside the fort. Bouweries, or farms, soon appeared as the employees of the Dutch West India Company settled in for what all hoped would be a self-sustaining and prosperous colonial venture. Although the English Crown also claimed the area, the Dutch had the advantage of occupancy. For the next forty years, a rhetorical game of imperial and commercial bluff between New Amsterdam and New England continued, but in practice, the Dutch settlement on Manhattan had established its primacy.

The West India Company sought profits for Amsterdam by imposing commercial order on New Amsterdam and the New Netherlands. Its directors quickly realized that Verhulst was a bungler, and on May 4, 1626, Peter Minuit (1580–1638) arrived as the new steward of corporate interests. Minuit brought with him two hundred more settlers as well as instructions to strengthen the company's corporate position by purchasing Manna-hatin from the Indians. Within three weeks, Minuit had made a deal with the Canarsie Indians, giving the Dutch title to Manhattan's twenty-two square miles. The price, sixty guilders, or $23.70, certainly marks Minuit as one of the shrewdest real estate operators of all time, for the land is today valued in excess of $60 billion. In fact, however, Manna-hatin was not really "owned" by any tribe, and on top of that, the Indian negotiators gave Minuit a worthless deed. The Canarsie lived primarily on Long Island and used the island between the rivers only as a hunting and trading site. Later, the settlers had to negotiate additional purchases with Indian tribes living near the Washington Heights area, Indians whose claim to the land was at least equally questionable. In any case, Native Americans played little role in the development of New York.

The legalities settled, the Dutch settlement around New Amsterdam slowly expanded beyond areas directly protected by the garrison's guns. An inlet at Broad Street was widened to serve as the Heere Gracht, a canal that soon had bridges across its width and provided the growing town with reminders of Old Amsterdam. Some thirty houses along the eastern shore of the island were erected by Minuit's contingent of settlers, and farms along the Hudson's banks provided food for the town. In November 1626, Minuit sent back to Holland on the *Arms of Amsterdam* a substantial cargo of beaver, mink, and other skins, as well as samples of New World lumber. Minuit also tried to expand trade relations with the English settlers at Plymouth, but his attempts were not successful. Nevertheless, by early 1628, the town of New Amsterdam had a population of three hundred and had sent another 7,520 beaver skins to Europe.

In Amsterdam, the company directors were pleased with the early returns from New Netherland, and recognizing that hired labor alone could not effectively colonize the enormous tracts of wilderness land held by the company, decided to accelerate the population growth. Accordingly, on June 7, 1629, the company drew up the Charter of Freedoms and Exemptions establishing the first government for its colony and offering large tracts of land to any rich Dutch investor who promised to settle fifty adults in New Netherland within four years. Although these *patroons* would hold the land as a "perpetual fief," they were required to purchase all Indian claims to the lands. By January 1630, five great patroonships had been organized, but except for Rensselaerswyck near Albany, all proved to be commercial failures. Even after 1640, when the size of patroonships was reduced, Dutch attempts to transplant European feudal attitudes into a virgin wilderness made the experiment a costly fiasco. By the end of the Dutch tenure in New York, all but two of the grants had been repurchased. Ultimately, the very word *patroon* itself came to symbolize the futility of transporting European land systems to America. Michael Pauw's Pavonia grant, which by 1637 had failed, was renamed Staten Island to honor the Dutch States General. Some modern residents of that borough still believe they suffer from alien customs, only now these emanate from City Hall across the harbor.

Although it accomplished little, the patroonship experiment demonstrated the West India Company's concern about the future of its colony. But New Amsterdam was only one part of wide-ranging corporate affairs, and the directors trusted Peter Minuit to handle the details of its development. In other words, the colonial governor had to produce profits, keep the colonists happy and working, secure the settlement against Indian attack, and be alert to potential incursion by other nations. All this he was to accomplish without adequate communication or support from home. Furthermore, because a governor's decisions were reversible after they were examined in Holland, Minuit's position was always vulnerable.

Minuit was a shrewd and determined man who insisted that the Indians be treated fairly, but he also had to be responsive to his own people. He knew that merchants in his town could complain to the company about his decrees and also that he would have to cater to the wishes of the patroons from whose estates so much was expected. In 1628, the company sent a minister to see to the settlement's spiritual welfare, but it never offered Minuit unstinting support. He was recalled in 1631 to answer accusations that he overly favored the patroons and was unable or unwilling to halt the private trade in furs in which all sensible settlers clandestinely participated. Not for another fifteen years would so capable and loyal an administrator preside over New Amsterdam.

Minuit's first replacement was Bastiaen Jansean Krol, an administrator who proved to be no friend of the powerful patroons in the one year he ruled the colony. It was hardly a surprise when, in the spring of 1633, a new governor arrived. Twenty-seven-year-old Wouter Van Twiller's primary qualification was that he was a nephew of the patroon Kiliaen Van Rensselaer. The new director-general brought with him 104 soldiers, who soon began work on a guardhouse, a new barracks, and the deteriorated fort. The growing settlement soon had its first church and minister—the Reverend Everardus Bogardus—three sawmills, and a brewery. The company's plan to expand its trade was indicated by the construction of Fort Good Hope on the Connecticut River and by Van Twiller's ouster of a party of Virginians who had camped in abandoned Fort Nassau. A garrison was stationed in the Delaware Valley to protect the trade of that region from foreigners, and the settlement of Long Island was begun in Flatlands, Brooklyn, with the issuance of grants to Jacobus Van Curler and Wolfert Geritsen.

Van Twiller's New Amsterdam resembled its mother city in many respects: gabled houses, bridged canals, the Dutch Reformed Church, and pipe-smoking burghers. By 1636, company laborers had constructed five large stone houses used as shops, as well as refurbishing the fort and the windmill. A school had opened in 1633, but Adam Roelantsen proved so ineffective as a master that he supplemented his income by running a "bleaching ground" at the edge of Fresh Water Pond where women could dry their linen. The area today is known as Maiden Lane. The waterfront area predominated in New Amsterdam; the several farms, such as those run by Roeloff and Annetje Jans, Jacob Van Corlaer, and Maryn Adriaensen, were located far beyond the town. Agriculture developed slowly because there was more immediate profit to be made in furs, whereas raising crops on virgin land was hard work. But opportunity was creating a more varied town. New Amsterdam already had a few blacks among its population, and in 1635 it acquired its first Italian resident, a Venetian craftsman named Peter Alberti. Overall, the colony was not as successful as the company directors had hoped. Physically, the town was "after the manner of Holland," but in ambition and profit it was very disappointing.

Van Twiller's main task as governor was to produce profits for his employer, but he saw his tenure in the New World as an opportunity to feather his own nest. Early in his rule, in 1635, the value of exports grew to 134,925 guilders, a return that had doubled in a decade but a barely profitable sum for the company. Van Twiller proved far more adept at adding to his own fortune than to that of his employers, especially by buying more land from the Indians. He purchased Nut Island—still today known as Governor's Island in his honor—and ran it as a successful bouwerie using company laborers. Van Twiller's greed even extended to extorting money from visiting ship captains. He feuded constantly with Dominie Bogardus (the minister), who demanded Van Twiller's dismissal. Ultimately replaced because of his one-sided thrift, Van Twiller remained in New Amsterdam where he had been so successful.

On March 28, 1638, William Kieft (d. 1647), a vain, rough, and venal Amsterdam merchant, arrived on the company ship *Haring* and replaced Van Twiller as governor. No one ever called Kieft "friend," and apparently the company had instructed him to lean on the settlers and make New Amsterdam pay greater returns. But Kieft alienated the people by issuing a series of edicts closing taverns and regulating the fur trade. He also ordered the refurbishing of company property, such as the fort and the stone houses, which were badly in need of repair, and replaced local officials without consulting any of the residents. Citizens were soon complaining that "under a king, we could not be worse treated." Then a ferry to Long Island began operating and a militia was organized, and the people's hopes rose. They were soon dashed, however, when Kieft imposed a series of measures designed to raise both revenue and population. He levied a tax on tobacco and told the residents of New Amsterdam that they would need official documents in order to leave and enter Manhattan. His revision of the patroonship system in 1640 sought to encourage new settlements, and a large land grant was awarded to Jonas Bronck, a Danish Lutheran farmer whose name was immortalized as the Bronx. Kieft also appeared to encourage Englishmen from Connecticut to settle in Dutch territory, a policy his burghers found incomprehensible and contrary to company interests.

Most damaging to the colony's future was Kieft's mismanagement of Indian affairs. During the summer of 1640, after a few pigs disappeared from Staten Island farms, the governor rashly decided that the Raritan Indians, who hated his newly imposed taxes on their corn, were responsible for the loss. Subsequent investigations showed that company seamen had stolen the pigs, but the militia that Kieft sent to Staten Island proved their mettle by killing a few Indians. An uneasy calm then settled on the province. The following summer, an Indian brave of the Wecquaesgeek tribe, who years before had witnessed the murder of his uncle by Dutch settlers, took sudden and fatal revenge on an innocent wheelwright, Claes Swits. When Kieft demanded the warrior's immediate surrender, the Wecquaesgeek chief refused, which emboldened the still angry Raritans to attack and avenge their honor. For the next year a series of bloody skirmishes made life in New Amsterdam extremely perilous.

In desperation, Kieft agreed to consult with twelve men—representatives of families rather than elected officials—who would serve as his advisory council during the uprising. "The Twelve" met with the Kieft on August 29, 1642, and gave their consent to a campaign against the Raritans, the Wecquaesqeeks, and the Indians of the lower Hudson Valley, the Algonquins. But the campaign failed, and late that year, under the auspices of Jonas Bronck, the Dutch negotiated a truce. The Indians did promise to "inflict [their own] justice" on Swits's murderer, but it is not known whether they ever did so.

With the abatement of the Indian threat, Kieft's advisers demanded that he reorganize the local governmental structure. On January 21, 1642, they suggested the creation of a five-man council to advise the governor, greater freedom of movement for settlers, and restrictions on the importation of both English cattle and settlers. Such impertinence was intolerable to Kieft, who informed his council that its services had been required only "to give advice respecting the murder of the late Claes Swits." On February 8, he thanked them for that service and for their unsolicited advice and ordered them not to hold any further meetings.

Although the first step toward representative government had been taken, the unchallenged position of the company director was restored by the end of 1642. Kieft used his recovered authority to perpetrate an atrocity beyond anything that had yet occurred. Mohawk Indians, armed by traders at Fort Orange who had exchanged guns for furs, had been pressing southward against tribes of the lower Hudson Valley. A mass of Indian refugees suddenly appeared among the Dutch settlers at Pavonia (New Jersey) and upper Manhattan. Disregarding the advice of the burghers and Dominie Bogardus, Kieft decided to use the West India Company's militia to kill the refugees, presumably believing that all Indians were his enemies. Accordingly, on the night of February 25–26, 1643, more than 120 Native Americans were massacred, with most of the bodies thrown into the rivers. A coalition of Indian tribes was immediately created, and only with great luck and considerable tact—the latter not supplied by an unrepentant Kieft—was another truce arranged in April.

By September 1643, the apparently never-ending Indian troubles once again erupted into open war. Kieft was not responsible for this conflict, which began in Connecticut and spread into the Hudson Valley, but that fact was little comfort to those settlers who lost their lives or property. Refugees flooded into lower Manhattan, where Kieft once again convened an advisory commission, this time labeled "The Eight," two of whom were English. Cornelius Melyn, a patroon with lands on Staten Island, served as president of this new council, which decided to attack the Algonquin tribes but seek peace with the Indians from Long Island. More important, the commission and Kieft decided to hire a veteran English Indian fighter, Captain John Underhill, and to build a line of city defenses that generally followed the line of today's Wall Street.

Immediate prospects were gloomy, however, and a November 3 letter to the Dutch States General from The Eight reported that "almost every place is abandoned . . . we are not safe even for an hour . . . all of us who will yet save our lives must of necessity perish next year of hunger." Yet almost against expectations, New Amsterdam survived. Successful counterattacks led by Underhill resulted in the massacre of hundreds of Indians in Connecticut and Westchester, and the danger passed. A settlement with most of the warring tribes was signed by Kieft in April 1644, and the province turned to the tasks of rebuilding their structures and assigning blame.

In the opinion of The Eight, it was Governor Kieft whose actions had turned the Indians against the Dutch colony. Yet peace seemed only to confirm his autocratic ways, for in June, Kieft decided that reconstruction costs required direct taxes on the settlers. But in accordance with the custom of the Dutch Republic, he had to obtain their approval, so he was forced to convene a session of The Eight. Meeting for the first time since the November crisis, Kieft ignored the advice of his counselors and imposed new taxes, including one on the Dutch beer brewed and consumed by colonists of all ethnic backgrounds.

Manhattan's population now included English auxiliaries, Dutch reinforcements from Brazil and Curaçao, Swedes from the Delaware region, blacks, Indian allies, and a myriad of others. In 1643, when Father Isaac Jogues, a Jesuit missionary rescued from Mohawk captivity, was recuperating in New Amsterdam, he counted eighteen different languages spoken in the town, the number having increased as a result of war. Father Jogues also noted that the nominal exclusivity of the Dutch Reformed Church had not affected the cosmopolitan atmosphere. Although the total population was probably only seven hundred, Manhattan's diversity already was apparent. Amid the bedlam, Kieft perceived an opportunity to make money. He opened his own distillery and loosened the restrictions he had recently placed on taverns. Soon one of every four structures was a tavern of sorts, and the Reverend Bogardus was preaching against Kieft's actions as vehemently as he had condemned Van Twiller. Since Kieft rarely attended church, he retaliated by having the town's militia drill, with drums, while Bogardus was preaching. This was too much for The Eight, who in August and again in October 1644 secretly petitioned the States General to recall their governor.

Kieft's tenure, however, still had two years to run, and it was not without accomplishment. On August 30, 1645, he presided in Fort Amsterdam as a general treaty was signed with all the Indian tribes in the area, a peace sealed by smoking a pipe "under the blue canopy of heaven." As the farms and villages were rebuilt, the Dutch presence on Long Island from Gravesend to Flushing also was restored. In 1644, Kieft also permitted English settlers to farm the community of Hempstead, in today's Nassau County. But as settlers from the Dutch colony moved northward toward Connecticut, they came into increasing conflict with the authority of English New Haven.

Kieft's diplomatic correspondence with the United Colonies of New England, carried on largely in Latin, is an interesting record of failure. New Amsterdam's political, moral, and business leaders were united against his policies, but the increasing numbers of English settlers to his north and east constituted an even greater danger to company control. Kieft himself informed Governor John Winthrop of Connecticut in April 1647 that he would soon be replaced. He set about preparing papers for his defense and, less than a month later, formally greeted his successor at Fort Amsterdam. It is history's loss that Kieft's defense was never heard, for on his return trip to Holland, he, Dominie Bogardus, and several other officials were lost at sea when their ship *Princess* sank in Bristol Channel.

"Lord General" Peter Stuyvesant (1610–1672) took command of New Amsterdam on May 11, 1647. Tall and vigorous, this son of a minister had forged a distinguished military career and lost a leg in the service of the company. He arrived in the colony armed with the power to liberalize existing trading regulations in the hope of stimulating the colony's agriculture, commerce, and ambition. Stuyvesant's moral strength, efficiency, and scholarly intelligence led him to honestly believe he could set New Amsterdam right within three years and then move on to his next assignment. In his first address to the townspeople, he pledged that all his actions would be "as a father to his children, for the advantages of the Privileged West India Company, the Burghers, and the Country." Certainly there was much to be done, from ensuring a smooth transition between governors to removing the cows and goats grazing on and around the walls of the fort. Discipline had to be restored, transgressors punished, the church repaired, and the town spruced up to Dutch standards. In sum, a general reform was necessary, and Stuyvesant set to work.

He ordered the taverns to close after 9 p.m., issued harsh new regulations to end the smuggling Kieft had chosen to overlook, and ordered that wine, liquor, and furs be taxed to pay for civic improvements. Soon the port hummed with the evidence of "building, laying masonry, making, breaking and repairing." The governor ordered that a dock be constructed (it was finished in 1648) and that a systematic land survey be completed. Finally, on September 25, 1647, Stuyvesant authorized the formation of a board of nine advisers from the burgher population. Although closely controlled by Stuyvesant, this body soon asserted its independence and in many ways deserves to be called the first legislative government in New Amsterdam. Its advisory position was, of course, dependent on cooperation with a governor whose proud nature made that difficult. Stuyvesant had a tendency to shout down his opposition, for his principal task was to serve the corporate interest. Inevitable misunderstandings and conflicts over what served the public interest soon led to political conflict.

In July 1649, "The Nine" dispatched a list of their grievances to the States General of the United Netherlands. They claimed that New Netherland had been weakened, if not ruined, by the mismanagement of the Dutch West India Company and the series of ineffective administrators that it had appointed to preside over the colony. The Nine argued that only a physical takeover by the national government would solve the "very poor and most low" situation and that local governmental authority should be given to the burghers. The petition requested greater security from "the insufferable arrogance of the natives," a condition that was correctly attributed to the meager colonial population. If the town were exempted from duties and taxes and if company authority were ended, New Netherland would prosper and all Holland would benefit. Although the petition was not primarily directed against Stuyvesant, it clearly viewed his paternalistic attitude as contributing to the colony's problems.

Not surprisingly, the Dutch West India Company opposed the petition, and a representative sent by the governor rebutted its arguments, yet it did stir the States General to action. On May 25, 1650, it issued an order easing immigration curbs to New Netherland and calling for the government to be reorganized, but the government refused to accept the task of running the colony. Its conclusions, however, made the corporate directors understand that concessions would have to be made, and they decided that Stuyvesant could be trusted to keep the colony under control while they negotiated with the States General. After two years of delay, the company was ordered to restructure New Amsterdam's municipal government, but even then the recall of Stuyvesant was averted owing to the outbreak of war with England.

In accordance with the States General's mandate, on February 2, 1653, Stuyvesant instituted a form of burgher government in New Amsterdam. He could name two burgomasters, five aldermen, and a new sheriff, and in fact he now presided over the first municipal council in America. Burgher rights were established, requiring the payment of fees to transact business in New Amsterdam. The city hall was placed in a tavern once owned by Kieft, and modifications of the fort and protective wall were intensified. By summer, a 2,340–foot defensive palisade across the island had been completed, along with six water towers and several gates. It never had to be used. England was victorious in a conflict that never spread to America, but New Amsterdam survived as a small Dutch island in a virtually English sea. The year 1654 ended with international peace and mutual pledges of domestic friendship between Stuyvesant and his council.

Stuyvesant governed New Amsterdam for a total of seventeen years, instead of the three-year term he expected. He came to embody the spirit of the community and made many improvements in a domain that never extended northward more than six hundred yards from the Battery. By the end of his regime, he had created a far more livable and efficient town than the one he had inherited in 1647. The land survey he ordered had managed by 1656 to properly align 120 houses on designated streets. Under the municipal arrangement of 1653, burgomasters became responsible for further highway construction. By 1664, the city's population grew beyond fifteen hundred, two dozen streets and seven paved major arteries cut across the expanding seaport, and a series of rudimentary traffic regulations were adopted for the protection of pedestrians as well as cart and wagon drivers.

The Dutch municipality also made a concerted effort to clean the streets. As early as 1647, Stuyvesant ordered that fines be imposed on residents who allowed their pigs, goats, sheep, or cattle to stray; the next year, any goat caught wandering without a keeper was ordered confiscated. Cleanliness was an ongoing problem, and in 1657 legislation was passed prohibiting the dumping of rubbish or litter into the streets; additional ordinances made home owners responsible for cleaning the street in front of their house. Attempts were also made to abolish or at least restrict the common practice of allowing bands of hogs to roam the streets at will. Pigs served a useful purpose as scavengers, but they also caused congestion and additional filth in the streets. Although ordinances were enacted to regulate this nuisance, they were unsuccessful, and the "ubiquitous hog" continued to vex municipal authorities into the nineteenth century.

Contemporaries frequently commented on the "noxious" odors of New Amsterdam, and the municipality was forced to concede that many residents dumped their garbage in the Great Gracht which ran through the center of town. In 1657, five locations were designated as general garbage dumps, and ordinances were passed regulating privies, slaughterhouses, and cemeteries. Although these laws somewhat helped the city's sanitary condition, New York was already acquiring a reputation for filth that has endured to this day. Medical facilities, too, lagged behind the town's growing needs. Although at least five trained physicians practiced in New Amsterdam, most were little more than barber-surgeons more adept at cutting hair than healing the sick. A small hospital opened in February 1659, but only after the English took possession of the city and additional doctors arrived did its medical facilities improve.

Manhattan also had to contend with the fundamental need for fire and police protection. In 1653, the municipality enacted a series of building regulations designed to combat the chief causes of fire, and by 1658, these codes were extended to cover roofs, chimneys, and walls. In addition, by 1660 Stuyvesant and his council had acquired firefighting equipment that included buckets, ladders, fire hooks, and storage sheds; several fire wardens were appointed to care for and repair the apparatus. The governor also issued a directive requiring every home owner to keep a bucket at his doorstep to be used in case of fire.

Equally important was the need for police protection. In the city's early years, there had been little need for such services because New Amsterdam's Dutchmen were basically law-abiding. Even though drunkenness was not unusual, robbery, rape, and murder were almost totally unknown, and everyone lived in fear of the Indians. As the port's commerce increased, however, so did the frequency of brawls and violence when sailors from ships other than the company's visited. In 1638, a law had been passed forbidding ships' crews from remaining in town overnight, but by Stuyvesant's time it was usually ignored. Finally in 1649, "Old Silver Nails" first organized a foot patrol to walk the streets at night, but the prosperous burghers found it expedient to avoid service. But as additional servants, slaves, sailors, and soldiers took up residence in New Amsterdam, more formal policing institutions clearly became necessary. In 1653, a jail was opened in the fort, and soon the aldermen and the sheriff who served as justices of the peace had much to do. By August 12, 1658, a "rattle watch" was created to police the streets at night. Although temporarily disbanded in 1660 for want of funds, it was resurrected in 1661 and continued to perform its duties until the English conquest.

During the settlement's early years, the Dutch Reformed Church—rather than the company or the town—accepted responsibility for caring for the indigent. By the time Stuyvesant arrived, the growing number of needy persons required more services. When New Amsterdam was granted municipal status, its first council appointed "orphan masters" to care for the children. Then, when a brief Indian war in 1655 created additional orphans, the town officials established a permanent "orphan masters court." In the same year, the Dutch Reformed Church opened both a poor house and a poor farm. The municipality issued a "poor code" in 1661, but civic leaders continued to believe that private philanthropy and religious charity were the best means of bringing aid to the indigent. With the exception of these meager beginnings, New Amsterdam devoted little attention to this widening problem.

Civic development in New Amsterdam was closely tied to trade and commerce, and as these grew so did the port's wealth, population, and problems. In 1648, a produce market was opened on Pearl Street, with Tuesdays and Saturdays used as market days during the Dutch era. The construction of the dock that Stuyvesant ordered had somewhat eased the process of off-loading cargoes, but because it was the only pier, the loading and unloading of goods remained slow and haphazard. Indeed, during most of the seventeenth century, New Amsterdam, despite its unrivaled harbor, never came close to competing with Boston in commercial importance. Nevertheless, most burghers believed that trade was the key to the colony's future and never lost their eye for the quick deal. Until 1664, Manhattan served as the point of entry for Holland's commerce, the place where all ships were required to unload their cargoes and pay the obligatory duty. New Amsterdam was the entrance to a vast and rich economic hinterland, and since the 1630s, a "packet service" had linked it to farms and towns along the Hudson up to Fort Orange. During Stuyvesant's tenure, meats, dairy products, furs, and liquors all were important commodities of trade. Despite chronic complaints from the Manhattan burghers that trade regulations kept them economically subordinated to the West India Company, business was good.

Manufacturing and retailing also were growing. After 1637, two windmills were operating to grind flour for export, and several bakers set up shops in the town. By 1664, ten bakeries were selling breads and cookies to an expanding clientele. Indeed, so many retail stores opened that in March 1648, the governor and the municipal council issued regulations concerning fair prices, weights and measures, and competition. In a fruitless attempt to restrict trade to Dutch citizens, nonresident merchants were prohibited from doing business in the seaport. These restrictive rules were expanded in 1657, when Stuyvesant required anyone wishing to engage in "trade or commerce" in Manhattan to obtain "burghers' rights." Counted among the artisans and tradesmen serving the residents at this time were several tanners, ten bakers, twelve butchers, a number of brewers, half a dozen grocers, a glazier, and three silversmiths. Common laborers, crucial to a growing city, seem to have been in short supply. The Dutch West India Company's constant attempts to recruit workers were unsuccessful because other opportunities in the New World dissuaded them from remaining in menial jobs. Nevertheless, ordinances were passed that regulated working hours and salaries for those who depended on ordinary labor. Another source of labor became available after 1646 when the first shipload of slaves arrived. Finally, Stuyvesant pleased his merchant constituency by reforming the complex wampum/beaver/gold/silver/trust trading system that had hindered commercial development until his administration.

By the mid-seventeenth century, a more sophisticated and urbane society was beginning to emerge in New Amsterdam despite efforts to preserve Dutch exclusivity. When he arrived in 1647, Stuyvesant banned all but Dutch Reformed religious services. He reasoned that in the New World diversity might mean danger. Then in September 1654, Asser Levy led a group of twenty-three Jews into the city. Dominie Johannes Megapolensis, representing the power of the established church, tried to have them expelled because "the obstinate and immovable" Jews would only bring confusion to New Amsterdam. But since the West India Company wanted the Jews to stay—to add to the population—his protests were of no avail. Although the Jewish community celebrated Rosh Hashanah in secret in 1654, within two years they were granted permission to have their own burial ground. Located a mile outside the defensive wall, part of that plot remains at Chatham Square and is the oldest cemetery on Manhattan Island. It took three years for the Jews to be granted permission to buy land, but soon afterward they were even allowed to join the rattle watch.

Levy's group joined the many Puritans, Lutherans, Catholics, and Quakers worshiping God in the privacy of their homes, for public services were restricted to the official church. Dutch Reformed authority was expanded beyond the East River to Flatbush in 1655, when Brooklyn settlers found it inconvenient to attend Sunday services in Manhattan. The governor permitted the Flatbush community to have their own pastor, but only on the condition that he preach on Sunday afternoons at Stuyvesant's farm. Stuyvesant's personal chapel stood on the site of St. Mark's Church, where the bones of "Old Silver Nails" now rest.

Stuyvesant's personal religious zealotry led him into unwise feuds with nonconformists. In 1656 he briefly imprisoned and then fined Lutherans on Long Island, an action repudiated by the company, which ordered him to show more flexibility. Stuyvesant's most infamous dispute was with the Quakers, an inoffensive but highly principled people who lived both in New Amsterdam and in larger numbers in Long Island villages. In the fall of 1657, Robert Hodgson, a twenty-three-year-old Quaker newly arrived from England, was arrested for preaching in Hempstead and was sentenced to a public whipping. Stuyvesant then had Robert Hodgson confined to his cell without food and hanged by his thumbs. Only after his own sister intervened did the governor exile Hodgson to a more permissive Rhode Island.

But Stuyvesant's troubles with the Quakers were not over, and his efforts against their presence in Flushing precipitated one of the earliest struggles for religious liberty in America. In the Flushing Remonstrance of December 27, 1657, a town meeting informed Stuyvesant that their patent (issued in 1645) guaranteed "liberty of conscience" to all residents. Flushing united in protest against the governor's edicts, arguing "Let every man stand or fall on his own." When the Flushing sheriff delivered the remonstrance to Stuyvesant, the enraged governor fired and ultimately banished him. Seeking strength from uniformity, Stuyvesant in 1662 arrested Quaker leader John Bowne after he openly convened services in his home. The governor then had Bowne transported to Holland, only to be mortified when the company directed Stuyvesant to "shut his eyes" to worship that was not socially disruptive. Bowne returned in triumph, and nine generations of his descendants lived in the home that still stands in Queens as a monument to religious liberty.

Although the governor's authority was absolute in theory, Stuyvesant did accept compromise in many areas except foreign policy, in which there could be no sharing of authority. Danger threatened the small colony on all fronts, for New Netherland was sandwiched between groups of English colonies, and the tension in regard to the boundary lines was constant. In addition, Swedes had settled on the Delaware River in territory claimed by the Dutch. Nonetheless, Stuyvesant was careful in his dealings with his neighbors, for he could expect little help from the West India Company. During the Anglo-Dutch War of 1653/54, for instance, his adroit diplomacy and the reluctance of Massachusetts to go to war had spared New Netherland. Then in 1655 Stuyvesant saw an opportunity to secure his domain and put an end to one of his problems. He quickly assembled an expedition against New Sweden on the Delaware River and, after a siege of ten days, captured Fort Christina on September 25. But even as the surrender took place, Stuyvesant's triumph was muted, for during the siege he had received word that Indian tribes, for the first time in his tenure, were on the warpath.

Just as New Netherland had the bad fortune to lie between English colonies, it also separated Indian confederations whose enmity spanned centuries. In September, while the governor was off conquering New Sweden, hundreds of Hudson Valley braves from at least three tribes appeared in New Amsterdam on their way to attack their traditional enemies, the Canarsies of Long Island. En route to battle, the war parties raided the farms along the Manhattan shoreline. Perhaps inevitably, a farmer named Hendrick Van Dyck shot and killed a squaw who was stealing peaches from his orchard. By the morning of September 15, angry Indians were roaming around Manhattan and were persuaded to withdraw only by the most tenuous agreement. New Amsterdam's luck became tragedy on Staten Island, however, and for three days, the angry Indians ravaged that area. Stuyvesant returned from the Delaware Valley to discover that the "peach war" had cost at least forty deaths, led to the capture of one hundred women and children, and caused the destruction of twenty-eight farms. The financial cost was put at 200,000 guilders. It took two years of negotiations before the Indians returned all the captives, and the governor had to pay a ransom for them in powder and lead. Stuyvesant was not present when the war began and showed great wisdom in refusing to wage a retaliatory campaign. To prevent further bloodshed, he forbade further farming of the Bronx, and only after the captives were returned did Stuyvesant permit new settlement of northern Manhattan. In 1658 he allowed a contingent of families led by Hendrick de Forest to create a town named New Haarlem.

Because Stuyvesant showed restraint, the late 1650s were a time of peace and contentment for New Amsterdam. As the Indian menace receded, the city's social life became quite lively, and picnics and fishing parties along the edge of Fresh Water Pond again became common. Children were expected to attend the Latin School established in 1652, and young adults enjoyed dancing, bowling on the green, and "pulling the goose." New Amsterdam loved holidays and celebrated the colony's first Thanksgiving Day in August 1654 when news came of the cessation of hostilities with England. Unlike the New England Puritans, the Dutch settlers regarded the Christmas season as both a solemn and a joyous time. One of the grandest legacies of the Dutch era is the "Sinter Klaus" figure, much modified by modern America, who distributed presents to small children on St. Nicholas's Day. The now defunct custom of making New Year's calls also was a Dutch practice, and New Amsterdam's anxious young women sat in front parlors to greet amorous young men. And May Day was so enthusiastically celebrated that erecting Maypoles was prohibited after 1655.

Unlike other administrators, Stuyvesant attempted to keep social order by imposing restrictions on liquor sales, though his edicts had little effect. New Amsterdam was a hard-drinking port where the social supremacy of the tavern "was contested only by the church, whose influence did not reach equally to all classes of people." Licensed taverns comprised the single largest contingent of shops, and illegal grog was easily available to the enterprising seeker. Visiting sailors, merchants, and hardworking citizens all at times enjoyed the solace of the tavern.

With peace secured and business booming, Governor Stuyvesant gave up his residence inside the fort and reestablished himself at a mansion named Whitehall, a name still used by a downtown Manhattan street. By 1660, his city had 342 homes, a population in excess of fifteen hundred, and several working windmills. But the small population reveals New Amsterdam's weakness compared with Britain's expanding domination of the New World. Demographers estimate that the population of New England grew 2.7 percent annually throughout the seventeenth century, a rate that doomed tiny New Netherland. Despite all efforts by the Dutch West India Company and the Netherlands' States General, the colony's population grew only slowly, and hundreds of Englishmen already lived peacefully within its formal boundaries in Connecticut, Westchester, and Long Island. New England's land patents overlapped Dutch claims everywhere, and ongoing boundary disputes were an onerous part of the governor's agenda.

In any case, Stuyvesant tried to maintain good relations with his neighbors and signed a trade agreement with Virginia in 1660, only to have it annulled by the British Parliament. Real protection, it appeared, could come only from physical possession of the disputed lands, and English settlers were far more numerous. In 1661, Stuyvesant issued charters to the towns of New Utrecht and Rust Dorp (Jamaica), but the Dutch remained little more than a third of the population of Long Island. Moreover, the English were angry about the Dutch trading monopoly with the Iroquois and the Mohawks and the high import taxes levied in New Amsterdam. Although the governor's strenuous efforts maintained his colony, Stuyvesant must have realized that its future depended on forces beyond his control.

In reality, New Amsterdam was but a minor pawn in the great commercial rivalry between England and Holland that dominated the last half of the seventeenth century. The city was necessarily involved in such conflicts because seamen recognized it as the most important port area on the eastern coast of North America. Whatever Stuyvesant's other failings might have been, strategic myopia was not among them, and he repeatedly petitioned the West India Company to send more supplies and soldiers. Instead of aid, however, the company sent only encouraging letters and news that its monopoly charter privileges had been reconfirmed by action of the States General on January 23, 1664.

Rather foolishly, the Dutch tempted fate by asking the British Parliament to confirm the Hartford Treaty establishing a Long Island boundary (bisecting the island from Oyster Bay south) that Stuyvesant had negotiated fourteen years earlier. Two hundred additional Dutch soldiers were dispatched to the colony, but with Connecticut encroaching into Long Island and a burgher population less than anxious to take arms in its own defense, the prognosis for New Amsterdam was not favorable. In the spring of 1664, Stuyvesant learned that King Charles II of England had granted to his brother James, the duke of York and Albany, a vast tract of land consisting of "all of Maine between the Croix and Kennebec Rivers and from the coast to the Saint Lawrence, all islands between Cape Cod and the Narrows, and all land from the western boundary of Connecticut to the eastern shore of Delaware Bay." Stuyvesant grimly recognized that the Dutch position in North America soon would be under attack.

James acted quickly, dispatching a task force of four frigates under Colonel Richard Nicolls to capture New Netherland. Fearful of assault by the English, Stuyvesant and his council ordered new defenses built, and fortifications were constructed in June and July 1664. James's fleet did not arrive off Gravesend until August 26, but when it did, English settlers on eastern Long Island willingly furnished it with both information and volunteers. To oppose the English, Stuyvesant had only four hundred soldiers and an inflexible determination to perform his sworn duty. On September 1, when Colonel Nicolls and Massachusetts Governor John Winthrop offered rather generous terms of surrender, the governor refused even to show the conditions to his burghers. Although outgunned and outnumbered, Stuyvesant was determined to hold on. On September 2, he proposed that both sides do nothing until they received orders from Europe. On September 4, Stuyvesant defiantly tore up yet another surrender demand, but his ability even to contemplate resistance was rapidly fading. Angry burghers pasted the letter together, and on September 5, ninety-three leading citizens and members of the council asked Stuyvesant to surrender and spare the city "absolute ruin and destruction"; among the signatures, the governor found that of his own son.

Although Stuyvesant had sworn that he "would rather be carried to my grave" than surrender, he now had no other options left. On September 8, 1664, he signed a treaty of twenty-three articles. With no shots fired and even before war between Holland and England had been formally declared, New Amsterdam had fallen. Under Nicolls's generous terms, the Dutch were allowed freedom of religion as well as their existing property and inheritance rights. According to the treaty, direct trade with Holland was permitted only for another six months, but in reality it continued until 1668. In addition, Dutch municipal officials were allowed to stay in office for a year until arrangements more suitable to James could be made. On October 20, all the citizens of New Amsterdam, Stuyvesant among them, agreed to take the oath of allegiance to Charles II. The conquest was complete, for in the interim, Nicolls's forces had taken control of all outlying Dutch garrisons. The report that the West India Company submitted to the States General on October 24 was more correct than it realized: The English had taken "the whole of New Netherland" and "immediately called the same by the name of York."

2

An English Town Becomes an American City

The second segment of New York's colonial history spanned more than a century, ending as it began with the clash of arms. The virtually uncontested seizure of New Amsterdam by the private fleet of James, duke of York, was the prelude to the Second Anglo-Dutch War of 1665–1667. In this conflict, the Dutch embarrassed Charles II and the Royal Navy by defeating it at Lowestoft in 1665, and after two years of intermittent conflict, culminated their seagoing exploits by raiding the docks of London itself. Other inconclusive battles drained the treasuries of both nations, and the two countries were relieved to sign the Peace of Breda on July 10, 1667.

Even though each party retained the "places, cities, and forts" taken during the war, the Dutch considered this to be a victory, since they maintained their dominant position in the East Indies and the English recognized their possession of Surinam. But James's seizure of New Amsterdam was confirmed as well. Manhattan had become New York and was now ruled by Richard Nicolls (1642–1672) in the name of his lord, Duke James. Nicolls proved to be both a popular and an efficient governor, and in time, even Stuyvesant became his friend. Nicolls had the good sense not to mandate a completely new set of regulations and even retained most of the local officials so as to soothe popular feelings. But English ways of administration and laws were slowly imposed as the town made a place for itself within the British imperial system. Yet as New York became more prosperous, it became apparent that rule from across the ocean, be it English or Dutch, was unworkable. Accordingly, in 1775 New York joined twelve other British colonies waging revolution against Britain. The decades of English rule, however, had provided New York with invaluable commercial connections and trading experience. Under British control, New York began the inexorable rise that made it the premier urban center of the United States.

*

The city that Nicolls conquered in 1664 was three-quarters Dutch, but the burgher population proved to be quite adaptable to the change of rule. Company employees who had accepted Stuyvesant's autocratic rule and labored under the aegis of the West India Company, saw unexpected personal opportunity as the main result of English rule. It is significant that not a single Dutch resident took advantage of the free passage home that Nicolls offered; only the garrison that had so ineffectually defended Fort Amsterdam was repatriated.

During the first months of the transition, the only indication of new authority was the public celebration of Anglican services in September. Nicholls also encouraged a spate of construction work in homes, churches, and shops and, in February 1665, allowed sitting town officials to name successors according to the local practice during the last years of Dutch rule. But more drastic change was imminent after Governor Nicolls issued the Duke's Laws on March 1, 1665. Consisting of civil and criminal regulations drawn from New England models, the code ordered the election of overseers and a constable in each town in the colony, established a provincial court system, authorized the organization of a militia, and ensured freedom of conscience for all. At Hempstead, on March 11, 1665, an assembly of thirty-four delegates from seventeen English settlements gave their approval to the colony's new legal structure. New Netherland had never had a representative legislature, and although the promises of the Duke's Laws could be suspended by gubernatorial edict, the prospect of even limited self-rule was attractive.

Under the new framework, Governor Nicolls retained the privilege of naming officials, and in June 1665 he appointed Thomas Willett to serve as New York's first mayor. Willett was an honest man, as were the aldermen that Nicolls named, a trait not always found in the succession of appointed officials who governed New York until the 1830s. Nicolls kept careful watch over the regime and wisely awarded offices to such powerful burghers as Nicholas Bayard, Jacob Kip, and Johannes de Peyster. In essence, he tolerated a continued influence over local affairs by the wealthy Dutch oligarchy but made them govern by English rules.

Such enlightened tolerance should not suggest that Nicolls did not have firm control of his colony. Indeed, in 1664 he confiscated the farms and property of the West India Company on the grounds that its absentee directors had "inflicted all sorts of injuries on His Majesty's subjects." During the Second Anglo-Dutch War, he seized the property of suburban Dutch owners reluctant to take the oath of allegiance. Although Nicolls's reform of land tenure was well managed and was intended to raise revenues, in time the higher taxes he imposed caused discontent. Even New Englanders who had migrated to Long Island in search of more fertile land were angered by the patent charges that he ordered. Generally, all colonists resented the higher taxes and the duke's arbitrary power to appoint magistrates over them.

Perhaps the greatest difficulty that subsequent British administrators encountered was an inability to understand Dutch pride. A sense of self-worth and community kept Dutch influence strong in New York for at least another century. In March 1668, when Francis Lovelace (1621–1675) succeeded Nicolls as governor, he expressed surprise that the people of New York, though drawn from many ethnic groups, displayed the "breeding of courts." Manhattan's society was far from democratic, but its Dutch leaders were united in their opposition to the patronizing attitudes of their English masters. Their own economic domination permitted them to live in greater luxury than their conquerors, and they fully intended to maintain that advantage.

When Nicholls completed his successful tenure as governor and turned authority over to Lovelace, Manhattan abounded in both social and economic tension. Dutch prosperity must have irritated Lovelace, for he envisioned the colony as a means to make his personal fortune. Unlike Nicolls—a soldier and one of the few governors who left New York personally poorer—Lovelace came to the colony with a desire for wealth and two brothers dedicated to helping him succeed in his ambitions. At first, he continued his predecessor's conciliatory policy, and so the town, the commercial heart of the province, continued to flourish. Expanding organized territory became Lovelace's major priority, and in May 1668, John Arcer was given permission to settle families in the upriver area of the Bronx; in 1673, that community became the town of Fordham. For the sixth and last time, lands were purchased from accommodating Indians, and their latent threat to the settlement vanished. In addition, the first ferry between the Jersey shore and the island of Manhattan began to operate during Lovelace's tenure.

But the most important acquisition of his administration was securing the duke of York's title to Staten Island, an area bitterly disputed between his colony and New Jersey. In 1665, Nicolls had reaffirmed James's claim to the land by naming it Richmond after an illegitimate son of the duke. Early in 1670, Lovelace concluded an agreement between the two provinces that gave New York title to all islands in the harbor that could be circumnavigated in a twenty-four-hour period. In April, Captain Charles Billopp accomplished the tricky task of circumnavigation, thereby saving Staten Island for the city. Billopp was rewarded with a vast manor, which he named Bentley in honor of his ship. The house he built there, located in present-day Tottenville near the southernmost point in New York State, later served as the conference site where negotiations to avert the Revolution failed.

But all that was in the future when on April 13, 1670, Lovelace took official possession of Staten Island. His optimism was justified, for by 1700 at least two hundred families had established farms in New York's fifth borough. Lovelace's tenure brought other tangible proofs of progress. A wagon road was completed to Harlem, and a ferry connection with the even more remote Bronx began running. In 1671, Lutheran congregants, long oppressed by Stuyvesant, were allowed to hold services in the house of Cornelius Pluvier, thus removing one source of discontent. Recognizing that trade was the key to the city's growth, Lovelace encouraged the expansion of the merchant's exchange. More cargoes made profits for the governor, and ships increasingly sought the safety and services of New York's harbor.

Early in 1672, however, an oceangoing vessel brought the unwelcome news that the peace between Holland and England had been shattered and that the old adversaries were once again at war. In July, Lovelace ordered the construction of new defense works and established a postal service between New York and Massachusetts. He had no wish to share Stuyvesant's inglorious end and sought to ensure quick access to information and reinforcements from New England should they be needed.

Despite all his preparations, Lovelace was still surprised when a Dutch fleet commanded by Cornelius Evertsen suddenly appeared in New York Harbor on August 8, 1673. The governor was not in the city at the time, and his deputy, Captain John Manning, had been so lax that Dutch sympathizers were able to spike his best cannon. The promised aid from Long Island amounted to only a dozen men, and the surviving guns from the fort proved to be rusted. Once again, the greatest prize in the New World changed hands, virtually without a fight. Smiling Dutch burghers declared their neutrality, and after only a single English death, Captain Anthony Colve of the Dutch landing force took possession of Manhattan; on August 12, he was designated governor-general. The rest of the province was reoccupied; Dutch officials were appointed; and the province and city of New York temporarily became New Orange. But even as Colve's forces were destroying old Fort Amsterdam and building new defenses at the tip of Manhattan, European negotiators were once again settling the fate of New York.

Colve had little time to display his talents, for New Orange had little significance for the conflicting imperial goals of Holland, England, and France. The territorial claims of the West India Company were totally ignored in the Treaty of Westminster, signed on February 9, 1674. Under its terms, possession of New York reverted to England, and Dutch claims to North America vanished forever. In London, Charles II generously reconfirmed his brother's grant on July 9, 1674. James, angered at the colony's lack of preparation, recalled Lovelace after arranging the forfeiture of his English lands. On November 10, 1674, after a hiatus of fifteen months, James's ducal flag once again flew over the city that so far had brought him little return.

Still determined to exploit the potential of his colony, James dispatched an experienced military man to act as governor of New York. Major Edmund Andros (1637–1714), an honest but unlucky bureaucrat, played a pivotal role in the politics of the late seventeenth century. Quickly reissuing the Duke's Laws, he judiciously divided official appointments among all ethnic groups, reorganized the ineffective militia, and reemphasized the goal of increasing the city's trade. Andros recognized that the revolving government had weakened all authority and daringly recommended that an elected provincial assembly be created. Duke James's refusal to consider such an innovation quickly ended the initiative, but his decision did cause dissatisfaction among well-to-do merchants of the town who stopped paying import duties for a time. In other spheres, however, Andros made substantial gains. In November 1675, he granted the English equivalent of burghers' rights to propertied merchants. New construction projects included a Lutheran church (1676), an insane asylum (1677), better wells, and the first night lamps (1679). A vital commercial facility was completed in 1676 when a great dock at the foot of Whitehall Street opened for shipping; the structure served the port until 1750.

Even more crucial was Andros's decision to grant a flour-bolting concession to a few large merchants. Although revenues from the monopoly benefited the merchant elite far more than they enriched James, the policy was critical to New York's development. On January 7, 1680, the Bolting Act formally mandated that all grain for export from the New York area had to be sent to the city for grinding, processing, and packing. Moreover, the governor decreed that New York would be the sole port of entry for the province. The result was a sudden spurt in prices, ship clearances, and profits among the favored merchants. Exactly how valuable the concession was has long been disputed, but those merchants who were not part of the monopoly charged Andros with favoritism, profiteering with the Dutch, and official corruption. By 1681, Andros was forced to return home, where he won both exoneration and a knighthood. His economic legacy was the first real boom in New York's history: the flour monopoly fostered a tripling of the city's wealth and population before the end of the century.

The profitability of the flour concession convinced James that lessening political control might bring him economic gain. If he granted his colonists more self-government, they might work so effectively that his revenues would increase. Both Andros and William Penn advised James that permitting a limited assembly would ensure the merchants' cooperation and produce greater revenue. A somewhat skeptical duke decided to follow their counsel, and on January 27, 1683, James named Thomas Dongan (1634–1715) as his new governor, instructing him to create an elected assembly and to revise the province's tax structure.

When Dongan arrived in Manhattan that fall, he authorized the first provincial elections in New York's history. All freeholders were entitled to vote for the General Assembly, and after a short campaign, seventeen men elected from ten counties convened in Manhattan on October 27. The assemblymen had the power to pass laws and raise revenues, though subject always to Governor Dongan's approval. Within three days, the representatives produced the Charter of Liberties and Privilege asserting their rights to self-government, self-taxation, freedom of worship, trial by jury, and other privileges enjoyed by Englishmen. Even though they pledged cooperation among the "Governor, Council and the people," the tone of the charter presaged the far more strident revolutionary voice of future English colonists. Duke James at first consented to the charter, but after his accession to the throne and the transformation of New York into a royal colony, he declared it abrogated.

Dongan proved to be both a strong and a skillful executive. Although the merchant aristocracy of New York, both Calvinist and Anglican, initially distrusted him because he was a Catholic, Dongan quickly overcame their fears. He had in fact arrived with several Jesuit priests who presided over the first public masses in New York. But the religious uneasiness abated once the community leaders recognized that Dongan was no fanatic; they then concentrated on the commercial privileges he could dispense. The new governor wooed the burghers by confirming both New York's monopoly on bolting and its position as the sole port of entry. Merchants' coffers swelled when Dongan allowed Manhattan's traders an exclusive right of transport on the Hudson.

In December 1683, the governor gave New York, now designated as a provincial capital, a new municipal charter. It divided the city into six wards (North, South, East, West, Dock, and Harlem), provided for the election of an alderman and an assistant for each ward, but retained the governor's right to appoint the mayor and the recorder. These fourteen officials together constituted a common council empowered to enact ordinances for the city in accordance with England's statutes. While reorganizing the city, Dongan purportedly named Queens County in honor of Catherine of Braganza, the consort of Charles II.

New York's privilege of self-government drew immigrant groups like the French Huguenots to the town in the 1680s. Although the new residents weakened Dutch hegemony, some visitors found the city still three-quarters Dutch in 1685. Political liberalization continued, and annual ward elections and a local court system were prominent features of a second Dongan charter, which took effect on April 27, 1686. Governor Dongan and the varied merchants who filled city positions enjoyed a comfortable working relationship. Long-standing disputes regarding real estate titles and wharfage rights were settled amicably, and cooperation and prosperity seemed to lie ahead. Yet despite real improvements in polity, tolerance, and economics, in 1688 the city joined in the Glorious Revolution against King James that toppled the House of Stuart.

The origin of that sea change in English and American life was the sudden death of King Charles II on February 6, 1685, and the accession of his Catholic brother as James II. James's imperious inclinations, as well as the advice of his lords of trade, convinced him that the Crown should exert greater authority over its colonies. For New York, this meant the cancellation of the Charter of Liberties and the recall of Dongan. James then ordered Andros out of his comfortable retirement and appointed him governor over a consolidated provincial unit composed of New York, New Jersey, and all of New England. The Dominion of New England would serve as a bulwark against French expansion from Canada and become a model for new trade policies. James intended to force all his American colonies to adhere to imperial trade regulations. Although merchants throughout the colonies resented James's actions, New York suffered more than other cities, since the stricter law enforcement threatened the revival of its trade. Along with Massachusetts and Connecticut, which also lost their charter rights, the city longed to see the Stuart "tyranny" overturned.

Once again, politics in the Old World stimulated events in the New. England's Anglican establishment was incensed by James's Catholic excesses and his political insensitivity. In 1688, the Glorious Revolution expelled King James and his offspring from Britain. Almost as swiftly, Governor Andros was imprisoned in Boston as the representative of a failed monarch. Andros's deputy in New York, a tactless martinet named Francis Nicholson, was bereft of both orders and guidance. In April 1689 a foolish remark by him made restive merchants fear that he might burn down the city rather than surrender to new authority, and rumors began to spread that Nicholson might even deliver the port to Catholic France. Impelled by a surge of popular anger, a committee of public safety was organized, and a well-to-do merchant, Jacob Leisler (1640–1691), took charge of the militia.

During Dongan's tenure, Leisler's reputation had risen when he refused to pay import duties on a cargo of wine because the port's tax collector was a papist. In the confused atmosphere of 1689, Leisler thus became a symbol of colonial liberty against monarchy, Protestantism over Catholicism, Dutch life against English regulations, and, perhaps most important, the popular spirit against all "grandees." On the night of May 31, 1689, Leisler's militia seized control of the city, expelling Nicholson, former Governor Dongan, and the few priests remaining in New York. On June 28, a convention endorsed Leisler's actions, and in the name of the people, he proclaimed the reign of William and Mary, the new Protestant monarchs. Merchants were shocked, however, when their man abrogated the flour monopoly, which, Leisler maintained, resulted in higher food prices for the public. Ruling as virtual dictator, Leisler granted city residents their first and only opportunity during the colonial period to choose a chief magistrate. On October 14, Peter Delanoy, a man from Harlem, became New York's first elected mayor, and its last for 150 years.

Leisler and his supporters believed that their seizure of New York would please Parliament and preserve English liberty. Citing constitutional authority, Leisler claimed the right to rule because letters that had arrived from England in December 1689 were addressed to Nicholson or "such other person [who] for the time being may be in authority." He naturally interpreted this to mean himself and so dismissed the provincial convention then in session. Resenting Leisler's unilateral actions, the aristocratic families of New York and their envoys, including Nicholson, soon appeared at court to denounce this "son of the people." Alarmed by these reports of "democracy," the monarchs appointed Colonel William Sloughter to replace Leisler as governor.

Unfortunately, Sloughter's subordinate Richard Ingoldsby arrived in the city before the new governor, but without official documents to prove his legitimacy. When an increasingly paranoid Leisler refused to step down, clashes between his militia and Ingoldsby's troops followed. Sloughter's belated arrival in March 1691 put an end to the disturbances as Leisler dutifully surrendered New York to its legitimate governor. The surrender came too late, however. His brief reign had both offended English officialdom and alienated the ruling classes of New York. Leisler was accused of treason, arrested, and tried by a specially commissioned court that condemned both Leisler and his son-in-law, Jacob Milbourne, to death. Despite impassioned pleas to King William for mercy, both men were hanged near the modern-day City Hall on May 16, 1691.

Leisler's execution was regarded by ordinary New Yorkers as revenge by the elite on a man who dared to serve the people; it was nothing less than judicial murder. In 1694, after Leisler's supporters convinced Parliament that a great wrong had been committed, his property and good name were restored to his heirs. But the specter of class struggle implicit in his rebellion continued to have a political impact during the next half century. One tangible legacy was an expanded city franchise that threatened the merchants' supremacy. Although property requirements kept the very poor from voting, Governor Sloughter permitted the broadened electorate to name a representative assembly that first met in a tavern on Pearl Street on April 9, 1691. Fearful of social conflict, the apprehensive governor even reissued the Charter of Liberties after Leisler's execution. But the struggle for power among the monarchy, Parliament, ethnic groups, and wealth was still unresolved when Sloughter died suddenly in June 1691, after an extended bout of drinking. With its treasury depleted, its social classes in conflict, and Europe once again at war, New York faced an uncertain future.

In the spring of 1692, another governor arrived in New York. Colonel Benjamin Fletcher (1640–1703) was an Episcopalian who established the Anglican Church as New York's official religion; he built the first Trinity Church in 1698 with the donations of rich New Yorkers. Following the pattern that Dongan had established, Fletcher did permit the free practice of other religions. Tolerance was established as the rule, and the Jewish Congregation of Sheerith Israel was formed in 1695; its successor group still meets today on Central Park West. Like many of his predecessors, Fletcher intended to make his fortune in New York, so he made common cause with rich merchants, English, Dutch, and French. Even though the Bolting Act had been repealed and a representative assembly created, neither condition hindered the escalating prosperity of the elite.

Fletcher used Parliament's Navigation Acts to control the harbor, and he collected trading fees from legitimate ships and even more exorbitant ones from pirates. In return for these substantial bribes, the governor permitted buccaneers to use New York's workers to refit and repair their vessels and entertain their crews. In return, they spared from damage the ships leaving the port. Legitimate merchants, with tacit approval from Fletcher, used the convenient excuse of European warfare to justify their smuggling operations. Some upstanding merchants even established trading arrangements with the island of Madagascar, better known as a haven for pirates. Among the many legitimate traders who cooperated with the governor was William Kidd, whose activities as both an agent of the government and a pirate led him to the gallows in 1701. Many New Yorkers still believe that Kidd's storied treasure will one day be unearthed from some sandy beach; Gardiners Island in Long Island Sound is often mentioned as the most likely location. Fletcher's dubious conception of free trade did bring prosperity to New York. Great brick mansions soon filled the area below Wall Street, and oil lamps first appeared on New York streets in 1697, Fletcher's last full year as governor. It was the fact that New York was not producing enough revenue for Britain, in addition to complaints from the Leisler faction, that caused Fletcher's recall early in 1698.

His successor, Richard Coote (1636–1701), earl of Bellomont, governed New York from 1698 to 1701 and, on balance, was not a bad administrator for a city officially numbering 4,937 persons. Coote recognized that he owed his post to complaints by Leislerians, and accordingly he staffed his administration with Dutch supporters. Attempting to provide more citizen services, Coote built the King's Bridge to facilitate trade with the Bronx and made yet another effort to clean Manhattan's streets. Construction began on a second city hall located at Wall and Nassau Streets, the site of the Subtreasury Building in today's New York. The ceremonial opening of Trinity Church under Rector William Vesey made New Yorkers proud regardless of their religion, which was fortunate, since taxes on all residents made its construction possible. Even in such arcane areas as the provisioning of troops, Coote reached agreement with both the populace and the merchants. His sudden death in 1701 led to the appointment of Edward Hyde/Lord Cornbury (1661–1723), a man of totally different talents.

Serving as governor of New York and New Jersey until 1708, Hyde presided over corruption and maladministration rarely equaled. Reputedly a transvestite and surely a thief, Hyde owed his position to the fact that he was a nephew of Queen Anne. He was probably not responsible for the yellow fever that swept the town in 1702, the first of many such plagues, but New Yorkers soon blamed everything else on him. In one case, Hyde simply put into his own pockets the money that the Assembly had appropriated to renovate the city's defenses at the Narrows. So flagrant were Hyde's personal excesses that New Yorkers of every political faction united to send to the queen a formal list of their grievances. In December 1708, the universally detested Cornbury was recalled in disgrace.

According to New York commercial records, Dutch economic domination was eclipsed by a coalition of British and French merchants during the first decade of the eighteenth century. Although the transition was inevitable, all entrepreneurs, regardless of ethnicity, were convinced that New York deserved fiscal independence. In the eighteenth century, successive royal governors each confronted seasoned representatives who controlled the provincial purse and were well schooled in ways of maintaining power. After 1708, the Assembly asserted that it had the right to vote annual appropriations for the colony and its officials. Governors fresh from London held back once they realized that the payment of their salary depended on their preserving good relations with the legislature.

In Manhattan, Abraham de Peyster, scion of one of the city's richest families, was named city treasurer in 1708 and held the post for the next forty-six years. Under his guidance, municipal finances were regularized and soon reflected the city's growing wealth. Lord Cornbury's successor, John Lovelace, who died in 1709, less than a year after taking office, did not govern New York long enough to have problems with the merchant-dominated Assembly. But the issue of salary payment clearly emerged during the tenure of Major General Robert Hunter (1710–1719).

Hunter (d. 1734) is often cited as the "best" colonial governor, and he presided over improvements in the municipality's finances, ferry services, and street construction. As a soldier, Hunter strengthened colonial defenses against French Canada, and as an author, he is credited with writing the first play printed in North America (*Androborus*, 1714). Also, a large influx of refugees from the Germanies swelled the city's population to almost seven thousand during his rule. Despite his popularity, Hunter refused a salary for several years to protest the Assembly's control over the governor's purse. Although he insisted that long-term assignments of money be appropriated, it was not until he left that an admiring Assembly settled his personal accounts. Notwithstanding all the pressure, the New York Assembly maintained control over the governor's annual salary until the Revolution. In 1756, Parliament conceded New York's right to vote annual appropriations, a major victory for self-government.

During the Hunter years, New York experienced its first significant racial troubles. The city population included many free blacks and a large number of Angolan-born slaves who occupied the lowest stratum of society; some accountings suggest that in 1710 a fifth of the city was black. Whites generally believed that black New Yorkers had too much freedom of movement, and some feared that insurrection was being plotted. Early in April 1712, a series of unexplained fires focused attention on the dangers posed by an unregulated black minority. Historians agree there was some substance for the public's anxiety, and it appears likely that some organized violence was planned. Details of the goals sought remain uncertain, but ten whites died violently and increasing panic ruled the city for two weeks. As troops scoured the city, a few blacks fled while others committed suicide. In time, nineteen black prisoners were executed by order of Governor Hunter. The racial fears first evidenced in the plot of 1712 often reappeared later in the city's history.

After Hunter, most of the men sent to rule New York were inexperienced, ill-informed, greedy, and unsuited to the office of governor. Nonetheless, each contributed to the growing wealth and power of the great marketplace at the mouth of the Hudson. Hunter was followed by William Burnet (1720–1728), who attempted to regularize the fur trade by negotiating directly with upcolony Indian tribes. A statesmanlike program later instituted by Sir William Johnson, Burnet's initiative enraged the powerful New York fur aristocracy. They defeated his plan in the Assembly and tried to isolate him from the commercial elite. A notable event of Burnet's tenure occurred on November 1, 1725, when New York's first newspaper, William Bradford's *Weekly Gazette*, began publication.

Colonel John Montgomerie, a genial Scottish crook, succeeded Burnet in the spring of 1728 and governed New York for the next three years. A personal friend of King George II, Montgomerie allied himself with the merchants against the Popular Party, the remnants of the Leislerians led by Judge Lewis Morris (1671–1746). He solidified the city's revenues by imposing quit rents and license fees. During Montgomerie's tenure, exports from New York exceeded those of Boston or Philadelphia for the first time. Montgomerie is most remembered today for granting the municipality a charter that lasted for a century. Approved on February 11, 1731, the grant cost Manhattan's burghers a large bribe, but it did extend the city's boundaries and expand the Common Council's lawmaking powers. Once the cash basis had been established, it is likely that even more concessions might have been obtained from Montgomerie had not he, along with five hundred other New Yorkers, died in a devastating smallpox outbreak during the summer of 1731.

Rip Van Dam, a shipowner, led the municipal council that governed New York for thirteen months until Montgomerie's replacement arrived. Montgomerie's successor, William Cosby (1690–1736), was typical of the royal officials who hoped to make a personal fortune from their public service. After being appointed governor of the Leeward Islands, Cosby was actually on his way there when he received word of the far more lucrative opportunity in New York. Returning to London, he obtained the open commission and arrived in Manhattan in August 1732. Granted a gift of £1,000 by a merchant-dominated yet independent-minded Assembly, Cosby immediately alienated potential supporters by suing Van Dam, claiming that his predecessor owed him half the salary he had received as gubernatorial stand-in. The new governor created the special Court of Exchequer to hear his claim for the cash and was mortified when the handpicked body refused to grant him any compensation. Cosby blamed his public humiliation and financial loss on the influence of Chief Justice Morris, and on August 21, 1733, Cosby removed the sitting judge for "partiality, delay of justice, and oppression of the people." An undaunted Morris reveled in his removal, using Cosby's arrogance as a campaign issue to restore power to the waning Leislerian coalition. In 1734, Morris won election to the Assembly while his partisans swept the city alderman elections. Class rivalries, long thought buried, suddenly reemerged in New York, owing to Cosby's greed and authoritarianism. The Morris faction even founded its own newspaper in November 1733, to promote its version of electoral controversies.

The *Weekly Journal* was edited by an ambitious German immigrant named John Peter Zenger (1697–1746). During the next year Zenger unmercifully satirized the power lust and avarice of Governor Cosby with a wit that often verged on open slander. Finally, the governor decided on harsh repression. On November 2, 1734, copies of the *Journal* were publicly destroyed, and two weeks later Zenger was arrested for libel; he was kept in jail by means of an extraordinarily high bail. The prosecution of Zenger not only stirred New York but also had reverberations throughout the colonies. When the newly appointed Chief Justice James Delancy (1703–1760), a Cosby ally, disbarred the local attorneys who were to defend the printer, lawyers in the other colonies were appalled. Zenger was forced to hire a "Philadelphia lawyer" to take his case.

When his trial finally began on August 4, 1735, the defense was led by Andrew Hamilton, the most gifted of Pennsylvania's attorneys. Hamilton's defense of Zenger conceded that the editor had printed the attacks but claimed that all the facts printed by the *Journal* about Cosby were true. There could be no libel unless the criticism could be proved false. Chief Justice Delancy did his best for Cosby, instructing the jury that when seditious words undermined authority, their truth was irrelevant. Hamilton responded, "It is not the cause of a poor printer nor of New York alone which you are now trying. . . . No! It is the best cause; it is the cause of liberty." Hamilton argued that Zenger had published only facts and therefore could not be convicted of libel. The jury agreed, ignored the chief justice's instructions, and acquitted Zenger. New York City's unexpected defense of freedom of the press became the basis for the First Amendment to the Constitution. It was also typical of the spirit of civil disobedience that prevailed in New York until the Revolution. Zenger's trial established the rule that government officials can be freely criticized if the accusations are truthful. With freedom of the press vindicated, could other rights be denied?

An often overlooked result of the Zenger case was the emergence of the first real "boss" of New York City. Although he represented the "wrong" side in these proceedings, Chief Justice Delancy remained the most important voice in city politics until his death in 1760. A leader of the merchant elite, he demonstrated an ability to control electoral districts over the appeal of popular candidates and soon held *de facto* authority over the Assembly. Delancy, who was an Anglican with political influence in London, managed the ongoing Assembly battle against political appointees; most New Yorkers believed he had more power than any temporary royal governor. The Manhattan that Delancy ruled counted only 10,664 persons in 1737 but almost tripled in size by the Revolution. Commercial activity was strong, and the garment, printing, and publishing trades all began in this period. Fortunes were made in the fur trade, and during the long series of wars against France, powerful trading interests clustered in the city.

The provisions of the Montgomerie Charter facilitated the elite's domination of politics. Although "freemen and freeholders" could vote, they had to pay for the privilege. And Delancy saw that there was no reduction of suffrage fees until just before his death. New York was hardly democratic; its percentage of eligible white voters barely increased, from 7 percent in 1731 to just over 10 percent in 1761. Women and blacks were excluded from voting, as they were everywhere in colonial America. But even though the economic power of the merchant aristocracy usually prevailed, New York's elections remained lively events. On Election Day, enfranchised citizens in each ward voted for candidates by a show of hands. Ward elections were supervised by aldermen who sometimes manipulated the results to help favored associates. So comfortable were the procedures that the Assembly did not alter the system until 1771, when special election officers were appointed for each ward.

In the decades before the Revolution, the appointed mayors and their

Common Councils accepted greater responsibility for improving urban services. Ordinances to expand fire and police protection, regulate wharves and
docks, and operate public markets were issued. In addition, Bellevue, the
nation's oldest hospital, opened in 1736 to care for lunatics and paupers.
Regardless of all these improvements, Manhattan still could not enact any
taxes without the permission of the Provincial Assembly. Even though its
population numbered only one-fifth of the province, city commerce already
was responsible for one-third of all the colony's income.

Although trade was the lifeblood of New York, shipborne disease always
threatened the health of the port. Only in 1738 did the Council order a
quarantine on all incoming ships until visited by a physician. In 1744, a series
of ordinances designed to improve health and sanitary conditions in the city
was enacted, and in 1758 a pesthouse was constructed on Bedloe's Island.
Demands for a hospital for the sick were not met until May 28, 1771, when
the New York Hospital was incorporated. Manhattan also attempted to care
for its indigent citizens, opening a public almshouse in 1735 in what is now
City Hall Park. The two-story brick building housed not only paupers but
also beggars, tramps, and vagrants. Because it was quickly overburdened,
private philanthropy and church charity continued to shoulder the greatest
share of relief for the poor.

The city's treatment of criminals and prisoners was not good, as brutal
penal practices were common in this period. Manhattan's jail was located in
the basement of City Hall until October 1, 1759, when a prison was opened
on the Commons. Harsh conditions were perhaps inevitable, though, for
New York was a port city, and maintaining social order was difficult with
sailors on leave and large numbers of soldiers, slaves, and petty criminals
constantly at odds. Navy press gangs, always on the lookout for prospective
seamen, sometimes clashed with residents and contributed still further to the
disorder.

The fear of violence and riot was never far from the consciousness of
those men who ran the city. For unexplainable reasons, in 1741 rumors
abounded that militant blacks intended to burn the city. Hysteria against the
so-called Negro Plot lasted from May to August, and before it ended, thirteen blacks were burned at the stake; sixteen others were hanged along with
four whites. More than seventy blacks and a few whites were permanently
banished from British North America in the wake of a conspiracy that may
never have existed but that reflected the pressing need to maintain order in
the streets. Gambling, prostitution, and drunkenness remained the most
common crimes, but robbery, assaults, and murder were not infrequent. Fear

of crime led the Common Council to establish a watch, and each ward annually elected two constables. By law, all residents were required to serve on night patrol, and after 1742 a citizens' watch was reinstated, with every able-bodied man required to take his turn. Although this system lasted for twenty years, it was not efficient. Only in 1762 did the Common Council reestablish a paid standing force, at the same time expanding the system of oil lamp posts on city streets.

Although crime was endemic, the most dangerous threat to urban life was fire. New York's officials passed stringent building regulations, though their enforcement was sporadic and lax. In December 1731, two fire engines arrived from London, and gradually thereafter additional equipment was purchased and distributed among the wards. In 1737 the Common Council approved the creation of volunteer firefighting companies, and thirty men were selected as the first contingent. Eleven companies served the city by the time of the Revolution, and the informal system of volunteers lasted beyond 1865.

Closely connected to fire protection was the issue of water. Springs and private wells adequate for a seventeenth-century town were clearly inadequate for ten thousand persons, so the municipality authorized public wells financed by means of special assessments. The most celebrated of the six public wells was the Tea Water Font at Chatham and Pear Streets; after 1741, New York installed pumps at the various water stations. The Common Council finally recognized the need for a more efficient water supply and in 1774 authorized Christopher Colles to draw up a detailed proposal for a public water system. Construction actually began on Colles's project—a reservoir to be built on the east side of Broadway—but the outbreak of the Revolution ended that plan. Well into the next century, New York suffered from inadequate water supplies and endured the many diseases resulting from contaminated drinking resources.

As the city continued to develop, one of the few constants was the benign leadership provided by Chief Justice Delancy. Although he held his position at the pleasure of the royal governor, he used the Assembly's power of the purse to win concessions from each new incumbent. In 1744, for example, Delancy induced Governor George Clinton to make his judicial post a permanent "good behavior" appointment in return for a salary of £1,560. When the two men subsequently quarreled over New York's role in King George's War, the chief justice made Clinton's tenure so unbearable that the governor abandoned the province. Few leaders in colonial America could boast of such an accomplishment. When Clinton's newly arrived replacement, Sir Danvers Osborn, hanged himself on October 12, 1753, the chief justice became the acting governor of New York. Governor Delancy meekly accepted the right of the Assembly to set his compensation, thereby solidifying the shift of political power away from royal authority. Indeed, royal governors during Delancy's supremacy were unable to grasp the intricacies of New York politics, for they succeeded one another too quickly to master any of the problems of the emerging metropolis. Whether the issues were ferry service, the almshouse, the pesthouse, or the jails, London's representative was always less ready to act than was the Delancy regime.

In a city that was constantly changing, education was not as great a priority as social mobility. A large majority of the children had no education at all, and even the children of the wealthy minority received inadequate training. A few evening schools existed to teach apprentices reading, writing, and simple math. The Dutch Reformed Church in the city operated an elementary school established before the English conquest, but not until 1772 did its board acknowledge that children could be taught in English. Religious charity schools educated a few of the poor; wealthy families hired itinerant private tutors; and the bulk of the middle class sent their children to private academies.

Probably the single most important educational achievement of this time was the chartering in 1754 of King's College, now Columbia University. This institution obtained its original endowment from public lotteries and was constructed on land donated by Trinity Church. The sixth college to open in America, its goal was to prevent the growth of republican principles. In fact, its charter stipulated that its president always had to be an Anglican, and Presidents Samuel Johnson and Myles Cooper did their best to make the college a bastion of conservative attitudes. Nevertheless, in the years before the Revolution, a number of patriot leaders emerged from the student ranks, the most prominent of whom was Alexander Hamilton (1755–1804).

In other aspects of cultural life, New York clearly lagged behind both Boston and Philadelphia. In truth, its merchants were far more concerned with their pocketbooks than with their souls, and they spent their leisure time hunting or boating rather than cultivating their minds. Accordingly, when the city's first theater opened in December 1732, the stage performers and musical groups had to be imported from Britain. And when a subscription library was established in 1754, it was not overly successful. Not until 1753 did Manhattan enjoy a full season of dramatic entertainment, and even then it was provided by the Hallam Company of London.

Architecture, music, and painting in New York imitated English models. New York's architecture adopted the Georgian style, the best examples of which were found in the homes of the wealthy, whose furniture also was imported from England. Portraiture was the most popular form of art in the city, and merchants and government officials, vying with each other to display their prominence, commissioned such able artists as Robert Feke and John Singleton Copley to have their likenesses preserved for posterity. Although the study of science advanced in colonial America, New York could not boast of a single scientist as distinguished as Philadelphia's Benjamin Franklin. Probably the most outstanding New Yorker in science was Cadwallader Colden (1688–1776), a professional physician, amateur historian, philosopher, and sometime lieutenant governor. Lower-class New Yorkers, however, eschewed culture and instead spent their free time in the many taverns and grogshops scattered throughout the city. In 1772, on the eve of revolution, there was one tavern for every fifty-five residents in the city's population of 22,000.

During Great Britain's long struggle with France for the domination of North America, New York was primarily a business and shipping center. Its acquired expertise in the Atlantic trade made it the most vital commercial city in British North America at the time of the Revolution. The city's docking facilities were expanded in the 1750s as merchants and administrators continued to develop its magnificent harbor. Traders opened up the Hudson Valley, exchanging imported manufactured goods for agricultural products, meat, flax, hemp, potash, and naval stores. Lucrative triangular trade patterns in a wide range of goods linked New York City, the West Indies, and Great Britain. The Acts of Trade and Navigation, enacted to tie the colonies to Britain's commercial patterns, were largely ignored as the city elite built fortunes independently of London's strictures. The merchant community continued its profitable but illegal trade with Holland, as it had done since the transfer of 1664. New York sold flour, meat, and lumber to the French and Spanish Indies, earning enough money to pay for British manufactured goods.

Trade was trade, regardless of belligerency, and during the French and Indian War (1756–1763), New York merchants continued an extensive and profitable commerce with the enemy in Canada. In the 1760s, the city's population passed Boston's, and New York became America's second largest city, after Philadelphia. By 1760, some retailing procedures began to be specialized, although most merchants continued to sell on both the wholesale and the retail levels. Some Manhattan artisan-shopkeepers sold specialty items over the counter at retail prices, but most merchant establishments remained in the general-store category. Business was so good that merchants protested the many Common Council rules regulating the price of meat, the size of bread loaves, and the operation of the public markets. But Manhattan's business atmosphere was often subjected to wild fluctuations. An unstable currency, an unfavorable balance of trade with England, and a paucity of specie to carry on normal business operations were long-term problems. Occasional paper-money issues by the province helped ease monetary conditions. When the British government refused to allow further issues in 1764, Manhattan's merchants became enraged, their anger intensifying the revolutionary spirit in America.

After Britain's victory over France in 1763, the Crown and Parliament began to lose patience with colonies that refused to accept their proper role in the imperial system. Across three thousand miles of ocean, English politicians found it easy to believe their American plantations wanted all the benefits and none of the responsibilities of being British. During the French wars, even as its merchants openly violated the navigation acts, New York compounded their guilt by refusing to vote adequate money for its defense. Indeed, from 1762 to 1764, not a single measure suggested by the governor was approved by New York's recalcitrant Assembly.

Parliament, self-confident after victory over France, decided to end its "salutary neglect" of the colonies and bring them into a proper relationship with their homeland. The Sugar Act of 1764 was a judicious piece of imperial legislation, for it reduced the duty on foreign molasses from sixpence to threepence per gallon, allowed the duty-free importation of British rum, and levied new taxes on non-English West Indian imports. But New York's merchants, alarmed because a determined British effort to enforce the new act would damage their rich West Indian connections, protested to the Board of Trade. A few radicals even suggested a boycott of British goods but were persuaded instead to circumvent the act in time-honored fashion; they would simply smuggle in the goods or bribe the customs officials. Nonetheless, there was general uneasiness because any revenues from the sugar tax would support an increased British military presence in North America. Then from London came even more distressing news. In 1765, Parliament had passed the Stamp Act imposing taxes on forty-three necessities of ordinary life: marriage licenses, playing cards, newspapers, deeds, and a host of other transactions. At issue now was not only the merchants' profits but also all Americans' "rights."

New York took the lead in opposing the Stamp Act (which was to take effect on November 1) and orchestrated the colonial protest. James McEvers, the newly appointed stamp collector for New York City, quickly decided to resign his post, fearing violence from his fellow citizens. Whig merchants opposed to the act held a majority in the Assembly, and in the summer of 1765 they sent a formal protest to the king. Simultaneously, this group opened communications with the General Court of Massachusetts. The two colonies together organized the Stamp Act Congress to meet in New York City. On October 7–15, 1765, twenty-eight delegates from nine of the colonies met, denounced the Stamp Act, and adopted a series of protests. Three New Yorkers—John Cruger, Leonard Lispenard, and William Bayard— were responsible for resolutions declaring that "no taxes [will] be imposed on [Englishmen] but with their own consent."

During October 1765, the Sons of Liberty first appeared in Manhattan. Ultraradical, the group advocated forcible resistance to the stamp taxes. On October 22, when the British merchant ship *Edward* arrived in the harbor with the first cargo of stamps, the Liberty Boys led by Isaac Sears, John Lamb, and Alexander McDougall threatened to riot. The stamps were immediately removed to a British warship and then transferred to the fort where they were locked up under guard. On October 31, a group of merchants meeting in Brown's Tavern drew up a nonimportation agreement pledging themselves to boycott English goods until the Stamp Act was repealed. In addition, New York's angry traders established the Committee of Correspondence to exchange information and plans with the colonies of Virginia and Massachusetts. A colonial consciousness was beginning to take shape.

On November 1, the day that the act went into effect, the Sons of Liberty ruled the streets of New York. Ships in the harbor lowered their flags; business came to a standstill; and some newspapers were published with a skull in the spot where a stamp should have been. No stamps were sold, for the vendors had resigned, and that evening a mob burned first the effigy and then the coach of Lieutenant Governor Cadwallader Colden. All port activity virtually ceased for almost two weeks until the auspiciously timed arrival of a new governor, Sir Henry Moore (1713–1769). The only colonial-born governor ever to rule New York, Moore "caressed the demagogues," invited all the city to his inaugural, and suspended the operation of the Stamp Act (November 13).

Although the Sons of Liberty seized and burned another load of stamps in late November, Moore's wise actions put an end to the crisis. The city continued to conduct its business without using the hated stamps, while the merchant embargo on imports continued to devastate trade with England. Parliament thus reluctantly decided to repeal the act in March 1766, at the same time reducing sugar taxes on both British and foreign molasses to only one penny. When word of Parliament's retreat arrived, the triumphant New York Assembly ordered that a statue of King George be constructed. The Sons of Liberty erected their own memorial by raising a "liberty pole" on May 20.

Even though the Stamp Act crisis had been resolved, additional issues remained to create tensions. In 1765 Parliament ordered New York to pay the cost of housing British troops, a demand that many saw as yet another tax without the colony's consent. Under intense official pressure, the Assembly provided a building for the troops but refused to deliver straw for bedding, firewood, cooking pots, or rum. Fights and insults between the angry garrison and the self-important Sons of Liberty became frequent. On August 10, angry garrison soldiers cut down the iron-banded liberty pole, the first of six such incidents. So tense did the situation become that King George III himself labeled the city rebellious. After the Assembly voted winter supply money in December, Moore prorogued the body to restore a semblance of peace.

The calm that prevailed afterward was like that before a storm. The colonies did not immediately oppose Parliament's 1767 decision to enact new import duties, the Townshend Acts. Governor Moore permitted another Assembly to meet and took some comfort from the fact that the merchant community had established the Chamber of Commerce on April 5, 1768, the first such organization in the world. The governor appeared oblivious to the danger that such a group might be useful for agitation as well as trade. By the end of 1768, demands for trade boycotts were renewed; Moore again clashed with the Assembly over appropriations; and fights at the liberty pole again broke out. The tensions peaked on January 19, 1770, when the Sons of Liberty fought British regulars in a riot sometimes called the first battle of the Revolution. Although there were few casualties in this Battle of Golden Hill—which preceded the Boston Massacre by two months—after it ended, British soldiers were permitted to walk the streets of New York only in pairs. That April, Parliament repealed all the Townshend duties except for a tax on tea. Moreover, it granted New York merchants a significant concession by permitting the province to issue 120,000 in paper currency. Peace had been achieved, and not even the Sons of Liberty objected when the municipality's statue of George III was dedicated on August 16, 1770.

For the next several years, New York returned to its preferred occupation, the pursuit of trade and commerce. A new royal governor, William Tryon (1729–1788), arrived in 1771, and more than seven hundred ships cleared the harbor of British America's second city in 1772. But issues of imperial control continued to fester, and in 1773 Parliament approved the infamous Tea Act giving the British East India Company a monopoly of all tea sold in the colonies. New York merchants understood they would lose some revenue as a result of the measure, but since the fees were minimal, they had little real objection to the act. The Chamber of Commerce, therefore, was as surprised as Britain's Parliament was at the results it produced. The Tea Act provided the spark to ignite American anger with British authority. In Manhattan, the Sons of Liberty reorganized and called a public meeting at which excited speakers pledged to repel tea ships that appeared in the harbor. A boycott of all New York establishments offering East India Company tea was accepted. When Boston's "Mohawk" Indians dumped 342 cases of tea into their own harbor on December 16, the resolve of the New York radicals strengthened. When the tea ship *Nancy* appeared in the Narrows, the firing of the city cannon and a massive protest rally persuaded its captain to depart without unloading. By 1774, the merchant elite no longer fully controlled the anti-imperial movement. When a reckless city consignee elected to receive his cargo, the "Mohawks" struck once more. On April 22, 1774, New York had its own "tea party" as eighteen boxes were dumped into the waters of New York Bay.

The road to the American Revolution was a winding one, but its meandering was now at an end. Radicalism was ascendant and hard positions were being taken on both sides of the Atlantic. When Parliament punished Boston's violence with a series of so-called Intolerable Acts, New York's reaction went far beyond sympathetic indignation. On May 16, 1774, even before news arrived of the closure of Boston's port, the city created the Committee of Fifty-one chaired by Isaac Low. The majority of this group represented conservative, even pro-English opinion, but it nonetheless resolved to protest British brutality. Low's group suggested that a meeting of all the colonies be held to decide on a common course. One speaker advocating united action was a nineteen-year-old King's College boy named Alexander Hamilton. The conservative merchants of New York thus became the first public group to call for the Intercolonial Congress, which eventually did convene in Philadelphia on September 5, 1774.

As the colonies inched toward rebellion, New York's radical elements deposed those who favored accommodation with Britain. By late summer of 1774, New England delegates on their way to Philadelphia were given a tumultuous welcome. John Jay (1745–1829), a delegate from New York, wrote the Declaration of Rights adopted by the First Continental Congress.

Congress ordered the cessation of trade with England, and the program of the Continental Association was enforced in New York by the Committee of Fifty-one. In November, the Fifty-one were transformed into a more radical Committee of Sixty elected by all the males in Manhattan. When the sitting Assembly failed to sanction the work of the Continental Congress, the Committee of Sixty organized a rival convention that named New York's delegates to the Second Continental Congress.

War seemed imminent. The British government proposed that New York be exempted from all trade restrictions. This blatant appeal to the cupidity of the merchant classes was, however, overtaken by events. On April 23, 1775, a messenger from New England arrived in Manhattan with the news that battles against the British had been fought outside Boston. Wasting no time, a mob led by Isaac Sears and John Lamb seized muskets from the arsenal and organized a citizens' militia. On May 1, the radical Committee of One Hundred took charge of the municipality. By the end of the month, the new Provincial Congress convened in Manhattan to authorize both the mustering of troops and plans to defend the city. But protest was not yet war and royalism was still powerful in New York. Governor Tryon returned to cheers from consultations in Britain. To alleviate the chance of violence, Tryon ordered the evacuation of British troops to ships in the harbor. Although the decision was universally praised, Colonel Marinus Willett and the Sons of Liberty did intercept the departing British column on June 6 and liberated some supplies.

In 1775, New York's Provincial Congress appointed its Commission of Safety, a body that continued to function throughout the Revolutionary War. Although Manhattan eventually was occupied by the British, committee members often met in the Christopher House on Staten Island, within the present-day city limits. In this year of neither war nor peace, moderates on both sides still believed that reconciliation was possible. New York City merchants continued to supply all the needs of the British troops in the harbor. Then on August 23, as city militiamen repositioned several cannon, shots were exchanged between the opposing sides. The warship *Asia* then delivered a broadside against Manhattan. By the end of the summer, the entire city was in patriot hands and Governor Tryon was attempting to rule his rebellious province from a military headquarters on the British man-of-war *Halifax*.

The path to independence was a difficult one for many Americans, but no colony was so sorely tried by the experience as New York. The city's radicals held control in 1775, claiming to speak for the entire province, much as Paris did for France in its later revolution. But commercial and patriotic ties with England remained strong, and early in 1776, a Loyalist uprising in Queens incited by Governor Tryon had to be repressed. When the city elections on February 1, 1776, resulted in a rout of Loyalist groups, Manhattan prepared for real war. Everyone understood that Britain had to control the greatest port in America and the pivotal colony of New York. Proof of New York's centrality is the fact that a third of all Revolutionary war battles took place within its borders. And despite its enthusiasm and preparations, New York City was so ravaged by the Revolution that its physical scars took a decade to mend.

Manhattan's long ordeal began in March 1776 when after forcing the British to evacuate Boston, George Washington triumphantly made his way to New York. The general and his entourage arrived on April 13 and took up residence in the DePeyster Mansion on Pearl Street. Like the British, Washington considered New York to be of paramount importance, and he knew that retaliatory action would be aimed at the city. Although settled areas of Manhattan extended only a mile north of the tip of the island, all its surrounding counties had to be defended. Forts and redoubts were therefore constructed in lower New York and along Brooklyn Heights, but Washington and his staff recognized the difficulties of effectively defending the city against a foe with naval superiority.

In the city of Philadelphia, where the Second Continental Congress was discussing a formal break with England, New York's delegation remained uncharacteristically silent. Fearful of British reprisals, the state's apprehensive Provincial Congress refused to permit their representatives to take part in the debate. Ironically, it was on July 2, 1776, just as the Continental Congress acted on the proposal for independence, that Lord William Howe's army— the largest expeditionary force that England had ever raised—landed unopposed on Staten Island. Despite the danger, city residents cheered Congress's formal break with England. When the news reached White Plains, the Provincial Congress added its belated approval. On July 9, 1776, Washington ordered that the Declaration of Independence be read to soldiers on the Commons. Patriot crowds pulled down the still-new statue of George III, recasting it into 42,088 bullets. But the revolutionary excitement ended on August 22, when Howe moved his forces from Staten Island to the south Brooklyn shore. A revolutionary city already having lost its Loyalist population now faced the reality of war.

The defenders of New York faced a difficult test. Washington, obliged to disperse his limited forces to protect against a series of potential threats, had been strategically surprised. Howe had the advantage of mobility provided by the Royal Navy and so was able to obliterate Washington's defensive preparations in a single maneuver. Most of the American defenders had been entrenched along Brooklyn Heights, a position now meaningless given the British presence to their rear. Only seven thousand Americans, largely militia, were in position to defend New York against twenty thousand British regulars. On the night of August 26, the British advance across Brooklyn began, and by ten o'clock the next morning the patriot forces had been driven back. The Battle of Long Island was a crushing American defeat: almost two thousand men had been lost, and the British juggernaut had not even been dented. Only Howe's lassitude saved Washington, who successfully extricated his defeated army by rowing it across the East River. By August 30, all of Washington's forces had withdrawn to Manhattan.

On September 11, an attempt was made to settle the conflict by diplomatic means. John Adams, Benjamin Franklin, and Edward Rutledge met British representatives at the Billopp House on Staten Island, but their negotiations collapsed over America's declared independence. Accordingly, on September 15, the Battle for Manhattan began as Howe's naval forces began a bombardment against American positions on the East River. His regulars landed easily, routed the militia stationed around present-day Thirty-fourth Street, and leisurely advanced across the island. Again Howe's caution saved Washington, for most of the American troops were able to escape into the granite hills of north Manhattan. On the next day, September 16, a British probe northward was repulsed by the patriot forces. The Battle of Harlem Heights, fought near the present site of City College of New York, was not much of a victory, but it did much to restore the patriots' morale.

Once more, Howe inexplicably halted his advance. Washington needed information about British intentions, so a volunteer, Captain Nathan Hale, entered the city to find out Howe's plan of attack. Hale was captured just as a fire broke out that destroyed a quarter of Manhattan's buildings. Believing that the fire was started by the rebels, Howe arrested dozens of New Yorkers as suspected arsonists. Hale was the most prominent victim of the blaze. On September 22, he was condemned as a spy and hanged near Dove Tavern. Certainly there were good reasons for Howe's suspicions, since for months there had been rumors that New York's radicals would destroy the city rather than see it transformed into a British base.

Although the Continental Congress had explicitly ordered that Manhattan not be destroyed, those instructions might well have been a public relations ploy. Washington was quoted as saying that "Providence, or some good honest fellow has done more for us than we were disposed to do." America's commanding general was doubtless happy that Howe occupied a ravaged city. In the meantime, Howe resumed his slow-motion pursuit of Washington's decimated army. Leaving a small force under Colonel Robert Magaw at Fort Washington (183rd Street), the Americans retreated to Westchester. At Throgs Neck on October 12 and again at White Plains on October 28, Washington's troops were defeated. He had no opportunity to save the few Americans remaining in Manhattan, as four columns of British troops now converged on Fort Washington. Harsh surrender terms were transmitted to Magaw, and on November 16 the last American stronghold on Manhattan fell to the enemy. New York, so influential in pre-Revolutionary affairs, remained in British hands for the next seven years. When the city was finally liberated, on November 25, 1783, it had endured the longest military occupation of any American area.

During the Revolutionary War, New York was Britain's military headquarters and served as the base for frequent sorties against the coastlines of other colonies. Like most occupied towns, New York suffered physical indignities: its resources were plundered to supply the troops; its trees were cut down to fuel their fires; and its commerce stagnated. Manhattan streets were patrolled by Hessian mercenaries and the Light Horse Cavalry, but not even stringent British precautions could prevent the calamity of another suspicious fire. On August 3, 1778, an additional one hundred homes were destroyed, and in response military rule clamped down even harder.

In 1780, Governor Tryon was replaced by General James Robertson, who presided over a city beset by high inflation and constant rumors of espionage. Its soldiers were serviced by a large corps of prostitutes. As the primary British bastion, New York also became the major detention center for prisoners of war. At first, an old sugar house on Liberty Street was converted into a dungeon, but its capacity was soon exceeded. Ultimately, American prisoners were housed in ships anchored in the harbor; the *Jersey* in Wallabout Bay was the most notorious. Conditions were bleak, and privation and unsanitary conditions took the lives of almost eleven thousand soldiers; their sacrifice is marked by a column in Brooklyn's Fort Greene Park. Ordinary citizens also suffered, since all residents were required to tip their hats to British officers and were constantly subject to search. The city's population, perhaps thirty thousand early in the war, had been reduced to only twelve thousand by 1781 when peace negotiations began. Yet despite the long-term occupation, city merchants continued their trade with the West Indies and Europe. Privateering ventures returned vast profits, and several Tories in Manhattan made large fortunes during these years.

In October 1781, Lord Charles Cornwallis surrendered to Washington at Yorktown, thereby ending the military phase of the Revolution. By chance, Prince William Henry was making a ceremonial visit to royalist New York at that time. Although such visits ended after negotiations for peace began in Paris, not until April 1783 did New York City receive word that the hostilities had ended. Manhattan itself was not free of British troops for another seven months. New York City became the setting for the last act of the American Revolution after General Henry Knox's troops assumed possession of the British garrison on November 25. General Washington and Governor George Clinton formally entered the city as the British withdrew to Staten Island. As a contemptuous parting gesture, the English greased the flagpole from which the Union Jack fluttered, so a young American had to make a perilous climb to tear down the British colors and unfold the American flag.

During the second stage of its history, New York became, both commercially and militarily, the most important urban center of North America. When war finally arrived, New York's strategic position made it a prime target of attack. No American city endured so long an occupation or suffered more for the cause of independence. Its commerce was disrupted; half its buildings were destroyed by two disastrous fires; and its population was reduced by two-thirds. Nonetheless, when General Washington bid farewell to his staff at Fraunces Tavern on December 4, 1783, optimism abounded. The Revolution had been successful, and a new era was about to begin for both America and New York.

3

National Capital City

Although it was only briefly a focus of fighting during the Revolution, New York was occupied by Great Britain longer than any other
American city and was a mainstay of British supply. After 1783, the city's
well-established commercial ties to England remained the strongest in the
new nation, and independence did not alter those patterns. However, the
actual traders changed from Loyalists to Americans. Ushering in this transformation, on April 27 1783, almost five hundred Tory families sailed from
New York City to Shelburne, Canada, to rebuild their lives under the
Crown. Such substantial losses of population and expertise hurt New York's
commercial development as much as the great fires that devastated it physically. The British fleet left the harbor on December 5, 1783, sailing away
from a city whose population had been reduced to twelve thousand, whose
elite corps of business owners had been shattered, whose municipal system
was in ruins, and whose people were deeply scarred by memories of the
occupation. Yet within a generation, all these difficulties had been resolved.
New York became not just a national (1789–1790) and state capital (1783–
1796) but also America's great urban center. Within forty years, the city had
recovered to become the true heart and unofficial capital of the nation.

America's first priority after 1783 was creating a stable government. On the
national level, the difficult road that led to the Constitutional Convention
of 1787 is well known. Transforming colonial institutions into state govern-
ments was the second major area of development, and in this sphere New
York was more fortunate than the other states, for it was led by one of the
great statesmen of American history, George Clinton (1739–1812). From 1777
to 1795, Clinton served as governor and, consistent with his advocacy of
states' rights, established the basis for New York's prosperity in the nineteenth century. Part of the English heritage that remained after 1783 was the
governor's right to appoint New York City's mayor, and so Clinton selected
a prominent attorney named James Duane (1733–1797) to serve in the post

and to preside over the city's reconstruction. Even as Duane took his oath in February 1784, the legislature proclaimed that New York City would also serve as the state's capital, a position it held until 1796.

In addition, the Articles of Confederation Congress, which had been convened in Trenton, New Jersey, declared that as of January 1785, the national capital also would be located in New York. City Hall, on Wall Street, was offered to the nation to serve as the Federal Hall. Thus after 1785 three levels of government were housed in lower Manhattan. The ravaged metropolis, which encompassed less than four square miles, was now recognized as one of the country's most important areas and was a focus of politics during the nation's formative years.

Duane was mayor for five years, and his major accomplishment during that time was the rehabilitation of the city. The post of mayor was unsalaried; its incumbent received as compensation only revenues gained through the issuance of tavern licenses and excise stamps. Since Duane was already quite rich, the lack of a fixed income was not a problem for him. Working closely with the governor and with City Recorder Richard Varick, Duane supervised rebuilding efforts that went far beyond the simple task of renaming thoroughfares: Crown became Liberty Street, Queen became Cedar Street, and King was transformed into Pine Street. Duane also presided as the Anglican Church was disestablished and King's College officially became Columbia. American institutions then replaced the British establishment. The first bank in the city opened for business on June 9, with Alexander Hamilton as one of its leading sponsors, and a federal customs house opened in 1784. As commerce was revived, the population increased as well, and by 1786 the city's total had almost doubled.

The issue of wartime loyalty remained a problem for New York. During the war, the Chamber of Commerce had professed its loyalty to King George III, so returned patriot merchants felt little sympathy for their fellow traders. Accordingly, the Duane administration confiscated a substantial amount of Tory property, whether or not the owners had actually fled, and used the proceeds to finance the building program. Tories were also subjected to higher tax levies as well as social ostracism. Initially, New York law courts ignored the Tories' claims to legitimately owed debts. But Hamilton defended and secured their legal rights and also argued for the primacy of a national treaty in the landmark case of *Rutgers v. Wadington* (1784). The decision eased an explosive social and legal problem.

The principal strength of New York in the 1780s was the inventiveness and expertise of its merchants. Immediately after the peace treaty was signed, trade was harmed because America no longer received favored treatment from the British Empire and because British goods were dumped into the starved American market. Within a few years, though, traditional lines of trade had been reestablished, but not until the 1790s did the value of exports reach pre-Revolutionary levels. New areas of trade had to be developed, and the city's merchants were quick to accept the challenge. It was a New York merchant ship, the *Empress of China*, that became the first vessel to transport American products to the Far East, the first U.S. attempt to tap the elusive China market.

China and the rest of the Far East represented at best, however, a minor commercial gain. The greatest market lost because of the Revolution was America's exclusion from the West Indies and Canada. Only with time and gradually improving relations with Britain could this trading gap be bridged, for no amount of smuggling could make up for the loss of normal commerce. In a move to expand its coastal trade with other states, the city's merchants began to ship some southern farm products, the first steps toward the creation of the future cotton triangle. The Society of Merchants and Tradesmen was chartered in 1786, and within a year it extended its membership to thirty mercantile areas. Thus although commercial treaties with foreign nations and full diplomatic relations with England were still in the future, the strength and resilience of New York's mercantile position was apparent. For New York, the bleakest and most depressed year economically was 1786, and the city's unhappiness was a prime factor in support of a constitutional convention By the early 1790s, both government and economic conditions had significantly improved. When Europe again went to war, New York had revived enough to benefit from the conflict.

The main factor enabling the United States to surmount the difficulties of its infancy was the creation of a constitution in the summer of 1787. No amount of local economic gain was comparable to the stability and order implied by an agreement on the frame of government. In the 1780s, those political and business leaders with the ability to look beyond parochial state concerns believed that the American experiment might fail unless a more effective central government could be created. The result of the Founding Fathers' work was the United States Constitution, with Alexander Hamilton playing a significant role in convening the Federal Constitutional Convention. Equally important was Hamilton's role in the struggle to obtain New York's ratification in 1788. Hamilton's contributions during the actual drafting of the Constitution in Philadelphia were minor, but most scholars agree that George Clinton's New York would not have ratified the Constitution had it not been for the genius of Hamilton and James Madison, with John Jay, who explained the document to America in their *Federalist Papers*. The delegates who convened at Poughkeepsie in 1788 to consider ratification of the Constitution were at first overwhelmingly anti-Federalist, but slowly the reasoning and persuasion of Hamilton and his associates changed their minds. Not an inconsiderable factor in the deliberations was that New York City acted as a united bloc of support for the Constitution, as its business community saw in a stronger central government the stability it needed in order to prosper. Some Federalists whispered, and John Jay was reputed even to have voiced the threat, that unless the Poughkeepsie delegates approved the Constitution, the city would secede from the state and join the union on its own. Whether it was brilliance or logic or expedience that won ratification is still debated, but New York decided to join the United States as its "eleventh pillar."

Even before formal acceptance, the city had expressed its commitment by organizing the greatest parade in the history of Manhattan. On July 23, more than five thousand New Yorkers marched to demonstrate their support of the Constitution, and the line of celebrants extended more than a mile. The city's message was clear, and the Poughkeepsie convention was, in a sense, only ratifying the will of the people when on July 26 it narrowly—by a vote of thirty to twenty-seven—gave New York State's approval to the Constitution of the United States.

One issue that helped sway the anti-constitutional majority at Poughkeepsie toward federalism was the fact that New York City would certainly be selected as America's first capital. Once ratification was secured, Major Pierre L'Enfant (1754–1825) arrived to remodel the City Hall into a suitable meeting place for Congress. All that fall and winter, his workers busily redecorated the structure along Grecian lines while city officials pondered how they were going to pay his bills. The municipality finally decided that some common lands north of present-day Thirty-second Street should be sold off in five-acre parcels and that individual building lots farther downtown should also be offered to buyers to raise cash. Neither sale brought in much revenue, however, as the purchasers often defaulted and failed to improve the land. Sadly, L'Enfant ended up not being paid in full.

Nevertheless, the Federal Hall was ready for the first Congress by March 1789, although the House of Representatives did not actually achieve its quorum until April 1. By April 6, the electoral vote had been officially compiled, and George Washington was notified that he had been unanimously chosen as America's first president. On April 23, Washington arrived in New

York aboard a ceremonial fifty-foot barge and was escorted to the first presidential mansion, the renovated Samuel Osgood home at 3 Cherry Street, a site now beneath a pier of the Brooklyn Bridge. After a week of formal dinners, balls, and final preparations, the day arrived. On April 30, Washington was inaugurated president on the balcony of L'Enfant's Federal Hall, and the United States finally had a chief executive. John Q. A. Ward's statue of the first president still gazes out at downtown New York from the steps of the Subtreasury Building which now occupies the site. New York was not destined to serve long as the national capital, however. The famed "deal" between Hamilton and Thomas Jefferson in 1790 gave the nation both a financial plan and a capital site in the swampland of the Potomac River.

It was inevitable that leaders from New York City, men who shared the Federalist faith that dominated the first decade of the United States' national existence, should figure prominently in the Washington administration. The greatest of these figures was Alexander Hamilton, whose service as the first secretary of the treasury established the financial and credit systems that allowed the nation to achieve respectability. In addition, John Jay served as the first chief justice of the United States; Mayor James Duane was appointed the first federal district judge for New York; and Samuel Osgood was the first postmaster general of the United States.

Richard Varick (1753–1831) replaced Duane as mayor of New York in 1789 and served with distinction for the next twelve years, a record not matched until the twentieth century. Like his predecessor, Varick's major preoccupation was the physical reconstruction of the city, and to this he added the political task of keeping it a bastion of the Federalist cause. Varick succeeded in both of these endeavors, but his city was no longer to play host to the national government, for in August 1790, the capital was transferred to Philadelphia, where it remained for a decade. Perhaps the most telling comment on this move was made by Abigail Adams. Lamenting the capital's transfer to Philadelphia, she wrote that she had resolved to make the best of it, but "when all is done, it will not be Broadway."

There no longer could be any doubt that Broadway and its surrounding city were rapidly recovering from the effects of the occupation. The first federal census completed in 1790 showed a population total of 33,131, still some 9,000 behind Philadelphia but growing much more rapidly. There was a sense of vigor and implacability in New York that Philadelphia could never match, and few people even in the 1790s doubted which would be the ultimate winner of this urban competition. The systematic reconstruction of the previous decade had increased New York's housing by four thousand homes, and the first city directory had to be issued in 1790 to document the changes; by 1793, continued construction forced the introduction of a house-numbering system. It seemed that every year created a new landmark structure. In 1790, the rebuilt Trinity Church was dedicated by its congregation, and in 1791, New York Hospital reopened. A second—naturally Federalist controlled—bank opened for business that same year.

In 1792, an institution that in the minds of some Americans is still synonymous with New York was organized by the city's brokers. Since 1790, they had congregated to buy and sell government securities under the branches of a buttonwood tree on Wall Street, and on May 17, 1792, they formed an association to regulate their activity. By 1793, these stock traders were meeting regularly in the newly constructed Tontine Coffeehouse, and much financial history was made there over the next decade. In any event, the "Buttonwood Agreement" was an important precedent for the creation of the general stock exchange, organized in 1817. In 1794, Bellevue Hospital for the treatment of contagious disease opened, as did also the sumptuous City Hotel, for a long time the finest hostelry in New York.

So rapid was the pace of construction that the old Dutch and English fortifications along the Battery shoreline had to be razed to meet the demand for advantageously located commercial sites. A new set of defensive works were soon placed at Fort Jay on Governor's Island. An inventor named John Fitch tested a steamboat on Collect Pond in 1796 but failed to obtain the financial support the project deserved. When his vessel was pillaged after an accident, it broke Fitch's heart, and the credit for steamboat travel was instead claimed by Robert Fulton early in the next century. A total of nine newspapers already were available to city readers in 1790, but as the population doubled to 60,489 in a decade, their number increased, too. By 1807, more than twenty papers were available, and New York was the premier news center of the nation.

During this decade of growth, New York was identified with the cause of Federalism. Even after Alexander Hamilton's retirement from the cabinet in 1795, he and his supporters dominated the political life of both Manhattan and the nation. It is somewhat surprising, therefore, that the city's political future was being prepared not in Federalist salons but in the slow growth of a private club. The club was the Lodge of Tammany, and its development into Tammany Hall is one of the marvelous stories of American urban history. In 1783, the year of Revolutionary triumph, the officers of Washington's army organized themselves into the Society of Cincinnati, a benevolent association whose main function was to aid the widows and orphans of veterans. The Cincinnati also sought greater state cooperation during the 1780s and was a supporter of the constitutional movement. The membership of the organization was inherently elitist. After a few years, a New York upholsterer named William Mooney (1756–1831) created a lodge with similar fraternal purposes but whose membership would be limited to common soldiers.

The first meeting of Mooney's lodge was held on May 13, 1788. Mooney sometimes called his creation the Society of St. Tammany, or the Columbian Order, and quite naturally most of its early meetings were held in New York taverns. The society's namesake was a Delaware Indian chief whose real character somehow merged with that of the mythical warrior Tammenend, a figure responsible for creating the Great Plains and Niagara Falls, among other deeds. Mooney's hope was to build a "national institution," and the society's original constitution claimed as its goals "the smile of charity, the chain of friendship, and the name of liberty, and in general whatever may tend to perpetuate the love of freedom or the political advantage of the country." By 1789, Mooney was the Grand Sachem of a society with branches in thirteen states, and the organization sought a national membership until early in the nineteenth century, when leadership changes focused on New York City. All members were assessed an institution fee of $1.25 and contributed $1.00 for charity each year. In return, they were able to attend patriotic lectures, march in parades, and know that their money was indeed being used to help widows and orphans. The group even opened a museum in 1790, and the Indian artifacts displayed there later became part of the collection of P. T. Barnum.

In the 1790s, the social and philanthropic purposes of the Society of St. Tammany were slowly overshadowed by its increasing political activity, the first stirrings of the machine that dominated New York politics for the next century and a half. The architect of the change was not William Mooney, however, but one of the great "lone wolves" of American politics, the war hero and brilliant attorney Aaron Burr (1756–1836). Burr had a distinguished family background; his grandfather was Jonathan Edwards, and his father was the president of Princeton University. But in the familial and Federalist politics that ruled New York in the 1780s, Burr was an outsider. He longed for political success to match his thriving law practice. When Mooney was replaced by William Pitt Smith—there was some suspicion that funds intended for poor relief were misused—Burr saw an opportunity to become the voice of common New York men against the aristocrats.

Burr's cadre of personal satellites—later called his Tenth Legion—entered Tammany and began to change its orientation from charity and fun to more serious political concerns. The Burrites argued that the aristocratic Federalists who dominated the city displayed little concern for the common worker, that they were conspiring to prevent a widening of the suffrage in local elections, and that only by allying with George Clinton and his upstate supporters could ordinary New Yorkers ever hope to receive the benefits of democratic government. Even after New York City was reapportioned into seven wards in February 1791, the society protested that a thousand such restructurings would not help poor workingmen because the voting lists had not been expanded. An unsubstantiated story asserts that Burr consulted with Thomas Jefferson and James Madison during their famous "botanic" expedition of May 1791, when the foundations of a national opposition party to Federalism were supposedly created.

One political change that aided the new Republican coalition was Aaron Burr's appointment as a senator from New York, a post he obtained because of his alliance with the upstate Clintonians who dominated the legislature. He returned the favor in 1792 by preparing the legal brief that invalidated the election of the Federalist candidate and won for Clinton his sixth consecutive term as governor of the state of New York. Burr gradually changed Tammany's destiny in the early 1790s, transforming Mooney's social club into a dynamic part of the rising Republican coalition in both New York and the country as a whole. Little by little, lesser merchants and artisans adopted the views preached by the legionnaires of Tammany, which echoed the opinions of Aaron Burr. In fact, something new was occurring in Tammany, a development that affected all of America's urban history: Aaron Burr was becoming the "boss" of a political machine.

At first, Burr's organization had little success in a New York City essentially governed by Federalists and Alexander Hamilton. As secretary of the treasury, Hamilton was at the heart of the Washington administration, but in local matters he felt it "a religious duty" to oppose the career of the pragmatic, amoral Burr. In any event, during Burr's years in Philadelphia as a senator, Tammany made few gains in New York City. Not until after 1793, when great issues of foreign policy preoccupied American society, did the party of Jefferson and Burr make significant gains in New York.

In June of that year, the French frigate *Ambuscade* anchored in New York Harbor and brought news of the France's declaration of war against Great Britain. An extraordinary wave of enthusiasm burst forth from French sympathizers, and the still fresh memories of the Wallabout prison ships made it difficult for any citizen to remain neutral. Jeffersonian groups professed strong support of France in its struggle against Britain, a point of view that intensified when America's old enemy began impressing U.S. seamen on its neutral vessels into the Royal Navy. New York City Federalists, however, favored Great Britain; the violence of the Reign of Terror convinced them that the French experiment in "democracy" was running amok. The Washington administration decided that continued peace with Great Britain was its major priority and sent Chief Justice John Jay to negotiate a trade agreement with its former enemy. The resulting treaty was hated by advocates of France but gratefully accepted by merchants who still dominated the politics of the city.

By a margin of sixty to ten, New York's Chamber of Commerce endorsed the "Jay treaty" in July 1795, in the expectation that it would increase the port's cargo trade and stimulate its shipbuilding capacity. In Philadelphia, however, Senator Burr condemned the pact and voted against it, an act that ultimately cost him his Senate seat. Burr's southern patron, Thomas Jefferson of Monticello, Virginia, also opposed the treaty, and in 1796, both Republican leaders ran for the presidency on the basis of their shared opinions. The electoral results only confirmed the Federalists' control of both the nation and New York. Burr, however, did amass the fourth highest electoral vote and so qualifies as Tammany Hall's first national candidate.

From New York's viewpoint, the national Republican defeat in 1796 was significant because the Clintonian-Burrite alliance lost control of the state legislature. Early in 1797, Burr was refused reelection as a United States senator and temporarily lost his role in national politics. But he was almost immediately elected to serve in the state assembly and spent the next three years preparing the way for a Republican victory in the next election; the mechanism he used to achieve this goal was a strengthened Tammany vote. Burr understood that as long as Federalist-sponsored property requirements for voting limited New York's electorate, the chance of a Republican victory was small. A system had to be designed, therefore, to reduce the elite's control of the voting lists and to broaden the opportunity to vote. Whether Burr really had much sympathy with the common man is questionable, but in 1798 he sponsored a bill that enabled foreign citizens to own land in New York State. By 1800, some of those foreigners were certain to have become Americans.

Even more significant was Burr's sponsorship of the famous Manhattan Company. Both yellow fever and cholera were endemic in New York City, and each year many lives were needlessly lost to diseases that doctors—even then—suspected were directly connected to the polluted drinking water.

Republicans supported a proposal to pipe in clean water from the Bronx to Manhattan, since everyone recognized that the growing metropolis needed a larger water supply. Finally, on April 2, 1799, the legislature granted a utility charter to the Manhattan Company. New Yorkers rejoiced as a private corporation promised to provide "pure and wholesome water" to the city. So vital and long lasting was New York's interest that a municipal representative served on the corporate board of directors for a century.

Quickly beginning operation, the new corporation dug a well on Spring Street and ultimately laid about six miles of wooden pipe to supply more than four hundred homes with water. In time, the wooden pipes proved to be ineffective and unsanitary, but even after iron pipes were substituted in 1828, the quality of Manhattan water hardly improved. In the area of water supply, New York lagged far behind its great rival, Philadelphia, during the first four decades of the new century. Nevertheless, the Manhattan Company continued to pump water until 1900, lest it lose its most precious possession—not customers but its charter of incorporation.

The Manhattan Company charter not only established a public utility but also granted to that corporation the privilege of investing its surplus capital in "monied transactions or operations." Burr and the Republicans saw in that innocuous clause the opportunity to break the Federalists' financial monopoly of banking in New York and to create a bank that would serve the democratic interest. The charter's investment clause allowed Republicans to create the Bank of the Manhattan Company, an institution that broke the Hamiltonian stranglehold over New York's development. Burr's relatives and members of his legion ruled the Manhattan Company's board, and it is apparent that several Federalists provided votes for the utility charter in order to place themselves on the ground floor of a good business deal. Republicans now had their bank, but their company never drew a drop of water from the faraway Bronx River. Rather, the bank provided mortgage loans to men of democratic persuasion, and these new property owners were enfranchised in time for the national elections. Tammany also encouraged its members to buy forty-shilling freeholds in common and thus qualify to vote for assemblymen. Thus by several expedients, as well as the normal course of economic growth, Republican voting cadres were expanded before the critical election of 1800.

The election of Jefferson has sometimes been called a revolution, but if so, it was a revolution made in New York City and successfully orchestrated by Aaron Burr. As the leader of Tammany, Burr not only mobilized his new voters but also put together a slate of local candidates so studded with important and aristocratic names that it could not help but be victorious. Control of the state legislature guaranteed Republican presidential electors, and the party's margin of national victory was provided by the vote of New York State. Few historians have appreciated the irony that Jefferson's victory in 1800 was due to urban votes, even though many people know that he regarded cities only as "sores."

The Tammany campaign of 1800 is one of the most dramatic stories in New York history, but it is often overlooked in the attention given to Burr's purported attempt to wrest the presidency away from Jefferson after both Republicans finished in an electoral tie. Almost all historians agree that the attempt was made, but after Jefferson became president, Tammany Hall claimed credit for his victory. Burr served as vice president until 1805, but Jefferson considered him only a "crooked gun." New York Democrats froze Burr out of local patronage, so knowing he had no future in Washington, Burr ran for governor of New York in 1804. He was defeated, partly because of Hamilton's intervention; Hamilton termed Burr "a dangerous man." Their frustrations and anger culminated on July 11, 1804, in a duel. On the cliffs across from New York City, Burr shot Hamilton, who died the next day. Burr fled, leaving Tammany temporarily in disrepute. But another leader emerged from the chaos.

The man who dominated New York City in the first decades of the nineteenth century was the strong-willed nephew of the governor, DeWitt Clinton (1769–1828). In October 1803, Clinton resigned from the U.S. Senate to begin his reign as mayor, a position he held until 1815, with only two, year-long, interruptions. In the first decade of the century, the incessant European wars between France and Britain stimulated the rise of America's, particularly New York's, merchant marine, and a federal naval yard was constructed along the East River in 1801 to handle the increase in traffic. The Common Council and the mayor, afraid that war might ensue if the British seized American shipments to France, ordered the construction of new defensive works on Governor's Island and at the tip of Manhattan. But few merchants wanted war, and their farsighted leaders were already beginning to speculate about the impact of steam on their profession. Indeed, on August 17, 1807, Robert Fulton's *Clermont* made its first trip to Albany, thereby ushering in the age of steam navigation.

By 1807, the value of goods exported from New York City exceeded that of any other American city or state and promised to continue rising. Not surprisingly, therefore, the city was outraged when on December 22, 1807, Congress declared a total embargo on all goods shipped to European belligerents. Frantic efforts by owners and captains launched a fleet of ships by eight o'clock the next morning, but hard times suddenly loomed. By April, "grass had begun to grow on the wharves"; idle seamen depended on food and shelter at the navy yard and at specially created soup kitchens. The end of Jefferson's administration also ended the embargo, but President James Madison's alternative policy brought little relief to New York's merchants. The Non-Intercourse Act banned trade with both Britain and France but offered to resume normal trade relations with whichever country first withdrew its restrictions on American traders. This act lasted only fourteen months, however, and was replaced by an even weaker measure. By the end of 1810, the port once again was open for business. Merchants believed that even limited commerce, carried out under wartime conditions and incurring huge insurance fees, returned sufficient profits.

With a population of 96,373 in 1810, New York now far surpassed Philadelphia as the nation's largest—and richest—city. Physically, Manhattan extended almost two miles north of the Battery forts. Rich merchants' large homes were situated amid warehouses, business establishments, and shops at the southern end of the island. Elsewhere, there was "such a rapid increase of building as to make the city seem perpetually new." The avenue called Broadway was the chief tourist attraction. City Hall, occupied in 1811, was immediately recognized as one of the "most superb" buildings in the United States, and in 1812, the first building called Tammany Hall was completed, serving as both a hotel and a political meeting place.

War in 1812 was the least welcome news the city could have received; nonetheless, the United States declared war on Britain on June 18. Trade-conscious New York wanted peace, even though one of the main reasons for the war was the imprisonment of American sailors. The actual battles of the war, on both land and sea, took place far from New York City. But many New York-based ships stayed at sea for the duration of the war, because after 1813 the port was effectively sealed by a British blockade. The closest that the city came to conflict was in August 1814, when a British invasion fleet appeared off Sandy Hook. As Mayor Clinton organized the defense, thousands of New Yorkers and even volunteers from New Jersey worked on the fortifications. Tammany Hall competed with the Freemason Society to see which could build the stronger ramparts along Brooklyn Heights, and the entire student body of Columbia College fortified the defenses at 123rd Street. "Let us die in the last ditch," proclaimed Clinton, rather than "tamely and cowardly surrender this delightful city."

By November, however, it became apparent that Britain's blockading squadron had no intention of attacking New York and that the city's defenses were never to be used. Life returned to a semblance of normality; the schools reopened and the militia and volunteers returned to their neglected businesses. On February 11, 1815, news arrived that America's team of negotiators had arranged a peace settlement at Ghent, a treaty that expediently ignored all the causes of the war and merely restored the status quo ante. Nevertheless, New York greeted the pact with "expressions of tumultuous joy": the port could now be reopened, and the city could once again trade with the world.

Behind the ship that brought news of the peace followed a fleet of British ships which, from April to June, "dumped" enormous quantities of goods into a ravenous market. New York's auctioneers made fortunes, and the customs house took in unprecedented amounts of revenue, but the well-calculated dumping caused a business depression. New York held a near monopoly on imported British textiles, but America's domestic woolen and cotton manufacturers were almost wiped out; the nation's first truly protective tariff had to be enacted in 1816 to prevent further damage to the economy. New York's poor also felt the impact of the recession, and by 1820, between 15 and 20 percent of its population was receiving public assistance. But the city's economy weathered this brief storm magnificently, and with its commercial houses, port facilities, and manufacturing capabilities undamaged by conflict, prosperity quickly returned.

Phenomenal growth became the hallmark of New York life in the decade following the Peace of Ghent. Already the largest city in the United States, the 1820 census of New York City showed a population of 123,706. The city was often referred to as the London of America. Peace opened the commerce of the world once again to its inventive merchants, and despite the best British efforts to hinder trade, the American entrepreneurs' initiative soon proved to be irresistible. Commerce demanded more and swifter ships, and naval builders quickly got to work. In 1817, a group of Quaker merchants decided to initiate a new type of commercial venture, and within a year they had created the Black Ball packet service. For centuries, ships had sailed from ports only when they had full cargo holds and when the tide was right. Black Ball packets carried cargo and passengers from New York to Liverpool on a specific day, leaving whether they were full or empty and even in the midst of a gale. The Red Star line and the Blue Swallowtail line soon followed the example, and by 1824, service was expanded to both London and France. Perhaps even more important was the maiden voyage of the steam-driven, oceangoing *Savannah*, which made the transatlantic voyage to Liverpool in

1819. Although this first trip was a financial failure (there was too little cargo space and the machinery was inefficient), the future of commercial enterprise was set. For many years to come, sailing ships remained the stalwarts of the Atlantic trade, but once New York merchants broke the Livingston-Fulton steamboat monopoly in 1824, the metamorphosis to steam shipping was inevitable.

Reliable packet service became vital to the port in yet another sector of New York's economy. During the years surrounding the War of 1812, New York merchantmen achieved dominance in the nation's coastal trade, and far more vessels were engaged in this type of commerce than in more glamorous oceanic shipping. The enormity of New York Harbor allowed ample anchorages for both those vessels bringing foreign imports and those collecting the products of the eastern seaboard. The city quickly assumed the essential factoring role in America's cotton export trade and soon controlled the transshipment of southern cotton to European manufacturers. Many New York-owned ships sailed directly to Europe from the South filled with cotton and returned to New York laden with textiles, manufactured goods, and immigrants: they then refilled their holds and again sailed southward to begin the triangle once more. Many other ships simply brought cotton to New York, and the annual output of cloth manufactured there rose dramatically from only three thousand yards in 1812 to well over 1 million in 1825. In 1832, George Opdyke (1805–1880) built the city's first important clothing factory, selling his goods largely to southern plantations and creating the basis of a new industry. Through their expertise and initiative, New Yorkers had forced the transatlantic cotton trade some two hundred miles off its normal course and had made their city the cotton broker to the world. The control of coastal trade in conjunction with the packet service to Europe solidified New York's trade dominance. When coupled with the city's control of hinterland trade routes along the Hudson and Mohawk Rivers, the economic primacy of New York was assured even before the completion of the Erie Canal.

The extraordinary growth of foreign commerce also necessitated the creation or expansion of such enterpreneurial tools as insurance, banking, and auctioneering. Men such as Philip Hone (1780–1851) and John Haggerty made their fortunes by clearing goods from the docks and allowing wholesalers and retailers to market them across America. The primitive stock arrangement of the Buttonwood Agreement was organized into a permanent exchange in 1817, and a series of new savings banks were chartered to provide the capital that drove business expansion. Specialized insurance companies were established, soon ending the traditional British monopoly of marine underwriting. In 1820, the New York Board of Underwriters was created, and soon it boasted a worldwide system of agents. Sailors of a dozen nations filled the streets and drank and whored at the 2,500 saloons that served their needs. Righteous and God-fearing merchants and manufacturers might lament the presence of such men and their waterfront dives, but both groups were necessary for the increasing wealth of the city.

Urban land speculation also offered opportunities for instant wealth, and men of all stations maneuvered to buy choice city lots. Those persons with the skill or luck to acquire property in New York City made fortunes. Shrewd purchases of New York real estate made John Jacob Astor (1763–1848) one of the richest men in America. During these boom years, the city was selling its property at ridiculously cheap prices, but Astor correctly reckoned that continuous urban growth would sharply increase its value. Accordingly, each year between 1800 and 1818, he bought $35,000 worth of New York real estate, both choice waterfront property and land on the outskirts of the city. Astor's acquisitions made him a millionaire many times over when they later became midtown Manhattan. When he died in 1848, his real estate holdings alone were worth an astronomical $20 million. Other large investors in New York real estate were the Wendel, Goelet, and Rhinelander families, who systematically expanded their landholdings in anticipation of New York's future.

The frantic expansion of the postwar decade was bound to leave many ragged edges in the wake of its growth, but city boosters dismissed these as the "carelessness" of youthful development. Visitors were almost unanimous in condemning New York's dirty and crowded streets, its smelly docks, and its ever present pigs. John Palmer, an English traveler, complained in 1817 about "the number and nuisance of the pigs permitted to be at large," and Baron Axel Klinckowstrom of Sweden, who visited New York in 1818, wrote:

New York is not as clean as cities of the same rank and population in Europe: in spite of the fact that the police regulations are good, they are not enforced and one finds in the streets dead cats and dogs, which make the air very bad; dust and ashes are thrown out into the streets, which are swept perhaps once every fortnight in the summer, only, however, in the largest and most frequented streets, otherwise they are cleaned only once a month. . . . The drinking water in New York is very bad and salty. Even the so-called Manhattan water . . . is not good.

Filth and bad water combined to make disease as rampant as moneymaking. In 1815, the Board of Health urged New Yorkers to be vaccinated to prevent the spread of smallpox, which had appeared in the city. Early in 1816, the Common Council appropriated $31,000 for free vaccinations, and Bellevue Hospital—built on the Murray, Livingston, and Kip estates along the East River—expanded its facilities. The public Institution for the Instruction of the Deaf and Dumb was incorporated in 1817, and this step was followed in 1818 by laying the cornerstone of the Bloomingdale Hospital for the Insane. Despite all these advances, however, yellow fever reappeared in 1819 and 1822, with the epidemic of the latter year the worst that the city had yet endured. More than one thousand people died before the frost came in October, and those who could afford to do so fled the crowded city for the suburban safety of Greenwich Village or Harlem. The victims were buried in an open field, now Bryant Park at Forty-second Street, because the advancing city was encroaching on the old potter's field near present-day Washington Square.

New York's growing pains were accompanied by a growing cosmopolitanism. In 1815, the first St. Patrick's Cathedral opened on Prince Street, tangible proof of the growing influence of Catholic immigrants on the city. Most of these newcomers were quickly incorporated into the labor market, but some of their children were able to attend classes offered by the Free School Society. By 1824, more than five thousand students were enrolled in the society's six schools, and thousands of other youngsters were privately educated.

Although not yet ready to challenge Boston's cultural primacy, New York did reign supreme in several other areas of intellectual life. It had already surpassed Philadelphia in the volume of its printed materials and had become the center of the printing and publishing industry. Several of the more enterprising printers opened bookstores and reading rooms where patrons could examine new editions or read one of the city's two dozen newspapers. Library societies were organized, and in 1820 both the Mercantile Library Association and the Apprentices Library were established to circulate books to people of moderate income. Indeed, to many observers, by the mid-1820s, New York City had surpassed both Boston and Philadelphia to become the literary capital of the nation. Books by such authors as James Kirke Paulding, Washington Irving, and James Fenimore Cooper were published in the city and won large audiences. And Manhattan was becoming a literary mecca for other authors; William Cullen Bryant and Fitz-Greene Halleck now called New York home.

Even though the city could not yet boast of major accomplishments in sculpture, music, or architecture, by 1825 many of the country's leading painters had moved to New York. Portraiture was still the most popular means for artists to earn a living, and many of the outstanding likenesses of successful merchants, bankers, and government officials that survive today date from this period. Painters from Europe also gravitated to the city, and the works of Fevret de Saint Mémin and Francis Guy attest to the attraction of Manhattan. Guy's *Tontine Coffeehouse* depicts the bustle of commerce characteristic of lower New York. In the 1820s, native New Yorkers like Samuel F. B. Morse (1791–1872), displayed extraordinary talent. Morse's main interest lay elsewhere, however: he is remembered today not for his paintings or his political career but for his inventive genius. Perhaps the best artist in New York was John Trumbull (1756–1843). Trained by the expatriate Benjamin West, Trumbull became the first important painter to establish a studio in the city. The New York Academy of Fine Arts, first organized in 1802, became the American Academy, encouraging artistic endeavor, and Trumbull served as its president from 1817 to 1835. His artistic rivals created the even more prestigious National Academy of Design in January 1826.

In the artistic field with which New York is particularly identified, the theater, the early years of the century clearly foreshadowed future celebrity. Even in 1815, the variety of dramatic and popular entertainments available to residents and visitors was noteworthy. The Park Theater, under the management of Steven Price, was the showplace of the city and began the practice of bringing Europe's best-known performers to the United States. National tours invariably began in New York and then "went on the road" under Price's direction. Audiences were almost always more intrigued with the actors than with the plays, and America's leading performers of stage, song, and dance all gravitated to New York where a reputation could be made. In 1821, a rebuilt Park Theater, accommodating 2,500 persons, opened, and other large houses soon were constructed in a city that had a seemingly insatiable desire for more theater.

The first grand opera in the United States, Rossini's *Barber of Seville*, was produced at the Park in November 1825. In 1823, the federal government ceded to the city the battlements of the old Southwest Battery, and after extensive remodeling, Castle Clinton became Castle Garden. Balls, receptions, and plays were regularly held there. In 1824, when the marquis de Lafayette, on the invitation of President James Monroe, returned to the country he had served during the Revolution, citizens of all classes thronged Castle Garden to honor the old warrior. The occasion was a triumph, but the homogeneity of the crowds greatly puzzled Lafayette. He reportedly asked Mayor Philip Hone, "But where are the people?"

Lafayette's question identified perhaps the most striking aspect of New York society: It was a city in which rigid class lines had begun to blur and in which opportunity beckoned to everyone. The class separations of the past were beginning to be replaced by a more democratic society. To be sure, New York's "identifiable society" was still dominated by its commercial aristocracy, who lived graciously and well, yet the gap between classes seemed to be surmountable. The vigor of city business now derived from the many activities carried out by the middle classes, and they in turn were constantly aware of entrepreneurial pressure from below. Life for the laborers, sailors, apprentices, and blacks was hard, but New York offered the possibility of upward mobility.

This pervasive sense of egalitarianism was apparent in politics even before the national Jacksonian revolution. In 1821, a constitutional convention met in New York and drastically altered the definition of citizens entitled to vote. The old Constitution mandated strict and heavy property qualifications for the right to vote in state or local elections, whereas the new Constitution abolished the Council of Appointment, scattered the appointing power, and greatly increased the suffrage. To a great extent, the new document created, for white voters at least, almost universal suffrage for men. Moreover, in 1817, Governor Daniel Tompkins had signed a measure abolishing slavery in New York as of July 4, 1827. Although relatively few blacks could vote, their physical freedom added to the general sense of optimism pervading New York. The extension of the suffrage made politics less a gentleman's preserve than in the past, and as events proved, it provided the impetus for rebuilding Tammany Hall's power.

Constitutional change had expanded the number of potential electors sixfold, and these new voters had to be led and counseled and organized. The extension of the suffrage was vehemently opposed by conservative men such as Chancellor James Kent (1763–1847), who feared that the city might become a copy of Europe, where nations were governed by urban capitals and their mobs. "New York is destined to become the future London of America: and in less than a century, that City, with the operation of universal suffrage and under skillful direction, will govern the State." Kent deeply resented the presence in New York of large numbers of recently arrived immigrants, whose voting potential could be tapped through naturalization. Tammany also recognized this opportunity, and in the 1820s it began to develop the techniques that would soon give it control of the city. By enacting into law an ideal of equality and democracy, the Constitution of 1821 fostered a bloodless revolution that altered the history of both the city and the nation.

By 1825, the city of New York had achieved commercial dominance in a rapidly growing America. Its port handled almost half the country's imports and a third of its exports. Five hundred new businesses opened during this single year. More than three thousand new houses had been constructed in 1824 to accommodate a population soaring beyond 165,000, and the capital available in banking establishments had passed the unprecedented level of $25 million. Yet all this seemed only preparatory to the great event of the age: the long-awaited Erie Canal.

DeWitt Clinton's "Governor's Gully" was about to open. Clinton's services to the city as mayor have been noted, but surely his greatest contribution to New York was made during the years he spent arguing for and planning a canal that could tie the city to the rest of the continent. After his last term as mayor ended in 1815, Clinton was appointed to the state's Canal Commission, and in 1817 he became governor. On July 4, 1817, Governor Clinton turned the first spade of earth for the canal project, and during its construction phase he remained its driving force. Not all city dwellers shared Clinton's vision. Opponents charged that "Clinton, the federal son of a bitch, taxes our dollars to build him a ditch." Yet the governor held firm and completed the canal. It was "the longest Canal in the world, built in the shortest time, with the least experience, for the least money, and to the greatest public benefit." New York City would benefit the most, however, for it became the essential middleman between the farmers and trappers and the European buyers. Suddenly, New York's hinterland included the entire Middle West as well as the reinvigorated cities of Buffalo, Rochester, Syracuse, Utica, and Albany. The Erie Canal guaranteed that New York and not New Orleans would be the outlet port for the produce of mid-America, and it ended forever Philadelphia's hopes of overtaking New York as America's lead city.

Finally the canal was opened. On October 26, 1825, the canal boat *Seneca Chief* entered the canal at Buffalo, and a series of cannon shots brought word of its entry to New York City eighty-one minutes later. Not until November 4 did the barge and Governor Clinton arrive in Manhattan, but as he poured Lake Erie water into the Atlantic Ocean, the governor knew that he had achieved a miracle. Some New York merchants opposed his scheme as "upstate improvements," but he had held firm; when the voters rejected him because of the higher taxes he had imposed, he had persevered; and now he had been proved right. The commerce of virtually the entire United States would now flow toward New York. Already it was America's greatest city, but in the next thirty years, it would become one of the great world centers. As much as one man can take responsibility for such a historic change, the credit should go to DeWitt Clinton.

The key characteristic of New York life during the first quarter of the nineteenth century was rapid growth, and the city's physical expansion consumed outlying areas like Greenwich Village. "Such has been the growth of our city that the building of one block more will completely connect the two places." Even before 1820 that union was accomplished, and in 1824 alone the city added eight thousand more buildings. Even without the Erie Canal, New York had become the nation's leader in population, commerce, finance, manufacturing, and culture. Its development had been swift, but so solid were the foundations laid down during this period that few doubts remained as to its national preeminence or its future world destiny. The organizational and entrepreneurial skills displayed by the city's business leaders set the standard for urban communities throughout the nation, and the extraordinary success of the Erie Canal ensured New York's primacy. Walt Whitman's later judgment was correct: New York is "the great place of the Western continent, the heart, the brain, the focus, the main spring, the pinnacle, the extremity, the no more beyond of the New World."

4

Building a Modern City

The completion of the Erie Canal guaranteed New York City's future prosperity. By 1835, the entire cost of the project had been repaid, and upstate cities along its route had grown by an average of 300 percent. Canal traffic, only 218,000 tons in the first year of operation, was 1,417,046 tons by 1840, and more than double that by 1850. City merchants, even those who had opposed the plan, now basked in the prosperity created by the "Big Ditch" and competed with zest for America's widening western markets.

Additional areas were added to the metropolitan hinterland each year. In 1828, for example, the coal fields of Pennsylvania were opened to New York when the Delaware and Hudson Canal was completed. Railroads such as the New York and Harlem were built, and in 1836, construction of the Erie Railroad along the Hudson began. Cleveland in 1835 and Toledo in 1840 were soon tied into the expanding New York network. Although most consider the Erie Canal to be a nineteenth-century project, its peak tonnage was not reached until 1951. The canal was merely the most obvious of the many forces that were combining to make New York a city in a class by itself. With its commercial and manufacturing firms and its entrepreneurs and energy, the city seemed the natural base for those seeking modern enterprise. A practical electric telegraph and transmission code existed by 1837, and various other inventions that presaged a new kind of urban society were being exhibited in New York; among these were pumps, submarine devices, and continually improving steam engines. Each device created jobs and helped build America's most modern city.

By the 1840s, Manhattan was growing at such a phenomenal rate that it would soon contain more people than did Baltimore, Philadelphia, and Boston combined. Immigrants from Europe poured in by the tens of thousands, making New York even more cosmopolitan and heterogeneous. Gulian C. Verplanck (1786–1870), a prominent scholar and politician, saw his native city as a "sort of thoroughfare where almost every remarkable character is seen once." The great waves of immigration of the 1840s came after the city's government had been reorganized on a more democratic basis by removing the property qualifications for voters. City offices were elective after 1834, and politicians now courted the votes of new citizens. New York's municipal government, though far from perfect, was greatly improved. Despite the many problems created by the inrush of newcomers, a richer, more productive, and culturally diverse city had been created.

Five years after the Erie Canal opened, the population of New York was only 202,589, but it quadrupled in the next thirty years. The rising birthrate combined with the influx of thousands of European immigrants to produce this demographic explosion. Far slower growth characterized the 2.5 percent of black city residents, a percentage much smaller than that of the colonial period. To vote, blacks had to fulfill a property qualification higher than that required of whites. These property qualifications were still required for blacks long after an 1826 law removed them for white voters. An attempt to grant blacks full equality in suffrage was defeated in 1846, as it was in 1867. Only after passage of the Fifteenth Amendment in 1870 was the property requirement eliminated in both the state and the city. In addition, blacks in the labor market were being ousted by white newcomers. As Irish immigrants entered the city after 1820, the men took the menial carting and wharf jobs that blacks had held, and the women replaced blacks in domestic service.

European immigration remains one of the dominant themes of American history, but in 1825, New York was still largely populated by native-born citizens: only 11 percent of its population had been born outside the country. The city had already integrated immigrants from France and Santo Domingo in the 1790s and was coping with an influx of Irish in the 1820s. However, during the 1840s, economic and political changes in northern and western Europe led to the uprooting of populations. Artisans displaced by the Industrial Revolution and farmers who had lost their land came to America. In Ireland and Central Europe, disastrous harvests caused starvation and economic decline unmatched in the nineteenth century. In the Germanies, the failure of liberal reform in 1848 led to the exodus of an educated and privileged elite. For a generation, hundreds of thousands of economic or political refugees crossed the ocean to seek advancement and security for themselves and their families. The number of Irish and British immigrants rose from 267,000 between 1841 and 1845 to 750,000 over the next five years. In that same decade, German immigration soared from 105,000 to almost 330,000.

The greatest transfer of population the world had ever experienced, 35 million people in one century, had begun to move from Europe to the United States.

From 1820 to 1870, 70 percent of the more than 7 million immigrants to the United States entered through New York. By 1860, this influx so fundamentally altered the demography of Manhattan that foreign-born residents comprised more than 50 percent of the metropolis. New York's hospitals, almshouses, orphanages, and soon its prisons, were crowded beyond capacity with foreigners. When the newcomers landed at the piers and wharves in New York Harbor, they were met by an unscrupulous army of "immigrant runners." who while sometimes providing them with assistance, often robbed them as well. In 1846, William Frederick Havemeyer (1804–1874), then the mayor of New York, prohibited the runners from entering the immigrant depots, so they simply waited outside the gates to exploit the new arrivals. Finally, the state legislature created the Board of Commissioners of Immigration to deal with the situation. Although the board was not able to resolve the problem of the immigrant runners, in 1855 it did designate Castle Garden, near the Battery, to act as the central entry point for all incoming foreigners. Here, relatively honest and reliable ticket brokers, employment agents, and city employees dispensed aid and advice to the newcomers. Immigrant aid societies established by each ethnic group were on hand to help immigrants find homes and jobs.

The Irish constituted the largest group of immigrants. One million arrived in the United States between 1845 and 1855, and in 1860, 200,000 of them were living in the city. More than 100,000 German newcomers and smaller numbers of English, Welsh, Scots, Scandinavians, and Jews also settled in Manhattan. The Irish crowded into rundown housing on the Lower East Side, and the Germans carved out a community farther north, extending from the Bowery to Fourteenth Street, called Kleindeutschland. Similar but smaller ghettos emerged after later migrations, and over the years, nineteenth-century New York became an interlocking grid of ethnic neighborhoods.

Living conditions were abominable, and the "fever nests" greeting most newcomers were already slums. To meet the housing needs of the new arrivals, older buildings were converted into several apartments that were then partitioned into still smaller units by unscrupulous landlords. Although immigrants filled these reconstructed houses from cellar to attic, the housing supply could never meet the demand. In 1837, an old brewery in the Five

Points area was converted into what might be considered the first tenement house; the site rapidly became a horror. One estimate asserts that the brewery was the scene of at least one murder a night over a three-year period.

Gradually, buildings began to be constructed whose purpose was specifically to house immigrants. These were New York's first true tenements. Such buildings were four to five stories high with a narrow hallway opening from a street, courtyard, or alley. On each floor, including the cellar, several apartments opened into the hall and contained windows. But there also were tiny rooms in the middle of the building that contained no windows and whose only ventilation was an airshaft that ran through the center of the structure. In most cases, there was another tenement in the backyard. This combination of front and rear buildings on the same lot created a labyrinth of passages and alleys that were dark, dirty, and smelly. The average density per block in these areas was unimaginable. In the wards below Canal Street, the gross density of population per acre rose from 94.5 persons in 1820 to 163.5 in 1850, with the average block density increasing from 157.5 to 272.5 during the same period.

Rents varied widely, even within the same building. An apartment with windows cost between $3.00 and $13.00 a month. Single rooms in the middle of the building usually went to bachelors and cost $0.75 to $1.25 per week. In 1850, more than 29,000 immigrants lived in dark, dank cellar quarters and paid whatever the landlord demanded. The immigrant renter rarely complained, for his landlord held the threat of immediate eviction; someone else was always waiting for the rooms.

A typical tenement house apartment had three rooms. Two served as bedrooms, and the other was a kitchen, dining room, and living room combined. Water came from a street pump or well in the backyard, where the toilet was also located. Bathtubs and showers were nonexistent, and water for bathing or washing clothes or dishes had to be carried to the kitchen sink from the street pumps outside. Keeping clean was difficult under these circumstances. Tenants went to public baths or washing establishments built by private philanthropists; the "People's Washing and Bathing Establishment" on Mott Street was the first one erected, in 1852. There is little doubt that many of the tenants bathed in the rivers and then only during the summer months. Backyard wooden privies, through overuse and improper care, caused a constant health hazard. A contest to create a better apartment house led to the construction of a model tenement on Mott Street in 1855, but it influenced few builders.

Life in the tenements often seemed an endless struggle merely to survive.

The high incidence of infectious disease frightened city officials, yet in the overcrowded immigrant slums, quarantine regulations were impossible to enforce. Any communicable disease could become epidemic. Yellow fever visited the city five times between 1795 and 1822, and in 1832, a new strain of cholera swept into New York. The epidemic was concentrated in the warrens where the Irish workers lived, with more than a third of all cases reported from the Sixth "Irish" Ward. Unlike the rich, many of whom sailed off on Cornelius Vanderbilt's steamers to Connecticut, the Irish could only die in agony, and by the October frost, they had contributed by far the largest number to the city's four thousand deaths. Cholera reappeared in 1834, 1849, and 1855; typhoid fever ravaged the immigrants in 1837; and typhus erupted in 1842.

All available statistics show that immigrants were far more likely to die from disease than were the relatively better-off native born. For example, 83.9 percent of Bellevue Hospital's admissions between 1849 and 1859 were foreign born. The hospital's 1857 annual report showed that 60 percent of cancer deaths occurred among immigrants and that 656 more aliens than natives died of tuberculosis. Perhaps the most fearful statistic was that two-thirds of all New York City deaths in 1857 were the children of foreign-born parents. Nothing so graphically indicates the rigors of slum life than this horrendous figure.

The disastrous slum conditions were in part produced by the residents themselves. Neglect, the uncontrolled dumping of garbage into streets and airshafts, and the haphazard removal of refuse by city workers created a fertile breeding ground for disease. Few health officials had much desire to attend to the welfare of the poor, and the city's sewer system did not extend to the poor areas. Indeed, services were not provided for even well-to-do areas until after 1849. To compound the dilemma of health care, even when immigrants received sound medical advice, they often ignored it, relying instead on superstition and home remedies to cure every ailment short of broken bones.

New York was not a healthy environment, and disease was not a respecter of social status. The ailing public was always receptive to new therapeutic systems promising health. During the 1830s, the Botanic System, which used herbal remedies, was popular, and in the 1840s the "science" of homeopathy swept the city. The appeal of such fads was temporary but did illustrate the general desire for better health care. No additional medical institutions were built in New York between 1830 and 1850, although Bellevue underwent some expansion, but several immigrant aid societies began to provide itinerant doctor, dentist, and midwife services. Not until 1855 did a new hospital open its doors, the Jews' Hospital (now Mount Sinai), joined in 1858 by St. Luke's.

Because of their poverty, differing customs, or simply an inability to speak English, immigrants often clashed with the law. For the most part, these were petty offenses such as drunkenness, disorderly conduct, or perhaps robbery. There had been a vast statistical rise in the crime rate as immigration increased, and New York's streets did indeed become more dangerous as the century progressed. As is true today, however, the victims of these minor crimes were largely found among the immigrant population itself. Both the Irish and German newcomers had a permissive drinking tradition, and this, coupled with assimilation difficulties and familial chaos, often led them to the local saloon.

Even sober immigrants had difficulties with the native-born constables, who saw in foreigners a danger to social order and who picked up immigrants for petty misdemeanors. Even after Irishmen began to join the force, they too repeated the stereotype that their people were particularly given to violence, citing as proof the "flour riot" of February 1837 when a mob of hungry Irish laborers sacked warehouses filled with grain. Prostitution also was common among immigrant women, as poverty led many girls to the oldest profession; 60 percent of the trade was foreign born. Immigrant children who survived the rigors of their life often joined one of New York's many juvenile gangs. For young men living amid poverty, lacking familial guidance and educational or recreational opportunities, the gangs of the slums were the answer. The Bowery Boys, the Dead Rabbits, the Kerryonians, and the True Blue Americans each adopted "colors," as did youth gangs more than a century later. A major difference was that in the 1840s, there were no public agencies to deal with such discontents, and the police rarely challenged the gangs' domination of the Lower East Side slums. Police also estimated that 55 percent of all city arrests in 1859 involved Irishmen.

Yet even as the authorities despaired and elitists lamented this barbarization of their city, another New York was evident. By 1830, Manhattan was first in commercial, industrial, and financial endeavors, and in the three decades before 1860 it achieved cultural and artistic dominance as well. As the influx of immigrants strained the city environment to the breaking point, New York claimed the cultural distinction it had always longed for yet rarely enjoyed. One area of general improvement was the availability of literature. The period between 1840 and 1860 saw a large increase in the number of libraries available to adult New Yorkers, although most remained private or were by subscription only. The principal exception to this rule was also the finest single library in New York, the Astor Library, created by a $400,000 bequest in the will of New York's greatest real estate speculator. Astor died in March 1848, and in April 1849, a board of eleven trustees approved a public library to be constructed on Lafayette Place. The trustees obtained an act of incorporation from the legislature and held a competition for design proposals. From thirty submissions, the trustees selected that of Alexander Aelzer and awarded him a prize of $300. A contract for erecting the Astor Library was signed on January 2, 1850, and when the building opened four years later, it already had a national reputation. In the twentieth century, it became the nucleus of the New York Public Library.

The city's libraries served only a small percentage of the population, however, and for most New Yorkers the most accessible means to cultural advancement was the newspaper. During the Jacksonian era, New York City became the center of the nation's journalistic activity; it seemed there was a newspaper for every possible taste. The penny press, which began on September 3, 1833, with the publication of Benjamin Day's *Sun*, offered political and social information within the reach of all, and other editors were not slow to follow this example. James Gordon Bennett (11795–1872) founded the *New York Herald* in 1836, which was shortly followed by Horace Greeley's (1811–1872) *Tribune* and William Cullen Bryant's (1794–1878) *Evening Post*. All these papers offered a varied fare of sensationalism, news, essays on science, practical tips, and gossip. The papers also shared a modern, liberal philosophy—Bryant's *Evening Post* soon won a reputation as the most advanced publication in the city.

Almost all readers acknowledged Greeley of the *Tribune* to be the best editor of the age. Greeley supported many radical and eccentric causes but made his newspaper the most influential in America. Karl Marx contributed articles on European affairs, and the editor's often quoted "Go West, young man" inspired countless thousands during the age of manifest destiny. The *New York Times*, founded by Henry J. Raymond (1820–1869) in 1851, was more sedate in its coverage, but its readership grew rapidly, and by 1860, it had outstripped all its competitors. In addition, a hundred specialized newspapers were published during these years, aimed at particular ethnic readers, religious groups, or laborers.

As early as the 1830s, periodical writers and artists began to gravitate into the orbit of New York. Nathaniel P. Willis (1806–1867), the editor of Boston's *American Monthly Magazine* until 1831, moved to the city, explaining that despite Boston's many attractions, "a man who has any taste for cosmopolitanism would very much prefer New York." He soon founded the

Home Journal to report the news of the city. Manhattan was home to fifty magazines by 1847, including the *Democratic Review, Knickerbocker*, and the *New York Monthly; Harper's Monthly* was about to begin publishing and quickly surpassed them all. Charles Dickens made the first of several visits to the city in 1842 and was impressed with its commercial bustle and intellectual vigor.

Just as New York drew journalists, it also attracted artistic talent. Portraiture remained the most popular form of painting, but Samuel Morse, John Vanderlyn, Thomas Cole, Asher Durand, James Longacre, and Henry Inman were among those who found Manhattan a congenial site for their different genres. And surely the most successful artistic collaboration of the century was formalized in 1850 when Nathaniel Currier (1813–1888) and James M. Ives (1824–1895) entered into a partnership to produce lithographs. Originally sold at prices ranging from a nickel to a dollar, some of these lithographs today sell for more than $10 million; for almost seventy years, the firm's many artists documented a changing nation.

Old World architectural styles were also quickly adopted by New York, and in the mid-1830s the Gothic revival was as advanced here as in England. Richard Upjohn (1802–1878) was commissioned to build Trinity Church's third building in that style, and when the church was consecrated in 1846, it brought him immediate renown and many private commissions. Trinity's steeple, 260 feet high, was the highest point in the city. Upjohn then helped create the American Institute of Architects and served as its first president. Not to be outdone, Archbishop John Hughes (1797–1864), leader of the growing Roman Catholic population, called on his community to contribute funds to build a suitable cathedral for New York. "Dagger John" had the courage to hire a thirty-two-year old Episcopalian as his architect, and James Renwick (1818–1895) began construction of today's St. Patrick's Cathedral in 1853. The cornerstone was set in place five years later, on August 15, 1858, but completion came only in 1889. Classicists appreciated the United States Customs House, which opened in 1842, but the Gothic style was ascendant in New York by 1860.

Despite a somewhat limited clientele, both serious music and theater became more important in Manhattan during the antebellum years. Although most of the population preferred the saloon or the music hall, wealthier New Yorkers insisted on better music. Subscribers organized the New York Philharmonic Society, which gave its first concert on December 7, 1842. The attempt to introduce Italian opera in the 1820s had not been successful, but it still remained an annual attraction. The most significant effort to expose the city to opera was made by Lorenzo Da Ponte, who opened his Italian Opera House in 1832. In the early 1850s, opera was presented at Castle Garden before it became the immigrant staging area. Attempts to offer "finer" music continued in 1854 when the Academy of Music on Fourteenth Street offered its first series of concerts.

Serious music lovers might sniff, but the masses still preferred entertainment like that offered by the Christy Minstrels, who first performed in New York in 1846. In 1850, P. T. Barnum brought Jenny Lind, the "Swedish Nightingale," to America for a series of two hundred concerts at the unprecedented fee of $1,000 a performance. She appeared first on September 11 at New York's Castle Garden. Everyone who attended was thrilled, and some even thought the performance was worth the $225 top ticket price that Barnum had charged. The willingness and ability of New York's elite to pay such exorbitant prices made it possible for Lind and those who followed her to strike it rich in the city of opportunity. In 1852, singer Adelina Patti filled the Lyceum Theater; she was eight.

New York's already strong position in theater was reinforced in the two decades before 1860. The Park remained the most prestigious theater, but the opening of the Broadway and Astor Theaters in 1847 brought competition. Niblo's Gardens, the National, and the Bowery Theater also were handsome structures, but the Park remained the "fashionable house" that hosted Europe's best performers and Manhattan's best people. Fannie Ellster, Fannie Kemble, Marcia Maliban, and the brilliant English actor William Macready all played to packed audiences in the Park.

The stage also provided an arena for political statements, as it did in May 1849, when the Astor Place riot erupted because of the rivalry between an American actor, Edward Forrest, and Macready. Irishmen who had never seen a play had no doubt who the better actor was, and when their demonstration against Macready got out of hand, the police had to be called; more than thirty persons died before order was restored. By 1851, Edwin Booth had replaced both men as the matinee idol of the age, and he remained America's leading actor for a generation. Overall, there was little doubt that in every artistic field, New York reigned supreme; it achieved a cultural style that the rest of the urban nation consciously sought to imitate. The words of the *Broadway Journal* were prophetic: "New York is fast becoming, if she is not already, America."

But if New York was America, it was a land deeply divided by an economic and social abyss. What possible connection could there be between the horrors of slum life and the elegance of a merchant's residence? How was it possible for the unlettered drayman and the sophisticated broker to communicate? The answer then, as it is today, was through the medium of political life. The great revolution of this age was in the equality men enjoyed in voting. During the 1820s, property barriers for the suffrage and imprisonment for debt were eliminated in New York, and Tammany Hall already had demonstrated the potential power of the masses. By the turn of the decade, Tammany decided to mobilize the increasing numbers of Irish voters. Tammany was able to naturalize immigrants expeditiously; its local leaders made alliances with the gangs roaming the ward streets; it saw that saloons had no trouble with the police; and it even began to obtain city jobs for Irishmen as lamplighters, fire wardens, meat inspectors, and policemen.

Slowly, Tammany's power grew, and even though its leadership remained old-line merchant, its electoral strength was increasingly the product of the masses it cultivated. As newcomers to New York, the Irish tended to be clannish, deriving their enjoyment from the local saloon and the Roman Catholic Church. Because Tammany threatened neither of these outlets and even offered a way of advancement, the Irish became the rank and file of an organization still dominated by native-born New Yorkers. In time, though, the Irish moved into positions in which they could exert control. Although this process took several generations, it was inevitable, and the sequence of ethnic succession still is manifest in New York's ethnic and racial politics today.

New York had been the "child" of state government since colonial times, but the Jacksonian movement stimulated the common man's desire to control city affairs. This was especially true in regard to the office of mayor, which remained a gubernatorial appointment even after 1830. Excellent mayors had often resulted from this selection process; DeWitt Clinton had been succeeded by leaders such as Philip Hone, William Paulding, and Gideon Lee. New Yorkers now clamored for the right to choose their own chief magistrate, and in 1834 they won that privilege. In that year, Cornelius Lawrence, the Democratic candidate, was elected mayor for the first of his three terms. He was of course well-to-do, but in the words of the aristocratic Philip Hone, his role had changed from being a "respectable functionary" to being "the mayor of a party." Hone seemed perversely pleased when in 1837, during the traditional New Year's Day greeting in the mayor's home, "the rabble" of the Democratic Party actually took over the premises, turning it into "a Five Points tavern." Lawrence was forced to summon the police to clear the place. By that time, the workingmen of New York "looked like men who knew they were free," and their allegiance clearly would go to the party or organization that served them best.

Tammany Hall in the 1830s was not the mythical, finely tuned, highly organized political machine described in the works of some political scientists. Rather, it was a coalition of factions deeply divided over questions of leadership and national issues such as banking, westward expansion, and abolitionism. These issues split the Democratic Party in the city into radical and conservative wings. In 1835, the radical faction of Tammany Hall, calling itself the Equal Rights Party, attempted to gain control of the organization from the more conservative members representing the city's banking interests. Leaders such as the agrarian reformer George Henry Evans; the editor of the *New York Evening Post*, William Legget; Alexander Ming Jr.; John W. Vethake; and others met at Tammany Hall on the evening of October 29, 1835, to seize command of the party. During the meeting, the conservatives plunged the hall into darkness by turning off the gas lights, an old tactic used in Tammany decision making. But this time the radicals had come prepared. Pulling candles from their vest pockets, they immediately lit them with a new type of wooden match known as *locofocos*. The meeting of the rebels continued, and by the next morning all New York was chuckling at the new name of the radical wing of the Democratic Party, Locofocos. What the party stood for, however, was serious. Its members claimed to oppose monopoly in any form and were disillusioned with the elitist Tammany organization. Because they hoped to "democratize democracy," the Locofocos drew support from segments of society ranging from laborers to professionals. As hard-money men, they distrusted the paper money of the banks. The banks themselves were despised as agencies of oppression and corruption, and corporations were opposed as inequitable and dangerous. The party's members also viewed imprisonment for debt as unconstitutional. In short, they sought to free American democracy from any taint of privilege and to purge it of inequities.

Such beliefs seemed sacrilegious to the merchant aristocracy, which had long ruled both the economic and political life of New York. Indeed, Locofoco radicalism led many Democrats to defect to the opposition Whigs and intensified the growing class and ethnic divisions of local politics.

As immigration from Ireland and Germany continued to augment Democratic ranks in the late 1830s, the Whigs, who futilely opposed Jacksonian democracy nationally, now feared that control of New York was about to be taken from them. The newcomers represented not only a new class but also a new religion. The Whigs, who were both elitist and Protestant, saw the rising Democratic strength as a threat to their hegemony and to the traditional separation of church and state. Conservatives predicted meddling by the Catholic Church in politics and feared for the purity of American, or rather Protestant, institutions. The church's identification with Europe's despotic monarchies allowed some New Yorkers to suspect the existence of a far-ranging papist plan to subvert the free government of the United States. In 1834, for example, the artist and inventor Samuel F. B. Morse wrote a series of letters to the *New York Observer* in which he argued that the papal conquest of America was already under way. Whigs emphasized the economic competition that clannish, uncouth, criminal foreigners offered to honest, stalwart American workers. In this way, nativism and prejudice made a joint appearance in the city's politics.

Whigs benefited immensely from their economic argument because of the "disappointed hopes and dwindling opportunities" accompanying the nationwide panic of 1837. Early in that year, the high cost of bread led to the "flour riot" outside Eli Hart's warehouse, and by April, ninety-eight business failures in Manhattan had been reported. On May 8 and 9, there was a run on all city banks, and by May 10, all but three had suspended specie payments. In this chaotic situation, most voters turned again to Whig competence and elected Aaron Clark, a rabid nativist, to serve as mayor. That the new executive was a bigot did not concern the workers in this year of national ruin. More than six thousand men in the construction trades alone were unemployed, and despite Clark's prejudices, a phenomenal 70 percent of all city relief went to the Irish. By mid-1839, the Democrats' strength had recovered sufficiently to regain City Hall. Once again, jobs became available, and by the end of the decade, New York, its workforce, and Tammany Hall seemed poised to enter a new era.

For much of the 1840s, the Democratic Party controlled New York City's politics, but its position was never secure because the Whig opposition constantly resorted to bigotry and economic discrimination to win votes. Nativists believed that foreigners were subverting the nation's economic and moral foundations by depressing wages, causing the decline of the apprentice system, and blindly voting en masse for unqualified candidates. As a result, signs reading "No Irish Need Apply" appeared in New York shopwindows, and anti-Catholic literature and oratory became a staple of political discourse. In 1841, artist-inventor Samuel Morse openly ran for mayor as a nativist; although he lost, he established the mean spirit of the decade.

City inspections of slum areas in 1842 attributed the housing crisis to the immigrants and their habits. Even though reform-minded gentlemen organized the Association for Improving the Condition of the Poor in 1843, more of them were apt to vote their prejudices. In 1844, James Harper, a publisher, won election as both a nativist and a reformer. Harper won more votes than any other mayor elected before 1852, so appealing to voters' baser instincts made political sense. The struggle for their allegiance became a vicious battleground in an age of democratic suffrage. Voters might sometimes select men who appealed to their prejudices, but they preferred those who delivered services useful to all citizens. In the confused politics of the "common man," the obligation to upgrade the city's environment to benefit all classes became the one unchallenged goal. The result of this harsh party competition was a more modern New York.

The city's first priority was to develop an adequate and clean water supply, for both disease control and fire protection. When Mayor Cornelius Lawrence was elected in 1834, the city drew its water from only five sources, the Manhattan Company, public pumps, the famed Tea Water Pump, Knapp's Spring, and imported casks. The quality of New York water was so bad that many believed it to be the principal reason for the increase in public drunkenness. Since 1818, those few who could afford it had purchased carbonated "soda water" as a substitute. Brewing was a major New York industry, but companies were threatened with extinction because the water used to make beer was so unpalatable. Doctors warned that disease would continue until the water supply was substantially improved.

All these factors led the City Council to endorse in April 1835 the construction of an aqueduct and reservoir system to be built with public money. Whether the project would have been pushed to rapid completion is questionable, but fate now forced the city to act. Since New York was New Amsterdam, fire had been the most terrifying of all urban problems, and serious damage was caused each year by its ravages. The only existing mechanism to fight city blazes were poorly organized volunteer fire companies, using outmoded, inefficient equipment; firefighters were more interested in social and political activities than the dangers of fire fighting. Rarely could such companies do more than confine blazes to already burning buildings. But on the morning of December 16, 1835, in zero degree temperatures and with a virtual gale blowing, a fire in the warehouse district suddenly blazed out of control. Many companies responded to the call but discovered that the water pipes had frozen solid. The firefighters were thus forced to watch as the seventeen-block area below Wall Street—more than seven hundred structures—was consumed. The blaze was visible as far away as Philadelphia and did not burn itself out for three days. There were other giant conflagrations: one in 1845 burned for five days, and in 1858 a blaze consumed part of City Hall, but the "Great Fire" of 1835 was surely the worst in city history.

Losses were estimated at $18 million to $20 million, and several insurance companies were driven into bankruptcy. Later, several investors cited the fire as a fundamental cause of the panic of 1837. By 1839, however, reconstruction of the burned district had begun. So extensive were the changes that Philip Hone, ever the observant critic, remarked that New York was a difficult city to love, since it was "rebuilt once every ten years." The fire, terrible though it was, contributed much to New York's future, since it forced a revision of building codes on a once reluctant merchant community. Even more important, it encouraged and facilitated the task of those demanding a more reliable water supply for the city.

Until the fire, property owners had rejected all entreaties that they accept a tax levied for a public water system. Only in April 1836, with the tragedy still fresh in mind, did the voters agree to finance the Croton Aqueduct System. Charles King planned the project; thousands of construction jobs were filled by immigrant laborers supplied by Tammany; and the tunnels and dams necessary for the undertaking slowly took shape over the next few years. Among the special projects that were built as part of the system were the High Bridge across the Harlem River, the world's largest earth dam in Westchester, and an Egyptian-style reservoir on the site of present-day Bryant Park—for which 100,000 bodies had to be disinterred.

Finally, on July 4, 1842, two reservoirs were filled, and on October 14, a citywide celebration marked the completion of a project almost as noteworthy as the Erie Canal. The daily flow of water was measured at 35 million gallons, and by 1852, each city resident was using up to 90 gallons daily. Health conditions soon showed a dramatic improvement; the danger from fire was decreased; and property owners smiled at the higher real estate values and the lower insurance rates. New York's Croton System was the most modern in the United States and, as expanded over the decades, served as a model for the construction of other municipal waterworks. Croton also led to a public demand for sewers, which began to be fulfilled after 1849.

Perhaps the only area that showed little improvement was the volunteer firefighter system. Members of those companies adamantly opposed any innovation in an arrangement that guaranteed them income and importance. Since most fire-fighting companies were pillars of strength in the Democratic organization, Tammany successfully opposed all suggestions to create a metropolitan fire department. Not until 1865 was a paid, professional fire department created by the legislature and even then, only over the loud protests of the vested interests. Until that time, New Yorkers had to be temporarily satisfied with a few new fire engines, the installation of more efficient fire bell-warning stations, and greater cooperation among the numerous volunteer companies.

Even before Croton was completed, the next controversy involving public service had erupted, one made even more complex because of its relationship to the nativist issue. In 1840, Governor William Seward (1801–1872) had suggested that public money should be made available to support Roman Catholic public education in New York, an idea that attracted Bishop Hughes. On September 21, Hughes requested funds from New York's City Council and was informed that the Protestant-dominated Public School Society, a legacy of DeWitt Clinton, opposed the grants (as they had opposed grants to Protestant schools) as improper and probably unconstitutional. Hughes argued that the entire atmosphere and temper of the education available to Catholics attending public school was permeated with Protestant tenets, but his appeal was denied. For Catholics, the few schools built with parish donations were their only real alternative to a public education built on Protestant thinking.

Hughes's plea for public funds was rejected by a vote of fifteen to one. In retaliation, he organized a predominantly Catholic municipal ticket (the Carroll Hall slate) to demonstrate that Democrats could not win in New York if they lacked Catholic support. The alliance between the Catholic Irish and Tammany thus became solidified after 1841, even as the fears of city nativists grew. As a result of Hughes's pressure, a law was enacted appointing a public Board of Education to administer the city school system. It was tacitly understood that instruction was to become less overtly Protestant. The first ward school opened in 1843, and Catholics felt that they had won a significant victory, even though they had not won public financing of their separate schools.

During the years before the Civil War, the average schoolchild in New York City rarely went beyond grade school. Yet if quantity can be viewed as a mark of progress, by 1860 the public school system did enroll 90 percent of those children actually attending schools. There was, moreover, increasing demand that free instruction be offered at the secondary level, and in May 1846 the state legislature permitted the city's Board of Education to establish a free academy. Its first classes, which did not meet until 1849, were the precursors of the free City University system. The board also opened schools offering instruction for artisans and tradesmen specializing in practical subjects. The first free evening school was also established in 1849.

The 1850s saw the creation of several public high schools, and although their physical conditions and teaching standards were poor, they offered the first real alternative to private secondary education anywhere in urban America. In regard to higher education, only a tiny fraction of city residents attended college and usually did so outside New York. Nonetheless, a few institutions of higher learning were established. New York University was incorporated in 1831 as a nondenominational rival to Columbia's conservatism and Episcopal haughtiness. Union Theological Seminary was established in 1836 by "New School" Presbyterians as an alternative to the Episcopalian General Theological School, founded in 1817. Bishop Hughes founded St. John's College at Rose Hill in the Bronx in 1841, a school today known as Fordham University. These new schools had long paths of development before them, and with the exception of Columbia, New York higher education remained undistinguished until the late nineteenth century.

Regardless of which party elected New York's mayor or whatever that executive's personal attitudes, all candidates discovered that the demands of the public for more efficient municipal government had to be met. The best example of this new political reality was the nativist movement, formally organized as a political party in 1842 and successful in electing James Harper as mayor in 1844. Against all expectations, Harper spent little of his time excoriating the Irish or criticizing the cuisine of Kleindeutschland. Instead, his major preoccupation was creating a municipal police force. Until Harper's administration, residents of Manhattan were inadequately protected by an archaic police system that had evolved over two centuries. Among the defenders of public order were a night watch, one hundred appointed city marshals, thirty-one constables, sixteen daytime policemen, and an additional thirty-five men elected to serve as ward police. Although a legendary cop like High Constable Jacob Hays (1772–1850) might himself constitute a "one-man force," there was no doubt that a city of more than 320,000 people needed a more effective system of maintaining order, especially given the rise in public awareness of crime.

Some three years before Harper's election, the Common Council had authorized the industrialist Peter Cooper (1791–1883) to investigate the expediency of creating a corps of twelve hundred policemen. Cooper's proposals languished until May 7, 1844, when the state legislature gave final statutory approval to a municipal police system. The law abolished the night watch and gave Mayor Harper the right to appoint two hundred men to police the city. Because the legislation removed a time-honored source of local patronage and enhanced the mayor's power, New York's aldermen rejected the statute and substituted an ordinance that established three separate forces, each to be named by different levels of government. While the wrangling went on, the mayor selected his first two hundred men, and they immediately won approval as "Harper's police."

George W. Matsell, a bookseller turned police magistrate, was named first superintendent, and the blue-clad police began to patrol the streets. Because uniforms set them apart from ordinary citizens, the new officers found they often became the target of unprovoked attacks, and so they soon demanded the right to work in plain clothes. Exactly how Harper intended to develop the issues of police protection remains unclear, for in April 1845, he and his nativist allies were rejected by the voters. Democrat William Havemeyer took office, and on May 13, 1845, reorganized the entire police system, creating a force of eight hundred. Formal uniforms were temporarily abandoned, but station houses were established where patrolmen could be found and criminals detained. The city was divided into three districts, each of which had a court, magistrates, and clerks. The mayor appointed the chief of police and all captains with the advice of the Council, but the selection of policemen became a right of political leaders on the ward level. The New York Police Department had been born, and although its professionalization was still far in the future, there was at last reason to hope that city streets might become safe for the public.

Even though the streets might belong to the people, there could be no doubt that they were filthy. One of Havemeyer's major tasks was to overcome New York's well-deserved reputation for squalor, a reputation it maintained in disregard of innumerable regulations dating back to colonial days. Horses remained the main mode of transportation; pigs still scavenged in the streets; and cattle being driven to slaughterhouses contributed to the piles of manure that further fouled already dirty streets. Led by Havemeyer, the Common Council in 1845 enacted a comprehensive sanitation law that provided for the cleaning of the streets by means of mechanical devices and appointed an adequate staff of street and sanitation inspectors who would work conscientiously at their jobs.

For a few years, the law was obeyed, and real improvement was apparent. Garbage was collected and taken away in small carts; fines were levied on private citizens who did not clean their portion of the sidewalk; and health inspectors began to see to the proper cleaning, draining, and maintenance of privies and cesspools. Unfortunately, the political influence of private contractors who collected the garbage and refuse prevented the formation of a publicly owned and operated sanitation department until 1866. During this twenty-year period, the mayors who succeeded Havemeyer allowed his regulations to fall into a state of neglect. All during the 1850s, however, city-financed sewer construction and the systematic paving of Manhattan's streets generally improved the appearance of the city.

Such a basic amenity as paving was important because the city's growing population constantly filled the streets. New arrivals had overwhelmed the housing supply, and the lower part of Manhattan Island was filled from river to river. Immigrants settled as close to the existing job market as they could, and most businesses were clustered in the dock and warehouse area at the southern end of the island. Repelled by the hordes of laborers walking to work or seeking jobs, middle-class owners of homes and businesses began to relocate their families to the relative quiet of uptown addresses. Since real estate values were rapidly increasing, row housing replaced the traditional single-lot residence of earlier New York. The Washington Parade Ground was a preferred area for the new construction, and Gramercy Park was already an exclusive residential enclave. The turmoil of New York's traditional moving day, May 1, thus saw the uprooting of the old and the influx of the new as Manhattan's population groups rearranged themselves on their common island home.

Wherever the rich moved, they agreed that a better transportation system would be necessary to give them quick access to their place of business. The small six-passenger stages that once ruled New York's streets and made its traffic jams nationally famous were therefore replaced by omnibuses in the 1830s and by streetcars in the 1850s. Despite their larger capacity, traffic conditions continued to deteriorate. Moreover, railroads such as the New York and Harlem actually ran on rails laid flush with city streets until such traffic was banned in 1839. By 1858, the streetcar lines serving Manhattan carried 35 million passengers annually, the riders drawn from both workers and the upper classes. Although most New Yorkers still walked to work, as the century progressed the city inaugurated the age of mass public transport systems. It was evident that the growing transportation system demanded paved thoroughfares, and by the time of the Civil War, half the island had been covered over.

As New York extended northward, it eliminated forever its former rural quality. By the mid-1840s the ravages of the Great Fire had been eliminated, but tenements filled with immigrants had replaced the business warehouses of the Lower East Side. In that area of the city, grass and trees were virtually nonexistent. Although Bryant Park near the Croton Reservoir was enclosed in 1846 and Madison Square opened in 1847, both were small areas. It became suddenly apparent that no real public parklands graced the Manhattan landscape.

Many considered the salvaging of green space to be a private rather than a public responsibility, but as the city population (515,547 in 1850) continued to climb, the popular demand for common park facilities increased. Mayors Ambrose Kingsland and Jacob Westervelt both favored such an initiative, and in 1853, the state legislature approved the construction of a park of 760 acres on the wasteland "goose pasture" located north of present-day Fifty-ninth Street. In 1857, a national contest to design a Central Park for Manhattan was won by Frederick Law Olmstead (1822–1903) and Calvert Vaux (1824–1895). Andrew Green (1820–1903) was appointed president of the Park Commission, and work quickly began on what today is universally considered one of New York's most prized treasures. Much was accomplished in the first year of construction, since thousands of jobs were given to men unemployed because of the panic of 1857, but during the Civil War years, work virtually halted. It took twenty years for the vast project to be completed, but the grandeur of its design and the integrity of its implementation have made Central Park America's model for urban green space.

In antebellum New York, the primary concern of the party holding power was the creation of a suitable urban environment for the people of an important world metropolis. Whether a mayor won office as a Locofoco, Whig, Hunker, or Nativist, he found that his popularity and future prospects depended on his ability to bring water, sanitation services, police protection, or parks to city residents. The voters proved to be stern critics, and few mayors were granted more than a single reelection during these decades when New York became modern. Progress was not only a matter of municipal or mayoral initiative. In 1837, after eight years of experimentation, Samuel Morse exhibited the first successful electric telegraph; five years later, he supervised the laying of a submarine cable between Governor's Island and Manhattan. By 1846, a telegraph line to Philadelphia opened for public use. The nation had suddenly become much smaller, a shrinking that also became apparent as rail connections knit Manhattan to the nation. Perhaps a dozen railroads depended on the commerce of New York, and after 1853 Commodore Cornelius Vanderbilt (1794–1877), whose first fortune grew out of steamships, began to consolidate many of them into the Grand Central Rail System.

But the sea remained the key to New York's trade, and in 1840, one-fifth of all American shipping was owned by New Yorkers. The 113 docks on the East and Hudson Rivers provided thousands of jobs for both artisans and unskilled immigrants. Steam packet service with Europe had been established in 1838, and the Cunard Lines moved to New York from Boston a year later because the lucrative transatlantic business was now centered there. But despite the many smokestacks in the bay, the most envied workers on the docks were those artisans and sailors who worked on the famed clipper ships. Constructed and launched along the East River, the clipper ships were perhaps the loveliest of all commercial vessels. The clipper age was short (1843 to 1860) but immensely profitable for a few. Spurred by the repeal of Britain's Corn Laws in 1846 and the discovery of gold in California in 1848, fleet vessels such as the *Rainbow* could earn a 200-percent return on a single voyage. The *Flying Cloud* set speed records that caused people to shake their heads in wonder. South Street, that "forest of masts," illustrated the commercial supremacy of New York. It is interesting that modern Manhattan is attempting to recapture the glory of that age in its South Street Seaport Museum, which opened in July 1983.

Beyond its municipal growth, its economic development, and its cosmopolitanism, New York participated in the "democratic ferment" that marked Jacksonian America. Reform in virtually all areas of social life made the age one of change, and some city residents joined crusades against the evils of society. In New York the temperance movement probably aroused the most passion. Alcohol was identified with immigrants and condemned by reformers as the major cause of poverty, ruined health, and criminal behavior. Throughout the city, unlicensed establishments sold liquor to anyone with enough money for a drink, and "hole In the wall" saloons operated openly in defiance of statewide laws prohibiting the sale of liquor without licenses.

During the 1840s, as excessive drinking became commonplace among all classes, the temperance movement grew, especially among Protestants. In an inevitable counterstroke, it was Tammany that organized legitimate liquor dealers into the Protective Union to oppose ordinances against drink. The union successfully opposed any statutory action by the city fathers. The influx of whisky-drinking Irishmen and beer-loving Germans made distilling and brewing big business, and hundreds of New York hotels, boardinghouses, and restaurants relied on sales of liquor to turn a profit. The iron triangle connection among dealers, hostelries, and City Hall was strong. Meetings might be held and temperance rallies might evoke enthusiastic responses among the committed, but in the 1850s liquor interests mobilized foreign-born voters into a strong anti-temperance bloc. More than five thousand city establishments sold liquor, and many grogshop owners were ward heelers in political organizations. Thus despite the hopes of those reformers who hoped to banish "Demon Rum" and eliminate forever the "face on the barroom floor," New York City took no action to prohibit drinking.

New Yorkers also remained largely aloof from the abolitionist movement. Downtown Manhattan was home to Arthur and Lewis Tappan, owners of the *New York Journal of Commerce*, who contributed prodigious amounts of time, effort, and money to national abolition efforts after 1831, but most citizens were not interested in the antislavery crusade. Only in the 1840s, as the controversy became more heated because of territorial expansion, did more New Yorkers embrace the antislavery cause. The Democratic Party split after the Mexican War, and a radical group called the Barnburners formed within Tammany Hall. The Barnburners were hostile to banks, to increases in the state debt, and especially opposed to the extension of slavery into free territories. As their name implied, if they could not control the Democratic barn, they would willingly burn it down, and their principled split from the more pragmatic Hunkers shook the foundations of Tammany Hall. The party's division over abolitionism cleared the way for the election of the Whig candidate for mayor in 1847 and ushered in a period of Democratic decline. Irish voters were largely unsympathetic to abolitionism, as they were already competing for jobs with free blacks. German immigrants were more sympathetic to the cause, and in time, many left the Democratic Party and became Republicans. Thus the slavery issue, though peripheral to the daily concerns of the city and the majority of its citizens, nonetheless had a great impact on New York because it led to the rupture of the Tammany organization.

Temperance and abolitionism aroused the greatest interest, but they were not the only causes championed by progressive New York in the antebellum years. Many specific reforms derived from the sympathy of the "better classes" for the plight of recently arrived immigrants. For example, in 1836, John McDowell organized the New York Magdalen Society to help Manhattan's prostitutes, and six years later, Thomas Eddy and John Griscom founded the New York House of Refuge, the United States' first juvenile reformatory. A Catholic priest, Felix Varela, founded two churches, two schools, and an orphange to help Irish immigrants. In 1843, the Association for Improving the Condition of the Poor was established, and in 1848, the New York Ladies' Home Missionary Society of the Methodist Episcopal Church made plans to reform the notorious "Five Points" section. In time, the "Five Points" Mission and the "Five Points" House of Industry were created to serve the Irish. In 1853, socially aware New Yorkers established the New York Juvenile Asylum to cope with the problem of vagrant children, and in the same year, the Children's Aid Society was founded by Charles Loring Brace (1826–1890). For some dedicated Manhattanites, pauperism, relief for the poor, care of the insane, improvement of prisons and local jails, and equal rights for women all were urgent concerns. Although the reformers did not always achieve their goals, they did win some significant victories, and their personal commitment and public accomplishments contributed to the development of New York's social consciousness.

By the mid-1850s, New York had become the greatest city in the nation. In the generation since the opening of the Erie Canal, its population had risen beyond 700,000, and the influx of immigrants still showed no signs of abating. Phenomenal growth, continued economic strength, and cultural maturity were the hallmarks of the age. New York had been transformed from a cohesive geographical and economic unit into a sprawling, untidy giant. The diverse economic, ethnic, and racial groups making up its large population had little in common except that they all were New Yorkers and somehow had to learn to coexist. The municipal government, a product of eighteenth-century philosophy, suddenly was forced to cope with problems created by growth, technological change, and the need to acculturate thousands of new citizens. With a few notable exceptions, New York's public officials were undistinguished leaders forced to deal with unprecedented issues of crime, disease, poverty, and development. That they managed as well as they did and made significant progress in providing essential services to all New Yorkers is amazing. The city may not have been mastered, but at least there was hope that it might yet be controlled.

What seemed most urgently needed was the development of greater political and social coordination through effective leadership. Leaders had to be found who could respond positively and effectively to the city's changing economic and social conditions. No longer could municipal offices be staffed by one-dimensional, albeit public-minded, merchants or aristocrats. New York's leaders would now have to be men with a different views of municipal government, professional politicians who viewed public service as a legitimate career. Even leaders interested in power and personal aggrandizement might well be able to serve the varying economic, political, and social interests of New York's vast, heterogeneous population. Beginning in 1854, with the rise to political prominence of Fernando Wood, the city did begin to receive this new kind of leadership. New York's "bosses" had a greater effect on the city's society and government than did any other men of their time.

5

The Age of the Bosses

From 1830 to 1860, the city of New York quadrupled in size, becoming both America's dominant city and a major factor in the pattern of world trade, despite a ramshackle government and weak administration. The city had obtained the right to select its own mayor in 1834, but that official was not granted even a two-year term until the charter revision of 1849. Yet somehow Manhattan incorporated hundreds of thousands of immigrants, drew the commerce of the nation and globe toward its bustling harbor, and provided its citizens with a better quality of life than any astute observer would have thought possible. To a large extent, the city's growth resulted from the ambition of its individual members; the larger corporate body proved far harder to incite to action. The several New Yorkers who learned to manipulate and move the government effectively were awarded the label of *bosses*. The political careers of Fernando Wood (1812–1881), William Marcy Tweed (1823–1878), and "Honest" John Kelly (1822–1886) dominated the political life of the city for thirty years and gave it a reputation for municipal corruption and political chicanery that long endured. These bosses were opportunists, political pragmatists, and implacable enemies to those who opposed them, but each was more than simply a plunderer of the public.

Although there were many factors causing bossism, the increasing public demand for urban services was perhaps the most crucial to its emergence. To provide such innovations as sewers, clean water, transportation systems, and police and sanitation departments cost vast amounts of public money. In the twentieth century, we have become accustomed to "special-interest" politics and "iron triangles" of bureaucratic/business/ governmental influence. Thus it is hardly surprising that midcentury America created alliances between the city officials who awarded construction contracts and the utility franchises and businessmen who sought those lucrative plums. Bribery emerged as a variable but certain cost of business in Manhattan, and law enforcement officers closed their eyes to corruption and crime; it was not only profitable for them to do so but sometimes also necessary. New York's bosses found their most loyal support among immigrant voters. In return for votes, bosses provided the new citizens with municipal functions not usually performed by agencies of government.

In recent times, films, plays, and novels have tended to over-romanticize municipal machines and their great bosses, but the system that they operated arose from necessity. Often it performed nobly. In 1837, for example, the food baskets distributed by Tammany Hall—at a time when no boss ruled—kept hundreds of people from destitution. Charity and comradeship were as essential to the boss and his machine as were contracts and commissions. Democracy had transformed politics into a mass participation sport, and the bosses understood this before anyone else. They remained in charge as long as they met the public's demands. Because of their usefulness and insight, bosses ruled New York politics for a century.

The 1850s were a time of political disintegration and sectional animosity, culminating in the Civil War. New York was hardly immune to such epic concerns, and the disorder of national politics had a major impact on city life. As the decade began, the U.S. Congress agreed on the compromise of 1850, the last great attempt to settle the slavery and territorial issues dividing the nation. Although the national Democratic Party endorsed the compromise, many New Yorkers found the legislation unacceptable. Dissidents from the national consensus included not only abolitionists but also Democratic Barnburners and "conscience" Whigs.

Instead, it was the conservative, mercantile Whigs of New York—whose prosperity and future depended on continued trade with the South—who took the initiative of supporting the compromise. In October 1850, they sponsored a mass meeting which urged that the entire business community, regardless of political affiliation, endorse the provisions of the compromise as good for the city. After hurried consultations, a Union electoral ticket was agreed on, won the endorsement of ten thousand merchants and firms, and swept to victory on November 5, 1850. The theme of the merchants' campaign was Save the Union, and the appeal won citywide support because New Yorkers were deeply frightened by the divisiveness of the slavery controversy. The Union ticket, led by Mayor Ambrose Kingsland (1804–1878), restored calm to the city and initiated a period of four years of business domination.

New York had always been a "city of commerce," so it was natural that businessmen should seek and obtain a respite from conflict. But the larger reality of the early 1850s was that party lines across America were fading under the pressures that were beginning to convulse the nation. As the moral issue of slavery and unending discussions about the nature of the Union increasingly predominated, the ties of party loyalty snapped. By the end of the decade, only the Democratic Party was left as a national political organization, and its influence alone was not sufficient to prevent civil war.

The fragmented party structure was already apparent in New York's coalition election of 1850, and it remained broken for the rest of the decade. But unlike the national scene, which rewarded weak figures such as Franklin Pierce and James Buchanan, in New York the breakdown of party structure offered opportunities to stronger leaders. It was an unfocused, disordered, and confused age, one tailor-made for an independent and self-centered operator. Mayor Kingsland himself proved to be less committed to Whigery than he was to personal gain, and he soon allied with Democratic members of the Board of Aldermen to enrich themselves and their associates at public expense. Indeed, so blatant were the overcharges that by 1852 the city councilmen were better known as the "Forty Thieves." Compared with future depredations, however, the corruption of the Kingsland regime was relatively insignificant, and its padding of city accounts by thousands of dollars was minor. But so intense was the public reaction that Kingsland was forced into retirement in 1852. The Citizens' Committee, led by Peter Cooper, also saw that many of the Democratic aldermen were involuntarily retired. A revision of the municipal charter in 1853 removed franchise-granting powers from the City Council and restricted the appointment power of the aldermen. Perhaps the most inventive of those ousted officials, a young Tammany partisan named Bill Tweed, landed on his feet and spent a term in Congress from 1853 to 1855. There he discovered that his taste ran to municipal rather than national politics, and so he returned to Manhattan, where he set his sights on a level of power higher than that accessible to an alderman.

Temporarily, however, the purity of reform ruled in Manhattan, and the city could bask in both rectitude and continued growth. The 1853 edition of the *Stranger's Handbook for New York* listed 272 churches, 8 marketplaces, 25 Broadway hotels, and 7 theaters to serve tourists and businessmen. Tourists could visit Castle Garden, the newly opened Hippodrome, and Barnum's world-famous museum or even climb the 350–foot tower of the Latting Observatory. Built of timber and braced with iron, the observatory was the tallest structure so far built in America and perhaps qualifies as New York's first skyscraper. At its base, the observatory was filled with expensive shops, and a steam elevator took visitors to the upper landings where telescopes were installed for public use. Yet for all its tourist appeal, the Latting Observatory was only an adjunct to the major city attraction of 1853, the first American World's Fair.

This huge exhibition was opened by President Franklin Pierce on July 14, in a vast structure on Forty-second Street, the Crystal Palace. The fair had more than six thousand exhibits from the United States, Canada, the West Indies, and most of the nations of Europe. It ran for sixteen months, and after it closed, the palace was used for concerts, balls, banquets, and local fairs. Unfortunately, in 1856 the observatory burned down, and in 1858, in less than twenty minutes, the supposedly fireproof Crystal Palace became an "incandescent ruin."

In 1854, the disintegration apparent in municipal politics intensified, and the precipitating factor once again was national affairs, specifically the introduction into Congress of Stephen A. Douglas's Kansas-Nebraska Act. Since this measure virtually nullified the Missouri Compromise of 1820 and reopened all the debates regarding slavery, its condemnation by most New York merchants is not difficult to understand. Manhattan's business community led the anti-Nebraska opinion in America, yet despite all its arguments, Douglas's measure became law on May 30. Politically, the legislation wiped out the surviving remnant of Whigs, leading to the formation of the Republican Party, and forced the Barnburner Democrats to leave their party. The resulting chaos in the city provided the breeding ground for New York's first Tammany Hall boss. National crises and party structures might come and go, but the Hall's desire to elect the mayor of New York was a constant on which everyone could rely.

Fernando Wood was one of the most charming rogues ever to serve as mayor of New York. In his later years, he adopted a debonair and elegant bearing, but that pose was far removed from his origins and character. The son of a cigar maker, Wood successively owned a cigar shop, ran a dockside tavern, and operated a fleet of sailing vessels, managing to amass a fortune before the age of forty. He served a term in Congress as a loyal follower of Tammany, and in 1850, as an adventurer just back from San Francisco and the gold rush, he ran for mayor, only to lose to the Whig coalition. His already rather unsavory reputation did not help his cause, and diarist Philip Hone noted that "the incumbent of this office should be at least an honest man. Fernando Wood, instead of occupying the mayor's seat, ought to be on the rolls of the State prison."

By 1854, however, Wood had somewhat overcome his past reputation and was acting as conciliator to bring together all the diverse groups within the Democratic spectrum. Although his loyalty to Tammany was certain, Wood tapped into voters' anger at the Forty Thieves and spoke the language of reform. Historically, it was one of Tammany Hall's most endearing traits that it periodically demanded a purging of the system, a cleansing that only it could administer. In 1854, Wood's campaign promised to restore lost honor to city politics. He promised also to obtain from Albany greater home rule for the city, to limit both prostitution and gambling, and get animals off the city streets. On November 7, he was elected because the Irish Sixth Ward cast four hundred more votes for him than it had registered voters. The first of New York's modern bosses came to power in a fashion soon to become familiar.

Despite the fears of patricians who knew Wood's reputation and perhaps even in the face of Tammany's expectations, Wood's first term proved exceptionally beneficial to New York. The new mayor used the charter reforms of 1853 to justify a consolidation of executive authority, and he actually did prohibit the archaic practice of driving cattle through the city streets. More significantly, Wood effectively championed the cause of Central Park, created a "complaint book" for citizens' gripes, ordered that prostitutes spend at least one night in jail if arrested, and put the municipal police into uniforms so that it became more difficult for them to leave the scene of a crime without acting. The mayor made speeches endorsing temperance, but he did not enforce saloon closings because he believed, correctly, that the law was unconstitutional. His inaction won him Irish votes. He made city land available to the diocese of New York so that construction of St. Patrick's could proceed, thus obtaining Archbishop Hughes's support for his next campaign. He made the upper classes happy when he moved to prevent the immigration of paupers and criminals into the city, and in 1855, his administration facilitated the transformation of Castle Garden into an immigrant-processing station physically separated from the city. On August 3, the first shiploads of new arrivals were processed there, and over the next thirty-seven years Castle Garden was the reception area through which almost 8 million people entered the United States. In all, the apprehensions that had attended Wood's election seemed unfounded as he acted the part of a "model mayor." Although he had strengthened his executive power and authority, his efficient administration had won wide support.

The first Wood administration brought contentment and order to Manhattan, but there was no such respite in sectional tensions. The mayor's pro-Southern attitude was well known, for both he and Tammany Hall recognized how the city's prosperity depended upon the cotton trade and its credit needs. After the passage of the Kansas-Nebraska Act, however, more

New Yorkers than ever seemed to regard the South, its aristocratic leaders, and its "peculiar institution" as a national curse. Raising funds to "save" Kansas and oppose slavery thus became relatively easy in New York after 1854, and some city residents went so far as to actively support Eli Thayer's Emigrant Aid Society (which provided Kansas's settlers with guns called Beecher's Bibles) and participate in the clandestine operations of the Underground Railroad.

Henry Ward Beecher of Brooklyn's Plymouth Church was perhaps the most outspoken of the area's clergymen in his condemnation of slavery, but equally influential was the editorial support for slavery's limitation provided by Greeley of the *Tribune*, Bryant of the *Evening Post*, and Raymond of the *Times*. A metropolitan campaign to raise funds for "the suffering free men of Kansas" was successful in the summer of 1856, even though it won little support from any major political figure. Yet despite these changed attitudes, city voters in the presidential election of 1856 supported James Buchanan, the Democratic candidate. Although there might be increasing distaste for slavery, the city as a whole did not want the Republican Party to occupy the White House. The Republican platform seemed to menace both the Union and New York's trade. In fact, half of Wood's annual message of 1856 dealt with the dangerous national situation and with New York City's commitment to "free trade."

After a successful first term, it seemed certain that Wood would run again in 1856, but his achievements caused a falling out between himself and Tammany. The mayor complained that his commissioners—all originally drawn from Tammany—were too independent and unconcerned with efficiency. In May 1856, after his candidate for the grand sachem of Tammany Hall lost, he allowed his supporters to ask publicly if "the sachems or the people" should rule in New York. Vicious infighting broke out within Tammany that autumn as Wood struggled with the sachems. Wood also discovered that a strong Know-Nothing candidate was planning to enter the contest against him. November's mayoral race became one of the most complex in New York's history, as five candidates and their supporters literally fought for control of the city government. When the battles ended, Wood had won reelection, but his position in Tammany was shattered. Alienated from his parent organization, Wood now radically changed his attitude toward government. He adopted the accounting methods of the Forty Thieves and the organizational techniques of Tammany Hall. His second term thus featured the open sale of offices and contracts, the blatant padding of bills, and the use of his executive power to benefit the bank accounts of the mayor and his family. In addition to graft, Wood's tenure after 1857 was marked by controversy, riots, and economic disaster.

One crucial factor in Wood's transformation from model mayor to spoiler was the desire of Republican Governor John King to assert state control over New York City. King wanted to reduce the home rule that Manhattan had gained in the charter of 1853 and so decided to focus on creating a new police system, one that "the legislature will hesitate to entrust" to Wood. Municipal reformers in New York, most of whom now were Republicans, did believe there had been an increase in police corruption in Wood's uniformed force and thus supported the governor's plan. Accordingly, on April 14, the legislature abolished the Municipal Police and created the Metropolitan Police, to be run by five commissioners (appointed by the governor with the consent of the state senate).

In effect, the city was denied its own police force and the patronage opportunities it provided. Then the legislature went even further and decreed that a special mayoral election be held in December 1857, arbitrarily cutting Wood's term in half. All this constituted an unwarranted attack on metropolitan home rule, and Wood—with the support of many concerned New Yorkers—decided to resist. When the new law became effective on May 25, he refused to surrender any police stations or to order the disbanding of the "Municipals." When King's newly appointed officials attempted to take control of the force, they were expelled from City Hall by Wood's loyal Municipals under Chief George Matsell. Matters came to a head in June when the "Battle of the Ms"—Metropolitans versus Municipals—took place in City Hall Park. Peace was restored only by the intervention of the Seventh Regiment. For a time, "criminals ruled the streets," and there were gang battles in the Bowery while the two police forces did their best to avoid acting against anyone except the opposing faction. Not until the court of appeals rendered a decision in July did Wood disband his force. Although the Metropolitans won a belated civil judgment against Wood, the bill for mayoral transgressions was paid by the city taxpayers. It is interesting, however, that five of the six judges who upheld Governor King's action were Democrats. Wood's independence and greed had totally separated him from the Tammany organization by the summer of 1857.

Summer also brought economic trouble to the regime of the once model mayor. In the decade since the end of the Mexican War, America had experienced a speculative boom in railroad construction, expansion of wheat acreage, and state banking institutions. The opening of the California gold fields and the nationwide growth in manufacturing capacity made entrepreneurs dream of quick wealth. New York investors plunged into the expansion of manufacturing and the construction of clipper ships. Then in August, the liberal credit policies that had fueled the boom suddenly ended after the unexpected failure of the Ohio Insurance Company. The collapse of the Cincinnati concern rippled throughout the East, and business failures in Manhattan alone numbered about a thousand. City banks were forced to suspend specie payments, and one estimate stated that one-seventh of the city was receiving charity. Several thousand unemployed artisans marched through the streets demanding that they be given bread and that construction jobs in Central Park be made available to them. The militia had to be mobilized several times to reinforce the Metropolitan Police, and not until December 12, when the banks resumed specie payments, did the disturbances end.

But the greatest of Wood's troubles was his feud with Tammany Hall. The mayor, taking full advantage of his right to name the heads of executive agencies, filled them with men loyal to him and not to the Tammany society. Scores of offices had been virtually auctioned off to the highest bidder, with the tacit understanding that the buyer could recoup his investment at the expense of the city. Fraudulent street-cleaning contracts and dozens of unsavory real estate transactions provided lucrative returns, but only for Wood's adherents, not for Tammany Hall politicians.

Although Wood controlled the official Democratic nomination, Tammany Hall and its rising young leader, William Marcy Tweed, decided that he had to be stopped. In a stunning reversal of the club's traditional party loyalty, Tammany decided to oppose the "regular" Democratic ticket with its own nominee, an alderman named Daniel Tiemann. Thus in the special election of December 1857, Wood had to fight the influence of the governor, the effects of the panic, and the combined opposition of Tammany's sachems. Tiemann was presented as a reform candidate and obtained some Know Nothing and even Republican support, but even more important was the fact that Tweed mobilized the Bowery Boys and other Irish gangs against Wood. In a bitter and violent election, Wood was defeated by 2,327 votes. After Tiemann took office in April, the "model mayor" announced his withdrawal from Tammany and the creation of a personal political organization he called Mozart Hall. He told Democratic leaders, "I am henceforth and forever against Tammany . . . now let them beware."

Nothing was sweeter to Tammany Hall than the opportunity to run for office under a cloak of reform, but a problem it had not anticipated was that Tiemann, a rather well-to-do man, actually believed the rhetoric. Although personally honest, the new mayor quickly proved himself to be a political incompetent, incapable of carrying out reforms within the administration. While Tiemann was floundering about and opposing the demands of Tweed's Tammany organization, Wood meticulously constructed a rival machine. Tiemann was embarrassed when a fireworks display in August 1858, celebrating the completion of the Atlantic cable, also succeeded in igniting the cupola, dome, and roof of City Hall. His discomfiture was increased when a court decree approved the sale of City Hall in October to pay a debt that had been contracted by the Wood administration. Although Tiemann personally purchased the structure for $228,000, a sum for which he was later reimbursed, the incident brought him little honor and much ridicule. Not surprisingly, he was refused the Tammany Hall Democratic nomination in 1859.

The election of 1859 offered Wood a chance to return to power as a man who understood and cared for the common citizens of New York. By a strange quirk, he was the poorest man in the race, for the Republicans nominated millionaire clothier George Opdyke, and the Tammany ticket, still flaunting the label of reform, was headed by sugar millionaire and former mayor William Havemeyer. As a result, Wood was the candidate with the most appeal to ordinary people, who remembered his relatively effective public assistance programs in the bleak fall of 1857. The the "model mayor" who now bossed Mozart Hall won the support of most of the Irish and, by a margin of three thousand votes, became the leader of New York City for the third time. When Wood took office on January 1, 1860, his executive departments were led by Tiemann holdovers, and those jobs were secure, since the Board of Aldermen was still ruled by Tammany men. Thus, factional politics continued, and the government of a city with 814,000 citizens remained inefficient and corrupt. Wood claimed he had been reduced to a "functionary" in their service, but he nonetheless continued to make deals that added to his wealth. There is no evidence that Wood took to heart Abraham Lincoln's "House Divided" speech, which the president delivered at Cooper Union on February 21, 1860. Although he was mayor as the nation moved toward the horror of civil war, Wood seemed solely concerned with himself; "his patriotism never seemed to reach beyond the limits of Manhattan Island."

During the presidential race of 1860, both Wood and the Tammany organization agreed that abolitionism rather than slavery was the cause of America's difficulties. In good demagogic fashion, Wood denounced the Republican Party as a "fiend which stalks within the narrow barrier of its

Northern cage" and contrasted this with the nationwide support enjoyed by Democratic candidates. Both Wood and Tammany did their best to elect Stephen A. Douglas in 1860, and the "Little Giant" received twice as many votes in Manhattan as did Lincoln, although the Republicans carried New York State. Wood sincerely believed that much of New York's prosperity depended on its Southern connections and that an accommodation with the planter aristocracy was in the city's best interest.

After Lincoln's election—indeed after South Carolina had seceded—this belief led to an extraordinary mayoral message to the Common Council on January 7, 1861. Wood suggested that Manhattan, in combination with Staten Island and Long Island, secede from the United States and become an independent city-state. The financial basis of this new entity would be secure because of its trade dominance and the enormous tariffs it was certain to collect. Although most people ridiculed the idea, it did not become "outrageous" until war erupted in the spring and buried the plan.

When the South fired on Fort Sumter, Wood proved capable of reversing himself. He ordered Mozart Hall to organize a volunteer regiment and waved the flag of patriotism as fervently as anyone else did. But he never really seemed to favor active prosecution of the war, and the conflict marked the end of his career as Manhattan's leading political figure. His ambivalence toward the Union tinged Mozart Hall with treason, and when the mayor sought reelection in December 1861, he finished third. His only accomplishment was to cost Tammany Hall the election by splitting the Democratic vote. In time-honored fashion, Wood now made a deal with the organization he had so long fought. Tammany Hall agreed to pay Wood's campaign debts and to nominate him to Congress in 1862 if he removed himself from city politics. Duly elected to Congress, Wood became a leader of the nation's "Peace Democrats" for the duration of the war. He ultimately served eight terms in Congress and became influential in currency and tariff policy.

The Tammany sachem who negotiated Wood's departure was William M. Tweed, a leader who soon was the first Tammany man to be publicly acknowledged as "boss." E. L. Godkin (1831–1902) later wrote in *The Nation* that "if Wood was the Ring's Caesar, Tweed was its Augustus." Yet as with the model mayor, there was little in his early career that set Bill Tweed apart from other roughnecks laboring for Tammany Hall. Tweed was born on April 3, 1823, on Cherry Street, the youngest of six children born to Scottish parents. Young Bill was bored by school, and as an apprentice in his father's chair-making concern, he also had difficulty with hard work. His attempt to establish his own firm collapsed, in part because of his brother's drinking and in part because Bill was far more interested in the operation of the local fire brigade than he was in his own company. It was as the leader of the "Big Six" Americus Engine Company that the 270-pound Tweed found happiness. He had the knack of getting to the water supply first and worked harder at quenching fires than he ever did on the job. His fire brigade prospered, and bluff, gregarious Bill Tweed was soon contemplating a political career.

It was traditional for fire companies—compact units of men with lots of relatives and similar attitudes—to provide candidates for Tammany Hall slates, and by this route Tweed entered politics. In 1851, he served as alderman, and was given credit by most reporters for orchestrating the activities of the Forty Thieves. Later as boss, Tweed reminisced for the *New York Herald* that "there never was a time when you couldn't buy the Board of Aldermen." Tweed's single term in Congress had given him a dislike of Washington; he wanted only to manage New York. In 1855, he served on the Board of Education and discovered how money could be made from textbook contracts and teacher bribes. As a supervisor of public works from 1857 to 1870, his eyes were opened to magnificent vistas of unending payoffs. Tweed organized the Tammany Hall faction that opposed the Wood regime, and it was clear that his purpose was not good government but, rather, the replacement of one boss by another. He made alliances with men such as Peter Sweeny (1825–1911), Richard Connolly, A. Oakey Hall (1826–1898), and Judge George C. Barnard, and by 1861 the coalition succeeded in expelling Wood from New York. The cost was minor, only a congressional nomination and two years of Republican rule, and the prize was New York City. The nation was still fighting its Civil War, but Tweed was already victorious. The age of the Ring, "a hard band in which there is gold all around," was beginning.

In politics, the word *boss* is not considered an insult, and the title was being applied to Tweed even before Wood finally left. Tweed had been made chairman of the Democratic Central Committee of New York County in 1860 and set about making that group synonymous with Tammany Hall itself; it was the completion of this procedure that made him the boss. By astute political dealing, Tweed and "Brains" Sweeny won control of Tammany's General Committee, gaining dictatorial power over party nominations as well as appointments to judicial posts. In 1862, A. Oakey Hall became New York's district attorney to ensure the Ring's legal invulnerability. On January 1, 1863, Tweed was made permanent chairman of the Executive Committee of the Tammany Society; all the other sachems who were elected were his allies. Finally in July—even as riots against conscription convulsed New York—Tweed became the grand sachem of Tammany Hall. The structure of the Ring was thus in place, even though Tammany itself was out of power. In December 1863, the mayoral campaign resulted in the selection of a Democratic mayor, C. Godfrey Gunther, an "Independent Democrat" who was a poor politician. His replacement in the next election marked the final closing of the Ring.

The Tweed Ring is instantly identified in the minds of Americans as the epitome of municipal corruption, but no one knows how much money was stolen and almost everyone agrees that substantial contributions were made to city life during its ascendancy. Graft is never a one-way street. It is true that Tweed and his cohorts were greedy for money, but reputable companies and citizens had to pay them and willingly did so. What sets Tweed's Ring apart from the ordinary corruption was the order and coherence that this boss brought to the payoff process. Tweed succeeded in extending graft to virtually every corner of the system and saw that the benefits of criminal activity were widely dispersed. If everyone did it, how could there be guilt? Tweed's genius was to regularize and bureaucratize an empire of graft, an empire that for a brief time was all-encompassing.

In 1863, in addition to his Tammany duties and his place on the Board of Supervisors, Tweed assumed the post of deputy street commissioner. Each of these positions gave him an opportunity to name legions of workers, and a system of job-related payoffs was instituted. In his post as deputy street commissioner, for example, there were not only street-cleaning contracts to let but also substantial revenues to be gained in "fees" related to street openings. As the city expanded farther northward, these charges were lucrative indeed. The Ring elected its first mayor, John T. Hoffman (1828–1888), in December 1865, and its control of municipal finance was assured when "Brains" Sweeny became city chamberlain and "Slippery Dick" Connolly advanced to the comptroller's office. Contractors to the city soon understood that a 10 percent kickback had to be added to any bid they made. In time, this percentage rose—to 15, 50, 60, and, in some contracts, an astronomical 85 percent. The existence of the payoffs was an open secret yet initially it produced as little outrage as well-publicized Department of Defense "cost overruns" do in modern America. By 1867, Tweed was already a millionaire.

As the system of Ring levies became well established, a tacit division of labor formed in the organization. Sweeny was in charge of judicial nominations; Connolly took care of financial accounts; and Hall advised the group on legislation and legal matters. Tweed presided over all with the calm of a field marshal and the largesse of a potentate. When he was asked in 1870 to contribute Christmas baskets to the Seventh Ward, he gladly wrote out a check for $5,000, only to be begged for "another nought." Without a blink, Tweed added another zero, and the Seventh had quite a Christmas. The boss was lavish, fun loving, and generous, and many persons in the city he ruled shared in the benefits.

Between 1865 and 1871, the Tweed Ring enjoyed virtually complete control of New York City's financial life. All contracts were padded, and the face amount was paid by City Auditor James Watson to the contractor, who then repaid 10 to 85 percent of it in cash. Watson, who acted as the Ring's paymaster, then distributed specific shares of the stolen money to the various members of the inner circle. Probably the most notorious example of this system was provided by one of the Ring's favorite henchmen, Andrew J. Garvey, who did much of the plastering work for the city of New York. His bills were so high that it was said that he could have plastered all of Europe at the same price and still made a profit. In two years' time, Garvey charged the city almost $3 million for plastering work, nearly 60 percent of which was kicked back to the Tweed Ring. No wonder the *New York Times* called him the "Prince of Plasterers." But colossal frauds were also perpetrated in connection with stationery supplies, whose bills for two years were $2.28 million. Tweed personally profited from all the printing done for the city, for he owned the printing company that performed the work.

The most infamous example of the Ring's plundering took place in the construction and furnishing of the New York City courthouse, which still stands at the northern edge of City Hall Park. John Kellum designed a three-story structure to cost $350,000, and work began on the project in 1862. But the advent of the Ring changed the function of the building into a conduit by which public funds could be transferred to Tweed and his associates: before the building opened, its total costs approached $13 million. Thermometers cost $7,500 each; brooms were a steal at $41,190.95; and carpeting costs could have covered the entire expanse of City Hall Park several times over. Bills were paid on Sundays with checks written to men such as I. C. Cash, and at least five dead men were on the janitorial staff. Before its completion, the courthouse cost New York almost four times as much as the House of Parliament cost Great Britain.

The larceny and fraud that characterized Ring operations were possible only because of its total control of the electoral process. The decades-old alliance between Tammany and the immigrants, particularly the Irish, was now unbreakable. The first city election in which 100,000 votes were cast occurred in 1867, and the machine added to its vote totals each year by effecting mass naturalizations, a process simplified by the Ring's control of the courts. New York had always experienced rowdy elections, but in the Ring's heyday, ballots were stolen, boxes of votes were lost or deposited in the rivers, "repeaters" were imported, violence kept opponents from the polls, and several wards regularly exceeded their total of registered voters. Tweed had himself named to the state senate in 1867, made Hoffman governor in 1868, saw Hall become mayor in 1869, and smiled all the time.

Despite charges of gross electoral fraud, nothing could be proved, and by 1869 the Ring controlled not only New York City but also both houses of the state legislature. In 1870, when Governor Hoffman was reelected, Republicans reclaimed the legislature, but even this loss proved to be only a minor setback. Tweed believed that everyone had his price, and suitcases full of cash were soon on their way to Albany to purchase Ring domination. The municipal debt soared, as did taxes, but there was little demand for change or reform in these years of the Ring's hegemony.

How did Tweed get away with such blatant fraud? A good part of the answer seems to be that the Ring and its masters could "point with pride" to substantial improvements in the municipal government. In 1865, the old system of volunteer fire companies was abolished and the Metropolitan Fire District (Manhattan and Brooklyn) was created to be served by uniformed, salaried, professional firefighters. Early in 1866, the city became part of the Metropolitan Sanitary District, and the Board of Health was created to deal with the centuries-old issue of communicable disease. City money was made available to subsidize both Mount Sinai Hospital and Catholic education; in fact, Protestant Tweed provided more than $1.4 million for Catholic schools over a three-year period. State Senator Tweed introduced bills that incorporated the Metropolitan Museum of Art, the New York Stock Exchange, and the Lenox Library. As supervisor he saw that Broadway was widened, removed the fencing around public parks, constructed public bathhouses, authorized Riverside Park and Drive, and participated in the early planning of the Brooklyn Bridge. It was true that problems of poorly maintained wharves and streets, insufficient housing, ineffective public transit, and inadequate sewers continued, but these were problems that predated Tweed and outlasted his Ring. Citizens could boast of new clubs, the first elevated train, an extraordinary new Tammany Hall, and the Museum of Natural History as continued proof of their city's dominance. Inertia and the desire for calm and stability after the agony of the Civil War also played roles in the overwhelming acceptance that the Ring enjoyed.

On April 5, 1870, the Ring won its greatest legislative triumph when

Albany approved a new frame of government for the city, the so-called Tweed charter. This "reform" measure had been secured only by massive bribes to Republicans, but it had nearly unanimous support from New York City because of its home rule guarantees. The charter increased the authority of the mayor, who now could name his comptroller and department heads. It also consolidated many offices while ending the old Board of Supervisors and replacing it with a Board of Audit. By abolishing the Metropolitan Police Force, which had existed since 1857, the charter restored to New York the control of its own streets; the authority to complete Central Park was also awarded to Manhattan. Tweed lost his supervisor's post but was immediately named commissioner of public works (which made him a member of the Board of Audit), and his control over jobs and the city payroll continued without interruption. In fact, a good portion of the Ring's strength came from its ability to provide jobs for friends, relatives, and political allies. Few appointees complained when "kickbacks" of salary were extorted. In May, elections were held under the charter, and as expected, Tammany swept the city with more than seventy thousand votes, electing five judges, all fifteen aldermen, and their twenty-two assistants. The circle of Ring authority was now complete.

In 1871, Boss Tweed was at the peak of his power and prestige. He lived in a palatial mansion on West Thirty-sixth Street, served on the boards of a dozen corporations, and freely indulged his taste for fine food and fast horses. Millionaires enjoyed his lavish hospitality, and dockworkers and ward heelers competed for his favorable glance. An investigation of city finances conducted by John Jacob Astor III asserted that there was no substance to charges of past financial manipulation. And an incipient revolt within Tammany, the "Young Democracy" led by Jimmy "The Famous" O'Brien, had been crushed, so Tweed still reigned as grand sachem. The boss had more than enough time to concentrate on the marriage of his daughter, Mary Amelia, and spent $700,000 to arrange the social event of 1871.

One effort to please the boss was a campaign to erect a statue of him in New York Harbor, a campaign that Tweed himself had to halt because he was afraid he might appear ridiculous. The privately subscribed money was returned, but the boss kept the list of those who had contributed. He was certain to remember those who had and had not shown their affection. Perhaps the only troubling cloud was that for more than a year, *Harper's Weekly* and its brilliant caricaturist Thomas Nast (1840–1902) had published a series of cartoons highlighting the Ring's greed, arrogance, and plundering operations. Far more than the unproven charges of newspaper critics, Tweed feared Nast's pen. "I don't care what people write, for my people can't read, but they have eyes and can see as well as other folks." Yet even nasty cartoons could be ignored as long as public apathy made Tweed invulnerable.

But as often happens, a falling-out among thieves proved to be the Achilles heel of the Tweed Ring. In the spring of 1871, Tweed and his associates made a serious mistake. They made an enemy of the sheriff of New York, Jimmy O'Brien, when they refused to honor his claim that $250,000 was needed to carry out the "extra" functions of his office. O'Brien then threatened that unless his bill was paid, he would disclose and have published all the Ring's machinations. O'Brien had obtained the facts and figures from a friend in the comptroller's office who had made a duplicate set of all bills, vouchers, records, and transcripts. The Ring's paymaster, James Watson, had recently died in an accident, allowing the copies to be secretly made.

Faced with extortion by one of their own, the Ring refused to pay, and after his ploy collapsed, O'Brien turned over the evidence to George Jones (1811–1891), editor of the *Times*. The Ring, which had tried to buy off Nast with $500,000, now offered Jones $5 million not to publish the damning documents. Jones refused the offer and in July 1871 began publishing the transcripts. By the end of the month, every intelligent citizen knew that the Ring had stolen at least $6 million, with subsequent estimates by historians ranging from $30 million to $200 million. Mayor Hall protested his innocence. Tweed kept a brazen silence. Sweeny and Connolly vacillated between courage and cowardice. The political response, however, was predictable. Indignant public gatherings were held; the Council of Political Reform was organized; a mass meeting at Cooper Union called for action; and Samuel J. Tilden (1814–1886), the state chairman of the Democratic Party, openly condemned the Ring. In September, a committee of seventy civic leaders was formed to look into the operations of the Tweed Ring, whose members for the first time were thoroughly frightened.

Attacks on the Tweed Ring grew more intense as the *Times*, belatedly joined by other newspapers, kept up the editorial cannonade. During the next few months, the so-called Committee of Seventy, headed by ex-Mayor Havemeyer and including Samuel J. Tilden, uncovered additional masses of evidence against Tweed and his Ring. Nevertheless, Tweed won reelection to the state senate in November and still hoped to ride out the storm.

That dream faded, however, when a grand jury returned an indictment of 120 counts against Tweed, and he was arrested on December 16, 1871. Tweed also was replaced as grand sachem of Tammany Hall and so would have to face the law by himself. When asked his occupation by the prison attendant, Tweed replied, "Statesman." With the boss gone, the Ring disintegrated as quickly as it had been forged. Sweeny resigned as parks commissioner and left on a visit to Canada that turned into a "vacation" in Europe. "Slippery Dick" Connolly also hurriedly crossed the Atlantic and found refuge there. The Ring judges either resigned from office or were impeached. A. Oakey Hall was still the mayor, and when indicted, he conducted his own defense and won acquittal by a hung jury. After some foreign travel, Hall returned to become city editor of the *New York World*. The elections of November 1872 resulted in a repudiation of the Ring when William Havemeyer, twice the reform Democratic mayor in the 1840s, was elected for the third time to serve as chief magistrate of the city. Reform was now in power, and the former boss had to pay for his crimes.

The trial of William Tweed began over a year after his arrest, on January 7, 1873, before Judge Noah Davis. Despite all the alleged thievery of the Ring, Tweed was not accused of any felony, but rather of the technical misdemeanor of failing to adequately perform his auditing responsibilities. Although the legal case was quite flimsy, the verdict was foreordained because an example had to be made. On November 19, 1873, Tweed was found guilty, sentenced to jail for twelve years, and fined $12,500. The former boss served twelve months both in the Tombs Prison and on Blackwell Island but was released when the court of appeals threw out the trial decision on technical grounds. Tweed's legal troubles were not over, however, because a civil suit for $6 million had been brought against him, and he was arrested and confined to the Ludlow Street Jail. There he was treated with a great deal of consideration by his jailers. He even was permitted to drive out in a carriage in the custody of deputy sheriffs and to dine with his family. On the morning of December 5, 1875, the city was startled to read in the newspapers that Tweed had failed to return to prison after one of his frequent carriage rides. After a variety of adventures, the boss made his way to Spain, only to be imprisoned upon his arrival. The Spanish government shortly thereafter returned Tweed to New York, where he was again imprisoned in the Ludlow Street Jail.

Few of the stories that Tweed told while in jail have been published; many were "lost" because of the embarrassment that they represented for still prominent leaders. But the boss never was tried again and died in prison on April 12, 1878. In various proceedings, New York City recovered $876,241 of the many millions that the Ring had stolen, but with Tweed's death, the public outrage ended.

Although one boss had fallen, Tammany Hall survived, along with the ideal of boss rule. Augustus Schell, the sachem who replaced Tweed in December 1871, was a former collector of the port and a leading businessman, but he was old and not interested in picking up the fallen Tweed's mantle. Schell presided over the lost mayoral race in 1872 and tried his best to restore Tammany's public image by negotiating an accommodation with Havemeyer, who, after all, was a Democrat. Although the organization had been hurt by the loss of patronage and factional disputes, Schell managed to restore a semblance of order.

The Havemeyer regime quickly turned to the task of reforming Manhattan: garbage was picked up twice daily, the system of public markets was rebuilt, police officers' pay was increased, the *City Record* was founded, and the public debt was reduced. Tammany could not ask for more. A new city charter replaced the Tweed charter. Meanwhile, in Tammany Hall, the search was on for a leader who could perform the miracle of making the machine acceptable once more. The man who accomplished this improbable task was certain to become the new boss; his name was John Kelly.

Kelly, Tammany's first Irish Catholic boss, was born in 1822 and had given years of service to Tammany. The son of immigrants, young Kelly worked at a variety of jobs, including that of office boy at the *New York Herald*, grate setter, and stone cutter. Like Tweed, he served in his ward's volunteer fire company and built up a political following. He was an alderman in 1853 after the expulsion of the Forty Thieves, a congressman for two terms, and the sheriff of New York County for three terms. In the 1850s, Kelly had opposed Wood and allied himself with Tweed before the Ring was created. As sheriff, an office that entitled the occupant to fees but no salary, Kelly grew rich and won for himself an invaluable designation: he became "Honest" John Kelly. Relatively well off and devastated by the tragic deaths in his family, Kelly left his office. During the excitement of the Tweed exposures he was in Europe, insulated from scandal and rumored to be entering a monastery. Only the solicitations of "hundreds of leading men" persuaded Kelly to return to New York and attempt to pick up the pieces for Tammany. His rise to leadership was deserved but took place because he was one of the few Tammany leaders not tainted by the Tweed debacle.

Kelly's genius was organization, and his epitaph might well read: "He found Tammany a horde and left it an army." One of his first moves was to restore probity to Tammany's image by persuading men of impeccable reputation to serve as sachems. Schell was already the grand sachem, but leaders such as Samuel J. Tilden, August Belmont (1816–1890), and Abram S. Hewitt (1822–1903) also agreed to become chiefs. The new regime was hailed as "a congregation of the city's honest men." But the irascible Mayor Havemeyer was not convinced, and in a letter in 1874 he accused Kelly of being a thief. "I think you were worse than Tweed, except that he was a larger operator." Havemeyer believed that the city should be run as a business enterprise, much as he had managed his American Sugar Refining Corporation, but Kelly held that a modern municipality must be more concerned with the welfare of its ordinary citizens and its jobholders. In 1874, he and the mayor fought a series of patronage wars over election inspectors, representatives to the Police Board, and the appointment of magistrates, which only added to their personal bickering. Kelly finally decided to sue Havemeyer for libel, but on the day that the trial was to begin, November 30, 1874, the eighty-year-old reformer died suddenly of a stroke.

The fireworks of a libel trial would surely have been entertaining, but Kelly had already won his battle to control New York. Ever the "inventive mechanic of party building," Kelly had already elected a new mayor of New York by appointing thirty-three new district leaders who had delivered the vote of their areas to the regular Tammany candidate in 1874. Even before Havemeyer's death, Kelly's man, William Wickham, won the mayoralty in the election of November 3, 1874.

A pliant servant of the new boss, Wickham named Kelly as city comptroller, and over the next five years New York's debt was reduced by more than $12 million. Kelly's Tammany Hall organization now was in control. His biggest difficulties in city politics for the next decade occurred only when district leaders forgot how they had received their posts and attempted to rebel. Wickham was succeeded as mayor in 1876 by Smith Ely, an election in which the smoothly running Tammany organization virtually doubled the Republican vote. Under Kelly—really for the first time—a party machine had been organized.

Kelly believed that Tweed's avarice had been outrageous and that both money and power could be collected safely through "honest graft." His organization would always countenance some bribes, kickbacks, and gifts, but for the most part, these were unnecessary as long as there was real estate to be sold, franchises to be awarded, and contracts to be let. Legitimate money could be made from all these transactions as long as there were no scruples about using "insider" knowledge. The machine also controlled two New York newspapers, the *Star* and the *Evening Express*, which kept up a drumbeat of praise for the boss. In addition, Tammany employed "spouters" on other papers who could be relied on to place events in the proper light.

Kelly as boss, however, was never unopposed, and his imperious orders were often ignored by Democrats in the districts. Secessionists formed the Irving Hall Democracy in 1878 and, with Republican support, actually elected Edward Cooper mayor over the aged Augustus Schell. But in general, Kelly's will prevailed. He was intelligent enough to compromise with his enemies and share patronage, and thus he maintained mastery of city politics until his death. In 1880, he elected William R. Grace (1832–1904) as mayor, the first Catholic to lead New York since Dongan had served as governor almost two hundred years earlier. When Grace refused to dole out patronage jobs to Tammany hacks, Kelly made certain he was denied reelection. Reformers might complain that Manhattan "without a steady body of civic opinion" was ill managed by ward politicians, but it still prospered. Herbert Spencer, visiting in 1882, asserted that "New York, like the Italian republic of the Middle Ages, was losing the substance, if not the forms, of freedom," but Kelly carried on. Without graft Kelly padded his personal fortune yet maintained his reputation as an honest man. Tammany also thrived by avoiding major scandals. In general, Kelly's reign as boss was considered eminently successful by the machine, by the city, and by himself.

Only when Kelly's ambitions moved beyond New York City's borders did he invariably fail. During his first years as boss, Kelly had clashed with Samuel J. Tilden for control of the state party organization and had been defeated. Later, Kelly became incensed by the shabby treatment that state Democrats accorded the jailed Tweed; he launched an independent gubernatorial race that cost his party the the state house in 1879. In 1883, Kelly decided to oppose Democratic Governor Grover Cleveland, whose independence in regard to patronage the boss considered sinful. As a result of their clash, Kelly refused to support Cleveland for the presidency in 1884 and openly predicted his defeat. He concentrated instead on the mayoral race in the city, in which Grace was attempting a comeback. When both Cleveland and Grace won, something vital died in the boss. He became ill, lost his decision-making ability, and could not sleep without the aid of drugs. In 1885, he left Tammany Hall for the last time and spent the rest of his days sitting in his home on West Sixty-ninth Street, visited regularly by his protégé Richard Croker (1841–1922) and wondering what had gone wrong. The broken boss died on June 1, 1886. The mass in St. Patrick's Cathedral was crowded with workers and city officials who came to bid farewell to a man who had been a benevolent dictator.

By the time of Kelly's death, bossism was an accepted part of the New York politics. The heritage of Wood, Tweed, and Kelly made it simple for Croker to inherit the mantle. Nothing was said about his right of succession, for the leadership had been unobtrusively passed on even before Kelly's death. The leadership of Tammany had become "a growth and not an appointment," and the leader to whom the scepter had been given brought the city renewed corruption. As the "master of Manhattan," Croker was the culmination of a long process: he combined the flexibility of Wood, the avarice of Tweed, and the organizational know-how of Kelly. His reign, from 1886 to 1901, produced a totally different New York.

Tammany Hall cut across all the economic, social, and political aspects of city life, and its leaders were far more than personifications of evil. Each boss used the system to enrich himself, some more so than others, but each also claimed to speak and act on behalf of the people. Certainly, each advanced the idea of a centralized government administration and provided increasingly efficient municipal services. The cost was high, perhaps exorbitant, but as a result, Tammany became the spokesman for New York and provided urban America with a new vision of itself. Immigrants of every continent first identified with American society through Tammany ward heelers in every section of the city. Bossism provided them with jobs, food, friendship, and advice, and they in return remained loyal to the machine. The wealthier classes, too, supported Tammany bosses, for the legitimate profits to be made in fulfilling rich city contracts and franchises seemed boundless. Municipal government likewise benefited because Tammany's machine proved adept at cutting through the red tape of bureaucratic administration. In short, whether operating on the local, state, or sometimes even on a national level, Tammany and its leaders got things done.

6

America's First Metropolis

On the eve of the Civil War, New York was indisputably the leading city of the United States. Despite the dogged, inventive, and sometimes frantic efforts of its competitor cities, New York had steadily widened the lead in commerce and finance achieved by its businessmen since the opening of the Erie Canal. Goods carried along the "Big Ditch" had increased each year since its opening, and by 1860 the total stood at 4.65 million tons. Internal trade was more than matched by New York port's domination of the country's foreign commerce. By 1860 also, the city handled two-thirds of all American imports and one-third of its export trade. The city ranked first nationally in all but seven articles of exported goods, whereas the imports of Boston, Philadelphia, and Baltimore combined amounted to less than New York's imports in textiles alone. City merchants held virtual monopolies over the marketing of English woolens, Irish linens, and French lace as they crushed competitors and opened new areas of commerce.

In transportation facilities and in the crucial field of banking, New York City also held sway. Both the New York Central and the Erie Railroad Systems now serviced interior sections of the state, but both maintained terminals and headquarters in the metropolitan area. Despite heated protests from displaced members of the farming community, railroad service now tied Long Island's villages to Manhattan. Thriving shipyards along the East River, producers of the "Flying Clippers," continued to build the finest, fastest wooden ships ever constructed and provided employment for more than two thousand laborers. In 1861, during the first winter of the war, the Brooklyn Navy Yard used New York City's accumulated expertise to produce America's first ironclad warship, John Ericsson's *Monitor*. The banking fraternity of lower Manhattan, freed since the 1830s from restrictions imposed by the Bank of the United States, held substantial control over American finance. Wealth gained from the cotton trade, the extension of credit to inland jobbers, and a willingness to invest in manufacturing enterprise all solidified that position. In the 1850s alone, the city's capital resources doubled, and Philadelphia's banks were left far behind.

The New York City of 1860 also led the nation in business enterprise. The census of 1850 indicated that the state was first in the value of its manufactures, a surprising fact due in large part to smaller businesses clustered in the city. In the 1820s, immigrant craftsmen such as Duncan Phyfe (1768–1854) created masterworks in New York, and it became the center of the American furniture industry. The tradition of excellence continued when Henry E. Steinway (1797–1871) in 1853 opened a piano factory that launched a dynasty. Because the city ranked first in printing and publishing, not surprisingly it was the center of American journalism. But the fact that New York dominated both sugar refining and jewelry making seemed less probable. And its 162 cigar makers produced more than $1 million worth of smoke. In 1860, the total value produced by the city's 4,375 manufacturing establishments, factories employing 90,204 workers, was $159,107,369. New York, with a population of 813,669, was in size, productive capacity, and enterprising spirit the leader of America's economic life. Then, from 1860 to 1900, New York outstripped its already fantastic achievements; America's metropolis became one of the world's greatest cities.

It is one of the minor ironies of history that when cannon fire at Fort Sumter began the Civil War, the loyalty of America's biggest city was much in doubt. In the 1860 presidential campaign, Manhattan did not support Abraham Lincoln for president, and on January 7, 1861, Mayor Fernando Wood proposed that to protect its commercial predominance and its excellent trading relationship with the southern states, the city withdraw from the Union and declare itself a "free city." He believed that Manhattan's continued prosperity depended on its ties to southern plantations. Beyond that, Wood argued, wasn't a war on behalf of the inferior black man absurd? The mayor believed that an independent city would have no financial difficulties, since a modest import tariff could generate enormous revenues.

Wood's extraordinary proposal seemed strengthened when the state Democratic Party, convening in late January, also endorsed the concept of peaceful secession. A massive petition to Congress drawn up by many Manhattan merchants went so far as to suggest giving to the South half of all United States territories. But it was not merely Wood and the merchant elite that caused anxiety for the incoming Lincoln administration. New York City was home to 386,345 foreign-born residents. Would they be willing to fight for something called the Union? Why should New York's despised and oppressed Irishmen, whose number was estimated to be 204,000, be loyal to America?

With the fact of war, appeasement proposals and fears of disunion were quickly dispelled. Manhattan rallied to the Union cause as ardently as did the rest of the North. Wood reversed himself in good political fashion and led the chorus of "Union forever." On April 20, 1861, more than 100,000 New Yorkers gathered in Union Square to pledge money and soldiers to the national cause. The Seventh Regiment marched out to "save" Washington, D.C., and after July, when the Union army had been defeated at Bull Run, the support of New York's population was no longer questioned. Indeed, at Bull Run, the New York City Garibaldi Guards and its Tammany regiment were greatly mauled; one-third of Northern losses in the first major battle of the Civil War came from New York State.

Mayor Wood himself proved surprisingly loyal to the Union and led a campaign that raised $1 million for the war effort. But too many voters had been alienated by Wood's excesses, and despite his rediscovered patriotism, he lost reelection to Republican George Opdyke. In January 1863, Opdyke proudly asserted that the city had already supplied more than eighty thousand volunteers for the war, an unprecedented showing. Many recruits were foreign-born residents who demonstrated their American loyalty by joining the service. The *Irish American* editorialized that immigrants could never "countenance the destruction of the government which naturalized, enfranchised, and protected them." Horace Greeley, editor of the *Tribune* and advocate of "On to Richmond," was frankly amazed at the number who volunteered to serve in city regiments. Psychologically and morally, the wartime sacrifices of New York's immigrant population helped integrate once despised communities into American society. Shedding their blood for America gave them a vested interest in the national destiny and helped overcome the prejudice against them. In the final analysis, no American city contributed as much to the Northern war effort as did New York, which supplied more than 150,000 enlistees and countless millions of dollars to help save the Union. War also confirmed New York's dominant economic power, increasing the gap in wealth between the city and the rest of the nation.

Although the magnitude of New York's wartime effort is unchallenged, it has been subordinated historically by the major crisis that occurred in the city during the war, the bloody draft riots of July 1863. Until the spring of 1863, the war, at least in the East, had seemingly resolved itself into a long series of lost, or at best drawn, battles with the armies of General Robert E. Lee. Moreover, the Emancipation Proclamation issued on January 1, 1863, expanded the meaning of the war beyond saving the Union to freeing the blacks. When Congress enacted a draft law in March 1863, New York laborers were faced not only with conscription, which threatened their lives, but also with emancipation, which would transform freed blacks into economic competitors.

Under the terms of the draft law, rich men could buy service exemptions for $300. For many laborers, the conflict suddenly became a war fought by the poor to benefit only the rich. Proof was evident in their daily lives, for since 1861 the cost of living in New York had doubled while wages lagged far behind. Irish dockworkers were particularly incensed when black scabs were used to end their strike attempt to win decent wages. Nerves were already strained from Lee's advance northward in June 1863, so when the draft was instituted on July 11, trouble should have been expected. Almost all troops had been removed from the city, and a heat wave was searing the streets. In addition, the invincible Lee was now in full retreat from Gettysburg, and news had arrived that General Ulysses S. Grant had captured Vicksburg. Relief, joy, anger, and anxiety contended for domination in the popular mind, with tragic results.

The role of Confederate agitators in provoking the crisis will probably never be definitively known. From July 13 to 16, huge mobs of unhappy men roamed the city, clashing with the Invalid Corps militia and 2,300 police. Forgotten were the huge city rallies of July 1862 and April 1863 promising sacrifice for the Union. Now angry crowds insisted that the war was ending, the draft was unnecessary, and white men should not die for black freedom. For two full days, random atrocities were committed—largely against blacks—and pitched battles were fought along both the East and Hudson Rivers. Without any doubt, the mobs were dominated by Irish workers, not the least evidence being the reluctance of Archbishop John Hughes to intervene until the violence was largely spent.

Extraordinary police bravery and the return of regiments from Pennsylvania battlefields ended the carnage, and the draft itself resumed in August without further incident. Historians differ widely in their estimates, but at least 150 persons died in the worst riots ever experienced by an American city. Millions of dollars in property damage resulted, and nineteen men ultimately convicted of rioting served an average of five years' imprisonment. The horror of treason and racial cruelties like the burning of the black orphanage masked the city's contributions during the four years of Civil War. Although the city remained staunchly Democratic—in 1864 it voted six to one against Lincoln's reelection—its military and financial services to the Union were enormous. A true sign of New York's loyalty was the five-mile cortege escorting the body of assassinated President Lincoln through the city streets on April 25, 1865.

It was a somber New York that returned to the routines of peace. The city retained its dominant position in trade and capital resources and accelerated its development in the postwar era. The National Banking Act of 1863, instituted after short-lived financial panics in 1861 and March 1862, had created legal tender greenbacks as a method of paying for the war. When Congress approved national bank charters in its 1863 legislation, bankers across America almost automatically turned to New York's conservatively run national banks as institutions where their own reserves might be secure, rather than trust their funds to state-chartered institutions. Ever since 1853, New York had offered a national clearinghouse for checks, and under the terms of the new law, local banks might count as reserves any deposits held by New York banks. In Manhattan, the local banks' money would be safe, easily managed, and close to the nation's most active financial market. By 1866, the city had fifty-eight chartered national banks drawing the nation's resources toward Manhattan. It was the national marketplace for bankers acceptances, call money loans, commercial paper, and government securities, as well as for stocks, foreign trade, and insurance. Moreover, since the national banks paid interest rates of 6 percent, they attracted more than 100,000 new depositors.

The end of the war thus found New York financially supreme, economically thriving, and intent on expanding its influence. Physically, the city now stretched up to Thirty-fourth Street, with additional settlement northward along the bank of the East River. In 1874, the first land additions to New York since the Montgomerie Charter of 1731 were negotiated. Portions of lower Westchester County (Morrisania, Kingsbridge, and West Farms) almost doubled the city's land area while adding more than thirty thousand people to the population. Wartime mobilization had temporarily reduced the total population of Manhattan and curtailed immigration flows, but with the coming of peace, the soldiers had returned. More important, new immigrants again filled the Castle Garden reception center. City merchants knew how to exploit vast reservoirs of unskilled labor, and the city soon extended its statistical lead in both the value of its manufacturing output and the diversity of its production.

The census of 1870 reported a population increase to 942,292, and 7,624 factories were producing goods valued at $332,951,520, more than twice the 1860 level. Profits depended on the availability of cheap labor, and it is

1. Manhattan Island in the 1620s illustrates the strong relationship between New York and the sea. Its superb harbor has always been the city's greatest asset. *(New York Public Library pictorial collection)*

2. New York on the eve of revolution was a well-developed city of thirty thousand people, more than half of whom fled when the British occupied the island. *(Museum of the City of New York)*

3. In 1789, George Washington became the first president of the United States, taking his inaugural oath in Federal Hall. The site today is occupied by the Subtreasury Building. *(New York University Archives)*

4. City Hall Park in the 1830s was part of the heart of commercial New York. The activity of 200,000 ambitious people is reflected in the many different conveyances. *(New York University Archives)*

5. The forest of masts along South Street in the 1830s gives some indication of the city's vast trade, a mercantile empire expanded by the opening of the Erie Canal. *(Museum of the City of New York, Edward W. C. Arnold collection)*

6. The Astor Place riot of 1849 caused dozens of deaths and demonstrated the growing role that Irishmen played in a city of half a million persons. *(New-York Historical Society)*

7. As early as the 1850s, reformers attempted to alleviate the evils of the slums by creating mission houses to aid tenement dwellers. *(Ladies of the Mission, Stringer and Townsend, New York, 1884)*

8. The parade ground in Washington Square provided a free show whenever the Seventh Regiment marched, as this plate from 1851 demonstrates. *(Museum of the City of New York, J. Clarence Davies collection)*

9. New York was the publishing capital of the nation, and during the Civil War, crowds gathered in Printing House Square to get the news. *(Museum of the City of New York, Edward W. C. Arnold collection)*

10. Completion of the Brooklyn Bridge in 1883 linked Manhattan to the city of
Brooklyn and probably made the consolidation of the two cities inevitable. *(Museum of the City of New York, J. Clarence Davies collection)*

11. The temporary arch that commemorated the centennial of Washington's inauguration was only a shadow of the real New York City landmark that soon was constructed. *(Harper's Weekly, 1889)*

12. Mulberry Street in 1890 displays the population density that made Lower Manhattan both vibrant and dangerous. *("The News, New York's Picture Newspaper")*

13. During hot summer evenings, the only relief to be found was along the waterfront, as this nursing mother discovered in 1901. *(Museum of the City of New York, Byron collection)*

14. New York was one of the first cities to approve a visiting nurse service for slum dwellers. Compassion for the unfortunate has always been a characteristic of New York. *(Public Relations Department, Visiting Nurse Service of New York)*

15. McSorley's Wonderful Saloon was opened in 1854 and is the oldest, most storied, and perhaps the dirtiest bar in the city. *(McSorley's)*

16. The grandeur of Madison Square Garden in 1903, near elegant homes, hints at the power of greater New York. *(Irving Underhill)*

17. Washington Square Park in 1926 featured mature trees and a great archway, which is part of the traffic pattern. *(New York University Archives)*

18. Left: The elegance of Upper Fifth Avenue is still to be found in the juxtaposition of Saks' department store and St. Patrick's Cathedral. *(New York University Archives)*

19. Below: The skating rink at Rockefeller Center is one of America's most photographed public places. *(New York University Archives)*

20. Right: Wall Street and Trinity Church reflect the coexistence in New York of the sacred and the profane. *(New York University Archives)*

21. Below: The United Nations complex along the East River added another vista to the world's most distinctive skyline. *(New York University Archives)*

22. Modern Manhattan Island—if you can make it here, you are a New Yorker.
(New York University Archives)

estimated that in 1867 at least thirty thousand women in the city worked twelve to fifteen hours daily for only thirty cents in daily wages. Given such figures, it is not surprising that the value of city property doubled between 1860 and 1870. By the latter date, nine ferries tied New York to Brooklyn, America's third largest city, and many entrepreneurs moved to Brooklyn to enjoy their success free of Manhattan's clutter. In addition, the New York Stock Exchange swelled beyond 1,060 members. Nothing seemed impossible for a confident and growing New York. In 1871, its harbor handled 71 percent of the total value of all U.S. imports and exports combined, an all-time high. Improvements on the Erie Canal between 1872 to 1876 enhanced the flow of midwestern produce to its wharves. Already the bellwether for national trade and commerce, the nation's largest city continued to outpace American growth rates for the next half century.

One area in which New York did not lead was in creating parkland for its citizens, but it arguably did complete the most famous park in America. The construction of Central Park had been authorized on September 11, 1857, and its first sections were opened to the public in 1859. During the Civil War, work on it effectively halted, even though the boundaries of the park were extended northward to the vicinity of today's 110th Street. In 1865, when the park already drew more than 7 million visitors yearly, the city reappointed the landscape team of Frederick Law Olmstead and Calvert Vaux to complete the work they had started. Olmstead saw his Central Park as essential to the "self-preserving instinct of civilization," and he was convinced that ordinary citizens should use the park as much as upper-class carriage owners would. When a small zoo was added to Central Park in 1871, it soon became one of its popular attractions. Yet despite Olmstead's expectations, common citizens' use of the park increased very slowly. Laborers preferred Jones Woods on the east side of the island as a site for picnics. Only after the Park Commission approved rides and a carousel did the park lose its elite status and become beloved by a broad spectrum of the population. In contemporary New York, defenders of the park created a century ago are legion.

We have noted that politics in post-Civil War Manhattan was dominated by the Tweed Ring. The "boss" controlled city appointments, held Albany in alliance with his "Black Horse Cavalry," and in 1868 dared to reach out to Washington. In that year, the magnificent new Tammany headquarters on East Fourteenth Street played host to the Democratic National Convention. Tweed was not a major force in the proceedings, but his organization went all-out to impress the delegates, even inaugurating an experimental elevated train that could attain speeds of fifteen miles an hour. Nevertheless, Democratic stalwarts complained of New York's "ill-regulated, badly paved, filthy streets crowded with vehicles."

After twenty-two ballots, New York won a Pyrrhic victory when former Governor Horatio Seymour (1810–1886) was selected to run against (and lose to) General Ulysses S. Grant. Tweed carefully observed the maneuvering and was sure that he and Tammany would be able to control the national party before the next convention. But the opportunity to test his theories never came, for the Ring collapsed soon afterward and Tweed fell from power. Yet amid crime and misgovernment, both Tammany and the city continued to thrive; no Republican held the mayoralty from Opdyke's wartime tenure until William L. Strong was elected as a reform candidate in 1894, a period of thirty years. The New York democracy invariably suffered far more from disaffection within its own ranks than from Republican opposition. During an age of economic revolution in which New York became a leading world metropolis, the city was almost always ruled by Tammany bosses.

Tammany Hall was significantly altered in the decade after the War. Long controlled by Protestant leaders like Tweed, an ethno-religious revolution was taking place within the Hall. By 1860, Catholics composed the largest religious group in the city, and church records counted 350,000 Catholics in thirty-two New York parishes in 1865. In 1866, a crowd estimated at 100,000 rallied in Jones Woods in support of Fenianism. And by the 1870s, the Irish— heirs of the destitute immigrants of the 1840s—finally attained political power in New York. George W. Plunkitt (1842–1924), a Tammany ward boss from the West Side who in 1871 was simultaneously collecting three public salaries, put it simply: "The Irish was born to rule and they're the honestest people in the world." The long-repressed fears of aristocratic leaders like Phillip Hone were now realized, and his elite class recoiled in horror as they recognized that political power now resided in the docile wards controlled by Tammany's leaders.

The Irish were given a major voice in 1871 when the *Irish World*, today the oldest weekly in New York, began to publish. In that same year on July 12, Tammany activists succeeded in preventing Protestants from celebrating the anniversary of the Battle of the Boyne; sixty-two persons died before civic order was restored. During the 1870s, the almost traditional Protestant attacks on Catholic Irish functions simply came to an end because the Orangemen were simply overwhelmed by numbers. An Irish-Tammany axis was being forged, and fundamental to its strength was the machine's unparalleled ability to provide care and service to immigrants already in New York and those who would arrive over the next fifty years. Boss Richard Croker later argued that Tammany Americanized the immigrant; it took "hold of the untrained, friendless man and converted him into a citizen." All it asked in exchange was his vote. The system that Tammany evolved worked well, and later history demonstrated its ability to fulfill the dreams of Italians, Jews, and blacks as well as Irish.

The pace of immigration to the United States had slowed substantially after 1857 because of economic depression and war, but a decade later, with the return of peace and prosperity, traffic resumed. In 1873 a temporary peak of immigration was attained when almost 400,000 newcomers landed in New York. The bulk of these arrivals were typical of the "old immigration": people from England, Ireland, Germany, and Scandinavia who were determined to improve their economic status. More than 2.7 million newcomers arrived in the United States in the 1870s—the last great influx of Irish coming after a minor famine in 1879—with northern Europeans dominating the immigration statistics. In 1882, despite passage by Congress of a fifty-cent "head tax," more than 788,000 immigrants arrived in the United States, most by way of New York.

The physical and territorial expansion of the underclass horrified the merchant entrepreneurs and bankers who dominated New York's economy. By the 1880s, the city extended up to the Forty-second Street area, and proximity to the lower classes was not desirable. Suddenly, life in the suburbs—Long Island, Brooklyn, or the Bronx—became an attractive alternative for many upper-class New Yorkers. For wealthy families who chose not to leave Manhattan, the far precincts of Harlem meant little inconvenience, for a surface rail system served their needs. In fact, urban transportation began to benefit the lower classes only after 1878 when three elevated lines began operation. For many, suburban Brooklyn offered the greatest attraction, despite the inconvenience of having to cross by ferry.

The geographic dispersal of New York's elite made the construction of the Brooklyn Bridge an endless topic of discussion for all classes. Building a bridge to connect Manhattan with Kings County was an old idea, but not until John Roebling (1806–1869) submitted a plan in 1857 did it appear feasible. After involved political maneuvering, construction actually began in January 1870, directed by John Roebling's son Washington, the engineer most responsible for completing the project. Most people believed it was impossible to span a sixteen-hundred-foot-wide river whose bottom was unknown, but for more than a decade, the bridge gradually grew in size and beauty. Poor residents of the slums and rich merchants on Brooklyn Heights watched its progress with awe.

Some Brooklyn residents, perhaps influenced by the preaching of Henry Ward Beecher in Plymouth Church, saw the oncoming bridge as opening a connection to Sodom itself. In May 1883—after thirteen years of work, at least twenty-six lost workmen, and his own incapacitating case of the bends—Washington Roebling (1837–1926) completed the task that had enthralled New York. On May 24, President Chester Arthur, Governor Grover Cleveland, and Mayor Franklin Edson dedicated the Brooklyn Bridge. Since by chance the celebration coincided with Queen Victoria's birthday, a riot by the Irish population was only narrowly averted.

The greatest engineering project since the Erie Canal, the bridge not only provided a convenient passageway to the fields of Brooklyn but also probably made the creation of Greater New York inevitable. For the fee of a single penny, anyone could walk across a bridge that connected the first and third largest cities in America. Despite the Memorial Day tragedy of 1883—twelve persons died of injuries when strolling crowds panicked—the bridge became a symbol of metropolitan New York City. Although Brooklyn had sponsored two-thirds of the project, the Brooklyn Bridge remains a city glory to the present day.

Despite the new bridge, deciding to leave the city was difficult for well-to-do New Yorkers, and not only in a business sense. The city offered more of the amenities of civilized life than did any other city in the nation. During the 1870s, museums of natural history and art opened, and a symphony orchestra led by Leopold Damrosch (1832–1885) was formed in 1878, the same year that Gilbert and Sullivan's *HMS Pinafore* was first performed in New York. The first licenses to the American Bell Telephone Company were granted in August 1877, and service was available beyond Manhattan by 1880. Thomas Edison's (1847–1931) incandescent lamp first illuminated New York, in the Wall Street area, in September 1882. The $2 million Metropolitan Opera House opened with *Faust* on October 22, 1883, immediately replacing August Belmont's Academy of Music as the standard of artistic greatness. Before the Civil War, Manhattan had accepted second place, behind Boston, as "the Athens of America," but after 1865 New York surged ahead into first place in music and the arts, a place that it maintains to this day. Symbolic of the transfer of power was the relocation of William Dean Howells (1837–1920) from Boston to New York in 1888. The city even had a three-ring circus, courtesy of P. T. Barnum. Never after the 1880s did it fall to second place in cultural affairs.

In architecture, brownstone facades sheltered the homes of many New Yorkers, but on Fifth Avenue, the homes of the truly elite featured a "chateau" style. Rich New Yorkers first lived on lower Fifth Avenue, but the May 1879 dedication of the newly completed St. Patrick's Cathedral by Cardinal John McCloskey (1810–1885) signaled that the center of New York had moved uptown. The result was another northward migration. The cathedral, along with nearby St. Thomas Episcopal Church (built in 1883) became a kind of magnet drawing the rich. Conspicuous consumption became the rule in architecture, and Astors, Whitneys, Vanderbilts, Goulds, and Huntingtons all built mansions on upper Fifth Avenue, where their wealth and good taste would be visible to all.

In addition to private housing, hotels like the Waldorf (1893) and the Astoria (1897) seemed to spring up everywhere. Even more impressive was the development of the skyscraper. Chicago and New York have long contended over which gave birth to that modern symbol of city life. Many technical controversies have been debated, including elevator service, plumbing, iron versus steel technology, and wind sheer. New York's Washington Building, even though it had twelve floors, was entirely constructed of masonry, so it failed the test of being a true skyscraper. But Bradford Lee Gilbert's Tower Building (1889) used steel for its metal skeleton frame and so perhaps was the first. The Tower Building became the first of hundreds of skyscrapers anchored into the solid bedrock of Manhattan. Improvements in electric elevators soon enabled the construction of taller structures such as the Manhattan Life Insurance Building (1893), new headquarter structures for Standard Oil, American Surety, and, most impressively, the twenty-five-story Flatiron Building (1902). All were precursors of the world's most distinctive skyline.

Of all the alterations in the cityscape, none was more symbolic of New York's future than its acceptance of a gift from the people of France. In 1865 a French admirer of American democracy, Edouard René Lefebvre de Laboulaye (1811–1883), decided to give the United States a monument to the friendship of the two peoples. Frédéric-Auguste Bartholdi (1834–1904) was hired to design the project, and in 1871, while sailing into New York Harbor, the sculptor was inspired by a vision of a gigantic welcoming statue representing "liberty." More than 180 French cities raised $250,000 so that Bartholdi could design and construct—around an iron framework created by Alexandre Eiffel—the most massive statue in the world. The woman named Liberty, 152 feet high with a 35–foot waist, a 3–foot mouth, and a 13–inch fingernail, slowly took shape in Bartholdi's Paris workshop.

At the 1876 Centennial celebrations in Philadelphia, more than 9 million visitors saw the statue's right arm and torch, which afterward were displayed in Madison Square Park. The French asked only that America provide a fitting pedestal for their gift. Typically, the federal and state authorities did not act quickly, although in February 1877 President Grant did approve a site on Bedloe's Island. It took nine years of effort and a final whirlwind campaign led by Joseph Pulitzer's (1847–1911) *New York World* before New Yorkers contributed enough money to complete the pedestal. When the Statue of Liberty was assembled, it towered 305 feet over its harbor site. Its dedication, on October 26, 1886, was attended by President Cleveland and the thousands of the ordinary New Yorkers whose contributions had made completion of the project possible. New York now possessed a more enduring symbol than finance, manufacturing, or architectural innovation, for the statue meant liberty, opportunity, and hope. In succeeding generations, "Miss Liberty" presiding over the harbor became the single most lasting memory for the millions of immigrants arriving in the United States.

Before 1883, 85 percent of all immigrants came to America from the countries of northern Europe. That year, however, marked so decisive a change in the new arrivals' lands of origin that historians consistently label the phenomenon *new immigration*. The primary source of immigration now shifted to southern and eastern Europe—Italy, Russia, Greece, and the Balkans—and the number of arrivals became greater than ever. The 1880s immigration alone was twice that of any previous decade. For the first time, great numbers of Russian Jews arrived, fleeing religious persecution begun by Czar Alexander II in 1881. In the following years, each subsequent pogrom brought a flood of Jewish immigrants to New York, and in thirty years more than 1.562 million East European Jews arrived in the city. The 1910 census reported that New York City's population contained 1.252 million Jews. The influx of these poor, persecuted, yet young and ambitious people fundamentally altered city life.

As impressive as the Jewish arrivals was the influx of southern Italians, a migration that has been labeled the "greatest and most sustained" population movement from one country to another. In 1880, the city had only twenty thousand residents of Italian heritage, most from the northern provinces, whereas new arrivals in the 1880s were largely agricultural workers from southern Italy. During the 1870s, Italians were held in low respect in New

York because of their religion, customs, and willingness to act as strikebreakers. As with most migrations, most of the first arrivals were males, many of them "birds of passage" intending to return to their homeland. Obviously vulnerable to exploitation, they often served as "scabs" to break up struggling labor unions.

Congress reacted to the problem by passing the Foran Act in February 1885, making it unlawful for anyone to import laborers specifically for use as strikebreakers. The statute was aimed at the *padrone* system, which enabled resident leaders to contract out the labor and arrange the lives of Italian immigrants. Although the padrone held social as well as economic power in his community, his influence soon waned under pressure from the law. The ministrations of Tammany Hall block captains also were a means for Italian workers to free themselves from neighborhood paternalism. As early as 1885, the New York Bureau of Labor could report that Italian immigrants—who at first worked for any wage—had become "sufficiently Americanized" to join and even lead strikes for higher wages. One of the first and most successful Italian labor leaders was Salvatore Ninfo, who organized the more than four thousand Italians who helped construct the New York subway some years later.

It was natural for new arrivals to settle near their compatriots. For both Italian and Jewish newcomers, this meant that they gravitated toward the low-rent, run-down areas of the Lower East Side. Their arrival encouraged the Irish and German residents to leave, with the latter group occupying the East Side district known as Yorkville. Within only a few years, new languages, foods, and customs prevailed in the southern areas of Manhattan. Jewish pushcart merchants were found on the sidewalks of Hester and Bleeker Streets, and orthodox worshipers constructed the lovely Eldridge Street Synagogue to serve a growing community. Certain streets of the Fifth Ward were not only Italian but Neapolitan (Mulberry Street), Genoese (Baxter Street), or Sicilian (Elizabeth Street). The resident northern Italian community itself migrated to Eighth or Fifteenth Ward streets west of Broadway. Not all Italians remained in the city. Many traveled to Brooklyn, Jersey City, Newark, and the rest of the nation. Nonetheless, the census of 1900 reported that New York had 145,433 residents of Italian descent, and the even greater migrations of the early twentieth century were yet to arrive. By 1908, New York contained more than 500,000 Italians, more than the population of Rome itself. By 1950, Italians constituted the single largest ethnic group in New York.

Immigration placed the city's social fabric under severe strain. As early as

1857, tenements that housed newcomers were denounced as "the nursery of increasing vice," and conditions had markedly deteriorated since then. Organized churchgoers saw the Tweed-dominated city as Sodom on the Hudson, and in 1866 Bishop Matthew Simpson (1811–1884) admitted that the city had "more prostitutes than Methodists." A problem seemingly beyond solution was the thousands of homeless children who roamed the city streets. Neither the New York Home of Refuge (1825) nor the Catholic Protectory (1863) claimed to have made much impact on the great numbers. A true pioneer in the field of juvenile care was Charles Loring Brace, who led the Children's Aid Society after 1853. Brace believed that children developed most successfully in more godly, rural environments and so began to place homeless juveniles outside the city. He also created the Newsboys' Lodging Home in 1853, the Girls' Lodging Home in 1862, and a system of vocational training schools that numbered thirty-three in 1853. Brace's lifetime of work ultimately relocated about 100,000 children to western locales and gave timely aid to thousands of others who remained in New York. Nonetheless, the plague of crime committed by this floating population of youngsters finally led to the establishment of a juvenile court in 1901.

The problems facing immigrants, adult or child, were so enormous that charitable societies finally decided to form a single umbrella organization. In 1882 Josephine Shaw Lowell (1843–1905) established the Charity Organization Society to give overall direction to the allocation of relief services. No state, federal, or city agency existed to care for newcomers, and whatever services were provided for them were paid by private donors. The sole alternative was, as already noted, the largesse of Tammany Hall and its coterie of ward captains.

Jobs and juvenile crime were almost minor issues compared with the perennial New York problem of finding adequate housing. A legislative investigation in 1857 had expressed horror at the conditions in New York's slums, but in thirty years nothing had changed. Deteriorated housing simply could not cope with the overwhelming demand. Despite code revisions in 1887 mandating plumbing improvements and fire escapes, the decaying tenements remained congested schools for vice and crime. Yet in those crowded rooms, entire families worked to make clothing, cigars, artificial flowers, and many other products. In 1890, more than 1 million New Yorkers occupied 37,316 tenement houses, and some estimates suggest that half of New York lived in tenements by 1893. In 1890, Jacob Riis (1849–1914), himself an immigrant from Denmark, published *How the Other Half Lives*. A reporter for the *Evening Sun*, Riis analyzed living conditions from "Jewtown" to "The

Bend" of Mulberry Street and into the Tenth or "Typhus" Ward and concluded that the East Side "is not fit for Christian men and women." His book inspired a generation of reformers from Theodore Roosevelt to Frances Perkins.

Whether New Yorkers were rich or poor, the services provided by the city constantly had to increase to meet their growing demands. The massive horsecar system, which carried 35 million passengers in 1858, simply could not be expanded rapidly enough to service passenger demand in the 1880s. Yet despite the sanitation problem of horse droppings, 50 million passengers were still using the system in 1900. Elevated train service had been initiated in the 1860s, but management and service was unreliable. In 1892, hoping to rationalize the elevated service, the Manhattan Railway Company was permitted to merge four existing lines into a single system. The passenger loads immediately increased, and the company was soon able to pay dividends to its investors.

In 1892 the growing city opened the tap on a much expanded Croton Reservoir System, which delivered 300 million gallons of clean water each day from several upstate reservoirs. The next year, New York became the first city in America to treat water with chlorine.

Garbage incineration began at a plant constructed on Governor's Island. Commissioner George Waring (1833–1898), who learned engineering working on Central Park, totally reorganized the sanitation system after 1895; his "white wing" cleaners provided the city with extraordinary service for several years during the reform administration of William Strong.

Completion of the Williamsburgh Bridge in 1896 opened an alternative route out of the East Side ghetto to Brooklyn and led to Brooklyn's rapid expansion. And going from Manhattan into the rural Bronx became easier after the Washington Bridge opened in 1889.

Settlement houses such as the Neighborhood Guild, the College Settlement, and the Henry Street House were established in the 1890s to help residents in tenement districts. Organized by progressive social reformers, the settlements offered individual attention and some education aid to Manhattan's immigrants. Their efforts were supplemented when the city school system, which had begun providing textbooks in 1877 and kindergartens in 1888, was expanded in 1895 to offer both free medical examinations and a high school education to upwardly mobile youngsters. The Board of Education's evening lecture series for adults, inaugurated in 1888, was always popular in lower Manhattan. In 1898 the Charity Organization Society offered its first courses in "social work." William S. Rainsford, author of *Christianity and the Social Crisis* and rector of St. George's Episcopal Church, organized both a community center and a boys' military company, and Grace Church sponsored a "boys' choir school."

New York in 1890 had a population of 1,515,301 and was fundamentally different from the city that had gone to war in 1860. Almost doubled in population, increasing streams of European immigration gave the city the unfinished, exciting quality it still retains. Additional thousands of small business establishments solidified Manhattan's ranking as America's prime manufacturing center. In 1890, New York's 25,399 factories produced 299 different industrial products, goods valued at $777 million. Indeed, Manhattan so totally dominated both the men and women's clothing trade that regional manufacturers found it necessary to establish themselves in the city to take advantage of the expertise and market knowledge found there.

By 1900, New York was the headquarters for sixty-nine of America's one hundred largest corporations. Manufacturers slowly developed sales, book-keeping, and credit-extension techniques and used mergers and consolidations to enhance their market position. New York's banking and legal communities also created new forms of business organization. Bankers such as Morgan, Lehman, Sage, Ryan, and Whitney were consolidators—architects of complex financial mergers—and it was their expertise that enabled New York to survive the Panic of 1893.

The mercantile field had a new generation of retailers. A. T. Stewart (1803–1876), an immigrant from Ulster, built the best retail store. In 1896, Stewart's famed "marble palace" was bought by John Wanamaker, who pioneered advertising campaigns that filled New York newspapers with announcements of sales, bargains, and savings. But Wanamaker's reluctance to advertise in the Sunday newspapers soon cost him his retail leadership, for Sunday advertising had become essential to mercantile success. New York City was the test market for advertising initiatives that are now the norm for twentieth-century America.

Whether it was effective advertising or the variety of goods they offered, the new-style department stores appealed to shoppers and had replaced the emporiums of the "Ladies Mile" before World War I. R. H. Macy, a dry goods emporium that opened in 1858, was the first store to move its retailing operations uptown to provide easier access to a richer clientele. Under the leadership of Oscar Strauss (1850–1926), the "world's largest store" was built on Thirty-fourth Street. Benjamin Altman (1840–1913), not to be outdone, began to construct a building two blocks east. Both stores opened early in the new century and others, such as Gimbel's and Bloomingdale's, followed them north.

Manhattan proved equally adaptable in catering to the entertainment demands of its varied population. The heart of the legitimate theater had been located between the "Rialto" of Fourteenth Street and Madison Square, where Edwin Booth (1833–1893) opened his theater in 1869. But late in the century the theater companies, too, slowly moved uptown. Vaudeville, once a source of disapproval or embarrassment, was "purified" by Tony Pastor (1837–1908) in the 1870s and emerged as the most popular entertainment. The concentration of music halls and gambling establishments in the West Twenties soon gave that area a dubious reputation. A police captain, elated by a transfer that would enable him to become rich from graft, labeled the section the "Tenderloin."

In the "gay nineties," entrepreneurs of the legitimate theater, led by Oscar Hammerstein (1847–1919), had to leap beyond the Tenderloin to the Longacre (Times) Square area in order to relocate the theater industry. But no matter where its theaters were located, New York remained a magnet for the world's great performers. The Lind and Dickens tours of pre-Civil War days were succeeded by visits from Madame Helena Modjeska, the "Divine" Sarah Bernhardt, Eleanora Duse, and Ellen Terry. Home-nurtured talent such as Ada Rehan, John Drew, Mary Anderson, and George M. Cohan entertained thousands. Few New Yorkers, however, took notice of moving pictures, which premiered in the city in 1896. Perhaps the greatest of all entertainment phenomena was Lillian Russell (1861–1922), a Damrosch student who who first became a star at the New York Casino. When she appeared at Weber and Field's Music Hall in 1898, she commanded a salary of $1,250 a week. For the cultural elite, Monday night at the Metropolitan Opera was socially obligatory, and the opera repaid their patronage by bringing Giulio Gatti-Cassazza (1869–1940), Enrico Caruso (1873–1921), and Arturo Toscanini (1867–1957) to New York.

Despite all its luster, New York's greatest daily challenge was the continued influx of European immigrants. Although Castle Garden served as a reception center until 1890, it was far too small to handle the flow. Accordingly, after January 1892, all newcomers entered New York through the federal reception center located on Ellis Island in the middle of the harbor. Although a fire swept the island in 1897, destroying immigration records dating back to the 1840s, the "island of tears and hope" remained the primary immigrant entrepôt for sixty years. Before it closed in 1954, Ellis Island had received more than 12 million immigrants. During its first decade of operation, the number of immigrants from eastern Europe increased dramatically. In 1892 in Russia, another great pogrom had encouraged the flight of 81,000 Jews to New York, and even worse persecutions in 1905/6 led to the arrival of 258,000 Russian immigrants in 1907. More than 1.28 million immigrants entered the United States in 1907, a number that remained a record until the 1990s.

For Jewish immigrants of the 1890s, life was a constant struggle. In 1895, the *New York Times* noted the Jews' "utter disregard for law," saw their "clothing reeking with vermin," and concluded "they cannot be lifted to a higher plane because they do not want to be." More dangerous than the complaints of the elite, however, was the rising ethnic conflict between immigrant groups already living in New York and recently arrived Jews. The tension and rivalry sometimes led to violence, such as when Irish workers stoned the funeral cortege of a rabbi in 1902. Still, the city assimilated the Jewish influx even as tenements on the Lower East Side became more crowded and loathsome than ever. Manhattan's incidence of tuberculosis soared. From 1896 to 1897, the Foundling Hospital on Randall's Island recorded a death rate of 97 percent among its 366 foundlings, with only twelve surviving the year. In 1900, the population density of the Jewish East Side ghetto reached 640,000 persons in a square mile, the highest such figure in world history.

Chaos was averted by the efforts—albeit uncoordinated for the most part—of social reformers, settlement houses, and city agencies. Perhaps the greatest need was replacing the medieval housing conditions of the ghetto. In 1879, a mass meeting at the Cooper Union resulted in the formation of the Improved Dwelling Association, but in 1897 seven-eighths of New York's population still lived in the slums south of Fourteenth Street. A commission chaired by James Watson Gilder documented the conditions and abuses of tenement life, and Jacob Riis published his photographs, but nothing was done. Housing code reform was aborted in 1896 by a Tammany Hall organization catering to landlord interests.

Only one person refused to give up the fight. Lawrence Veiller (1872–1959) believed that humans have a "God-given right to light and air," and he gradually formed a coalition to make the appropriate changes. In 1901, the New Tenement House Law was enacted, becoming a model for cities throughout the nation. The law ordered windows to be cut into 350,000 previously airless rooms and mandated minimum sanitary standards for all new construction. New York was primarily a renters' city, with only 12 percent of its residents owning homes in 1900. The legislation was thus designed to improve conditions for the majority. But 86,000 "old law" structures remained common housing stock in 1901, and landlords generally ignored the "new law" mandate of yearly inspections; the first full inspection of "old law" buildings was not completed until 1908.

Notwithstanding all the changes in architecture, the arts, life, and population in New York City during the last decades of the century, one institution remained stable and constant—Tammany Hall. Since Mayor Opdyke's brief wartime tenure, no Republican had served in City Hall, although reform Democrats such as Havemeyer, William Grace, and Abram Hewitt had briefly taken up residence. Since 1886, the title of boss had belonged to Richard Croker, a man whose career proved how talent and ambition could be rewarded in New York. Croker matured in typical Tammany fashion, from a vicious street fighter to leader of the Fourth Avenue Tunnel Gang, from volunteer fireman to ward captain, from courtroom bailiff to alderman. When John Kelly took power in the 1870s, Croker allied himself with the boss and was rewarded with the post of coroner, an office paying $15,000 a year in fees. As leader of the Eighteenth District, Croker regularly delivered to Tammany candidates one of the strongest Democratic votes in Manhattan. When "Honest John" died, Croker stepped behind the boss's desk without serious opposition.

In the election of 1886, Croker's first as leader of Tammany Hall, it somewhat reluctantly backed the candidacy of Abram S. Hewitt as mayor, a decision the new boss came to regret. A rich, opinionated, and difficult man, Hewitt proved to be too independent, and in 1888 the Democrats rejected him. Croker gave the regular nomination to his old friend Hugh J. Grant (1852–1910), and although Hewitt mounted a rival campaign, the machine voters elected Grant by a sizable majority. Patronage and lucrative contracts flowed to the faithful, and Croker, as the dispenser of city largesse, became a rich man. Not all or even most of the business was corrupt, for there was much money to be made from "honest graft."

Since the principal element in Tammany's effective control was the police force, special care was taken to ensure its loyalty. Tammany controlled 85 percent of all appointments to the force, and the police commissioner made transfers or promotions only after consulting with local district leaders. Policemen who received their positions through political influence felt no qualms about kicking back money to ward bosses or to the party headquarters on Fourteenth Street. They in turn extorted what graft they could from the prostitutes, saloon keepers, gamblers, and merchants of the areas they patrolled. From the Tenderloin to the Battery, from the Village to the Bowery, everyone was happy except for the reformers and possibly the people.

The genius of Croker's "wide-open town" was the unrestricted opportunities it provided for inventive looting; personal enrichment was acceptable as long as Tammany received some part of the proceeds. "Contributions" from local leaders, policemen, and legitimate businessmen intent on maintaining a working arrangement with Tammany swelled the party coffers. Croker's Finance Committee accepted all the bounty and did not even bother to keep records. Police corruption was everywhere, but it represented only a small portion of the municipal rot.

Businessmen found that a macrosystem of payoffs was necessary to do business in New York. Charles W. Morse (1856–1933) was an entrepreneur who created an "ice trust" in 1899 that held exclusive rights to land ice on city docks. Ice was a necessity in the city's sweltering summer streets, and Morse won his monopoly only after making gifts of stock to Tammany chiefs. He then recouped by permitting only hundred-pound blocks of ice to be sold. Naturally, few residents of the tenements could afford to buy ice, but who really cared? Municipal leaders appreciated such business enterprise more when they shared in the profits. City contracts for services such as water or transit development provided ample opportunities for poor men to become prosperous. Croker himself led the way, and by the 1890s he was already a very rich man.

Perhaps each generation of New Yorkers must discover for itself the dangers inherent in one-party control. During the last years of the century, public anger at Croker's excesses grew, just as it had at the greed of the Tweed Ring. Democratic mayors such as Hugh Grant and Thomas Gilroy (1839–1911) thrived, however, as the tacit alliance of Tammany, business, and the underworld went unchallenged; no one was concerned about serving the people's interests. Then in 1892, the Reverend Charles H. Parkhurst (1842–1933) of the Madison Square Presbyterian Church carried out a series of personal forays into the corruption of the Tenderloin district. His discoveries, delivered in passionate Sunday sermons, shocked the congregation, especially since their minister denounced by name the politicians involved. Parkhurst documented "Hell with the lid off," and his moral outrage at the extravagant corruption led State Senator Clarence Lexow to conduct an official investigation. As evidence of the municipal rot continued to accumulate, a sudden but quite convenient illness overcame Richard Croker. He sadly informed the Executive Committee of the Democratic County organization that restoring his health had to be his first priority. He then left New York to experience the restorative powers of Wantage, his newly purchased estate in Ireland.

The voluntary removal of Croker's guiding hand from the political arena came just as a coalition of reform elements began to do battle with the Democratic machine. The Fusion movement of 1894 represented a conscious effort to recreate, one generation later, the melodramatic atmosphere of the crusade against Tweed. Another Committee of Seventy was selected and briefly considered John Goff, chief investigator of the Lexow panel, as a potential mayoral candidate. But Goff turned out to be a Democrat, and reform could not compromise with a persuasion they detested. The committee instead selected William L. Strong (1827–1900), a respected banker and upright Protestant, to lead its cause. Strong's candidacy gained support from angry merchants, independent voters, and even the somewhat hesitant Republican organization. In the fall he won an easy victory, by 45,000 votes, over the leaderless hordes of Tammany. City Hall once more belonged to righteous, reform-minded men.

Strong gave New York three years of nonpartisan, businesslike, and puritanical government. Drawing on the talents of the best men, Strong's appointed commissioners were uniformly excellent and included George E. Waring, who reformed sanitation procedures so completely that Manhattan had clean streets for perhaps the first time in its history. At the same time, Strong achieved major improvements in a road system badly in need of repair. But by far the most distinguished of Strong's administrators was the flamboyant Theodore Roosevelt (1858–1919), who served on the Police Commission. Although Roosevelt represented participation by the elite in politics, when asked why he served, he responded, "So I can join the ruling class." As he attempted to combat widespread gambling and the many illegal drinking establishments, Roosevelt's nocturnal forays into the city streets to discover corrupt policemen became part of his legend, in time helping him win the White House. Roosevelt is so far the only president of the United States actually born in New York City.

Mayor Strong believed he had a mandate to appoint only the best men to carry out city business, but this attitude soon found him at odds with Republican machine politicians who hoped to benefit from their alliance with reform. Moreover, the zeal of Strong's anti-Catholic school proposals and his mounting insistence on total compliance with Sunday blue laws soon eroded his support among reform-minded Democrats. Increasingly isolated, Strong chose not to stand for reelection in 1897. Unfortunately, he is remembered not for the better government he delivered to New York, but instead as the mayor whose term preceded the creation of the "greater city."

The idea of expanding New York City by annexing surrounding areas had been around ever since the 1830s. After the Civil War, this idea was strongly identified with the career of Andrew Haswell Green (1820–1903), a lawyer, reformer, and preservationist influential in the construction of Central Park and the overthrow of the Tweed Ring. Green believed that a more efficient city government depended on merging New York with the surrounding municipalities and unincorporated lands. In 1868 Green chaired a commission that recommended—to no effect—such an expansion, and he made the crusade his own for the next thirty years. Green's only success came in 1874 when Manhattan annexed three Westchester towns west of the Bronx River: Kingsbridge, West Farms, and Morrisania became the city's Twenty-third and Twenty-fourth Wards. Even this small addition of territory virtually doubled the size of the city, adding 12,500 acres to the existing 14,000. Annexation also finally brought New York City onto the mainland of the United States and foreshadowed its transformation into a larger geographic unit.

During the 1880s, as Manhattan's population and economic power continued to expand, the city made a physical connection with the city of Brooklyn when the Roeblings' bridge was opened. The bridge only strengthened Green's belief that territorial expansion would guarantee the city's bright future. After winning endorsements for his crusade from Abram Hewitt and the Chamber of Commerce, Green in 1889 persuaded the State Assembly to approve a commission to study the issue of consolidation. However, opposition from Brooklyn legislators wary of Manhattan's intentions defeated it in the Senate. As president of the Consolidation Inquiry Committee, a private group including the mayors of the surrounding municipalities, Green returned to Albany in 1890 with a highly detailed and nonpartisan report showing the many benefits that would accrue from merging Kings, Queens, and Richmond Counties with an expanded New York City. On May 8, a law creating a study commission was authorized. All previous proposals had been anathema to the state's Republican Party, but Green and his fellow commissioners gradually won their support by convincing upstate Republicans that an expanded city might vote against Tammany. Early in 1894, after the legislature approved a popular referendum on the issue of consolidation, the measure was signed by Democratic Governor Roswell P. Flower.

In analyzing the success of the consolidation movement, it seems clear that a critical role was played by Thomas Collier Platt (1833–1910), the "easy boss" of New York's Republicans who gradually became a supporter of the proposal. Green's persistence, the growing reform sentiment in the city, and the conservative voting patterns of the municipalities around Manhattan led Platt to believe that Republicans might be able to wrest control of the city from Tammany Hall. Accordingly, the GOP's opposition to the referendum vanished, so it was added to the election ballot of November 6, 1894. Thus it was that as Strong won his reform victory over the Democrats, the voters of the region also endorsed the concept of New York's expansion. Final vote tallies showed a large margin favoring the nonbinding measure, with only eastern Queens and the Westchester town of Mount Vernon strongly opposed. Brooklyn voters were almost perfectly divided, however, reluctant to see their independence vanish. Many questions regarding tax rates and municipal debts remained to be clarified, but with Platt's support and reform sweeping New York, it appeared that circumstances at last agreed with Green's vision.

For more than two centuries, Manhattan had slowly stretched northward within its island boundaries and intruded into mainland areas only in 1874. But gains in the Bronx had whetted expansionary desires, and city voters in 1894 appeared confident that expansion would permanently secure their position as America's greatest city. Circumstances certainly were favorable. The Bronx had long served as breadbasket for the city, and its industrial areas would greatly benefit from a New York connection. The area was a strange combination of farms, heavy industry, and elegant country estates. It was in the Bronx that Leonard Jerome (1817–1891) had built a racetrack for his friends and where the Belmont Stakes was run every year until 1905. But in 1895, ordinary voters in lower Westchester County saw great benefits to be gained by joining their future with the economic giant to their south. And to the southwest of Manhattan, consolidators knew that residents of Staten Island (Richmond County), who had approved the referendum by a vote of four to one, wanted to be annexed. Although Staten Island would be the least populous section of the new municipality, the farmers and businessmen in that area were convinced they would reap profits by joining their future to New York's revenues.

Residents of Kings and Queens Counties held far greater anxieties regarding the merger. Brooklyn, granted a city charter in 1834 over the determined opposition of Manhattan, ranked as the third largest urban center in the country from 1860 to 1890. Rivalry was always present in relations between the two cities, and when Central Park was under construction, Brooklyn had enticed Frederick Olmstead to build its Prospect Park in 1866. In the 1880s, Brooklyn's wharves actually handled more tonnage than did Manhattan's, and its merchants deeply resented any implication that they were merely an appendage to New York's economic strength. Finally, the gala celebrations that marked the opening of the Brooklyn Bridge in 1883, hailed in Manhattan as ensuring future union, were less festive across the East River.

Over the next decade, Brooklyn moved aggressively to annex six towns whose independence dated back to Dutch days. The local Democratic machine—led by Hugh McLoughlin (1823–1904), the "sage of Willoughby Street"—simply did not want to join forces with Tammany Hall. Brooklyn's Republican politicians recognized that Philadelphia had completed a long recovery and now exceeded Brooklyn in size. They knew also that Brooklyn had reached the limit of its allowable debt, that additional bond sales were questionable, and that consolidation was wise. During the 1890s, it was the reform wing of Brooklyn's Republican establishment that endorsed the movement for merger.

Finally, the vast acreage of Queens County, fated to become more than a third of the greater city, had to be wooed by advocates of consolidation. With a growing population of almost ninety thousand, Queens had many commercial connections to Manhattan, especially in the industrial areas that had developed along its western shoreline. The company towns created by the Steinway family in Astoria and by Conrad Poppenhausen (1818–1883) (rubber products) in College Point were always oriented toward the west. But eastern Queens, then extending into today's Nassau County, was occupied by farmers who resisted big city attractions. In the 1894 referendum, voters in those areas opposed consolidation but were overwhelmed by the residents of Long Island City, Newtown, and Flushing.

The complexities of consolidation were both immediately obvious and totally unpredictable. Success would incorporate up to forty municipal entities under the single mantle of New York and make irrelevant any long-standing fiscal arrangements and existing political fiefdoms. Manhattan's tax revenues would suddenly have to be applied to an area five times larger, and patronage and job distribution for a similarly expanded payroll made leaders giddy with anticipation. In fact, New York's civil list would expand from twelve thousand jobs to more than sixty thousand. Every politician both coveted the prize and feared that such patronage would fall to the opposition. With such issues unresolved, it surprised few politicians when Albany's attempt in 1895 to approve a commission to draft a new city charter failed.

But New York City leaders were in no mood to be thwarted. In 1895, while the legislature dithered, they announced the annexation of the Westchester towns of Eastchester, Pelham, Wakefield, and Williamsbridge. These areas east of the Bronx River had a population of about thirty thousand and completed the city's unilateral northward march. Meanwhile, in Albany, Senator Clarence Lexow, with the approval of Boss Platt, maneuvered to break the statutory deadlock and create the final Consolidation Act. Under its terms, the legislature would name a fifteen-member commission to draft a charter for a Greater New York. It was hardly surprising that Governor Levi P. Morton appointed Andrew Green to lead the body or that it included among its membership such reform-minded luminaries as Seth Low (1850–1916), William Strong, and Frederick Wurster (1850–1917), whom destiny fated to be the last mayor of Brooklyn.

Within the commission, opposition to consolidation came from the sitting mayors of New York and Brooklyn; both Strong and Wurster were eager to prove themselves independent of Boss Platt. Strong went so far as to veto one version of the consolidation proposals. Seth Low, the president of Columbia University but also a former mayor of Brooklyn, emerged as the facilitator of a complex agreement. It was largely his work that won legislative approval and was signed by Governor Morton on May 4, 1897. The new charter for Greater New York centralized the city government under a stronger mayor. Each of the five newly designated boroughs (Manhattan, Brooklyn, Queens, the Bronx, and Staten Island) would have a "president" to administer neighborhood affairs and nurture "local pride and affection." The upcoming November election would select the first mayor of the consolidated city, the five presidents, and all the members of a bicameral city legislature.

During the summer of 1897, residents of the metropolitan area contemplated the imminent transformation. For decades, prophets of consolidation like Andrew Green had argued that expansion was needed if the city was to maintain its current supremacy over upstart challengers like Chicago. Yet the proposed changes were daunting. Greater New York would quadruple the size of the old city. Manhattan—for more than 250 years the entire city—became one of five coequal boroughs. Yet the historical aura of power attached to Manhattan was so strong that it dominated city politics far into the twentieth century. Even today, a century after consolidation, residents of the other boroughs speak of going to "the city" when they enter New York County. Most important, the new mayor of New York would have greater municipal responsibilities than any other mayor in America, affect the lives of more than 3 million citizens daily, and dispense more patronage than the president of the United States did.

Only the opportunity to rule such a magnificent empire was sufficient to lure Richard Croker back from his Irish exile. Emissaries from the Democratic establishment, William C. Whitney and Hugh Grant, visited Croker at Wantage to convince the former boss that his party needed him to run the campaign. Only Croker's expertise and wiles could guarantee that the new city administration and its quintupled civil list would become Democratic. Flattery worked wonders, and Croker returned in September, reasserted his authority over Tammany Hall by October, and then selected a magnificently acquiescent mayoral candidate.

Robert Van Wyck (1849–1918), a judge on the City Court since 1889, was nominated for mayor with the understanding that Tammany Hall would dispense patronage for the entire city. While Croker united contending borough interests behind a single candidate, Republicans and reformers were publicly committing political suicide. Municipal reformers first wished to select the incumbent Mayor Strong, but after he suggested that consolidation would be a "funeral service" for New York, support for his candidacy evaporated. Fusionists, calling themselves the Citizens Union, turned to Seth Low, but he was so piously upright that cooperation with Boss Platt became impossible. Platt in turn insisted on running his own candidate, the former secretary of the navy Benjamin Tracy, a fine man with little understanding of city realities. Finally, a fourth candidate revived nostalgia for a past era as Henry George (1839–1897) mounted an independent campaign on the issue of tax reform. Facing a plethora of reformers, the united Democrats of Richard Croker easily won election on November 2, 1897. Faithful members of the Tammany organization happily chanted "to hell with reform" as they prepared once again to occupy City Hall. Richard Croker, once the "master of Manhattan," pondered his control over the future of the greatest city in the world.

On January 1, 1898, Robert Van Wyck took the oath of office as the first mayor of Greater New York. If his name is hardly remembered today except for an expressway, it is because he was a mediocre judge, an inept administrator, and a mayor who willingly transferred his authority into the hands of a boss. His accession to power came just as the city had taken a quantum leap forward to become both the nation's and the world's most economically powerful metropolis. The Port of New York had the finest harbor on earth and dominated both the export and import trade of the nation; 67 percent of all American imports entered the country somewhere on the city's 578 miles of waterfront. The city ranked first nationally in number of factories, their capital valuation, gross domestic product, and number of employees. Commercial and manufacturing supremacy merged with financial domination. Yet all this was of little consequence to Van Wyck. Elevated by Boss Croker to preside over City Hall, he understood that patronage, policy, and politics were not his concerns. Not surprisingly, his brief tenure was marked by personal scandal, and he was accused of accepting tainted stock from the Ice Trust in return for official favors. Greater New York's first mayor was far less eminent than the city he governed.

7

Governing the World's Greatest City

The creation of Greater New York brought Tammany chieftain Richard Croker to the pinnacle of his power, but it also destroyed the credibility of "Easy Boss" Tom Platt. Platt's belief that New York might be turned into a Republican bastion by mobilizing the conservative voters of Brooklyn and Queens was shown to be an illusion. Victory by an obviously weak Tammany candidate over splintered opposition groups indicated that New York was a Democratic city and likely would remain so if facing fragmented opposition. Only when Tammany Hall became too greedy, when its excesses became public, when anger at its arrogance could be mobilized, would Republicans or reformers have an opportunity to win control of the city. Because Tammany leaders were often less than astute, such occasions occurred more frequently than might have been expected. But because Republicans and reformers had difficulty agreeing on programs of cooperation, their Fusion movements accomplished far less than good government advocates expected. Nevertheless, the twentieth-century political history of the greater city revolves around the tensions and clashes among these three shifting groups.

The struggle over consolidation illuminates and presages some of the political themes that continued into the new century. Consolidation would never have been attempted without constant pressure from good government advocates like Andrew Green and never would have been approved without the influence of Platt. Yet even with control of the first city administration as a prize, Republicans and reformers failed to create a joint ticket. Even though their competing candidates took 55 percent of the total vote, Tammany easily won the election of 1897. New York was the grandest creation of American urban society, but it was at best indifferently governed. Always there were demands that city politics be cleaned up, that reform be introduced, that the city's economic power be matched with enlightened government. During the first decades of the new century, the crusade to bring better government to New York continued, winning only intermittent success against the entrenched forces of Tammany Hall.

*

The city of Greater New York hailed its birth with a gala party on New Year's Day 1898. Newspapermen such as John Peter Zenger, William Cullen Bryant, Horace Greeley, and Henry Raymond had often prodded New York to greatness. If events seemed more sensational, more visceral, and more exciting there, it was perhaps due to their editorial skills. Yet never before 1898 had newsmen's concern for circulation helped create a war. In that year, the city's dominant publisher was Joseph Pulitzer of the *World*, a New Yorker only since 1882. His was a democratic newspaper that spoke for the masses against the "interests" and crusaded for public causes like the Statue of Liberty. The paper also provided jobs for thirteen hundred New Yorkers. Pulitzer had created a comprehensive illustrated and extremely profitable paper that, according to Frank Cobb, was "unmuzzled, undaunted, and unterrorized."

Newcomer William R. Hearst (1863–1951) dared to challenge the *World*. In 1895, driven by ambition and financed by his mother, Hearst had bought the *Morning Journal*, a scandal sheet referred to as the "chambermaid's delight." Soon he was ready to compete with Pulitzer. Both men admired Napoleon and, like him, sought to expand their empires. Hearst, the newcomer, was the aggressor and raided the *World*'s stable of reporters, hiring away Arthur Brisbane and making him his editor. Hearst then reduced the price of the *Journal* to only a cent, demanded sensational headlines, and opened his pages to the cartoon adventures of the "Yellow Kid." But all this had no effect, as Pulitzer kept the *World*'s circulation safely in front of the *Journal*'s and far ahead in advertisements.

To men such as Pulitzer and Hearst, the increasing tension between the United States and Spain over the insurrection in Cuba was merely another round in their battle. That the commander of the *Maine*, which exploded in Havana harbor on February 15, 1898, happened to be a New Yorker only added to the fervor of their editorials. Both papers, joined also by the *Herald* and the *Times*, established Caribbean news syndicates to supply a stream of often spurious stories to arouse the public and sell more newspapers. This was "yellow journalism." A single newspaper would publish up to forty editions daily, and prices rose to two cents to finance the publishing madness. Yet the press succeeded in its goals, for public outrage moved the nation closer to conflict. On April 25, 1898, Hearst triumphantly asked New York, "How do you like the *Journal*'s war?"

Some three hundred correspondents descended on Cuba, and Hearst himself sailed off in his yacht to join the *Journal*'s fleet of ten dispatch boats delivering the latest news. Hearst's efforts drew his paper abreast of the

World's daily circulation at 1.125 million, but the end of the brief war soon reestablished Pulitzer's primacy; it also saved both newspapers from bankruptcy. After the war, Hearst decided to return the price of his paper to a penny. The far less flamboyant *Times*, published by Adolph Ochs (1858–1935), matched the price cut in October, and in self-defense, fifteen other dailies followed suit.

The Spanish-American War dominated city news during 1898, but almost anything would have overshadowed Mayor Van Wyck. Totally ruled by Tammany Boss Croker, the pliant Van Wyck dispersed patronage as directed and turned his back as the police allowed vice to flourish. In return, Croker agreed to run his brother for governor, and Augustus Van Wyck probably would have won the state house had his opponent not been Theodore Roosevelt. Roosevelt refought the battle of San Juan Hill on speaker's platforms across the state and triumphed every time. He thus became governor, much to Croker's chagrin, and the boss had to be satisfied with control only of the city. Nevertheless, at Croker's appearance, the Metropolitan Opera's orchestra routinely played "Hail to the Chief" in recognition of the boss's supremacy.

No area of city government suffered more under Van Wyck than law enforcement. For deputy police commissioner, Croker demanded the appointment of William "Big Bill" Devery (1855–1919), reputedly the overlord of Manhattan's midtown vice. Devery's Bowery counterpart was "Big Tim" Sullivan (1863–1913), whose main interest was hardly law enforcement but whose name is honored anyway with the city's gun control law. In fact, the "Sullivan Law" was enacted so that Big Tim's police cohorts might easily dispose of his opponents by planting guns on them and then hauling them off to jail. Decorum and order became the rule in Sullivan's saloon empire; men were known to sew up their pockets in order to prevent arrest. In Greater New York, there was a tacit understanding among business, politics, and vice, each understanding the greed, necessities, and ruthlessness of the others. An honest official like Chief John McCullagh was replaced by the vice boss of the Tenderloin; a sitting district attorney led a chorus of the ever popular "to hell with reform"; and business leaders supervised Croker's speculations on Wall Street. Earlier, the Lexow Committee of 1894 found the police department in 1894 to be "an established caste" dedicated only to "the cohesion of public plunder." Despite reform's brief fling under Mayor Strong, the Van Wyck administration backtracked into familiar corruption.

Once again, however, corruption led to state action. In the summer of

1899, an investigative commission led by State Senator Ferdinand Mazet was able to document the revival of "dirty graft," organized vice, and police corruption in New York City. Mazet's report, issued in January 1900, also charged that the American Ice Company, a city-granted monopoly that refused to sell ice in less than sixty-cent blocks, had enriched such Tammany Hall luminaries as Croker, Van Wyck, and Docks Commissioner Charles Murphy. The depredations were startling only because they were made at the expense of the lower-class voters that Tammany claimed to represent. The impact of artificially high ice prices was understood by even the most ignorant slum dweller. Croker's delicate political antennae picked up the popular anger, Rather than control the demand for charter revision resulting from the Mazet revelations, Croker surprised everyone by retiring once again. After almost sixteen years as boss, Croker withdrew to Wantage, Ireland, where he happily bred horses, including the Derby winner of 1907, for the rest of his long life.

Croker left New York for Ireland in February 1901 amid signs that it would be a bad year for Tammany. Episcopal Bishop Henry Potter (1834–1908) had issued an open letter condemning the Van Wyck administration, and in one of his last acts as governor, Vice President-elect Roosevelt removed District Attorney Asa "To Hell with Reform" Gardiner. With the boss gone, the Democratic party organization became divided by territorial and patronage disputes. Indeed, the intraparty investigation carried out by Louis Nixon, Croker's nominal successor, was so damning that a public report could not be issued. Ambitious ward leaders now asserted that "Croker ain't the whole thing" and struggled to safeguard their fiefdoms against the rising tide of reform.

Special Session Court Justice William Travers Jerome (1859–1934) began to question police captains about covering up crime. He launched a series of "John Doe" raids that won popular acclaim and catapulted him to the post of Manhattan district attorney. Most ominous of all for Tammany was the slow march toward political accommodation between the good government forces of Robert Fulton Cutting's (1852–1934) Citizens' Union and the Republican followers of Thomas Platt. If that coalition could be achieved—and the experience of 1897 proved that it must be achieved in order to defeat Tammany—then New York might be saved. On September 5, 1901, the *Nation* editorialized that reform's cause was "not electing a mayor, but saving a city," and on September 10, the Citizens' Union called for a Fusion ticket (Republicans and Reformers) to oppose Tammany.

The demand for Fusion threw the political spotlight on the patrician figure of Seth Low, president of Columbia University, who had carried the banner of reform in 1897. A successful businessman and the formidable mayor of Brooklyn from 1881 to 1885, Low had dedicated his life to public service. His personality was cold, however, and he did not have the skills of a professional politician. Even in his career as president of Columbia, Low allowed his successor to claim credit for valuable academic reforms. Yet despite his lack of desire for recognition, Low was identified with the idea of the greater city. He had served on the charter commission of 1896 and had long promoted consolidation.

Although Platt found Low personally obnoxious, he could not ignore the possibility of victory that Low's candidacy presented. So he gave his grudging approval to a Fusion ticket headed by Low and Judge Jerome. Tammany countered with its own expedient reformer, Edward Shepard (1850–1911), but a united opposition, the public's revulsion against crime, Low's competence, and Jerome's demagogic rhetoric doomed the Democratic effort. Low proved to be a dull campaigner, but he nevertheless defeated Shepard and in January 1902 took office as New York's ninety-second mayor.

The single greatest irony of the Mazet investigation was that reform cost New York City two years of honest and efficient government. Senator Mazet had recommended, and the legislature had enacted into law, a charter revision that reduced the term of mayor by half and reorganized the city into five boroughs. Hence, Low entered office with only two years in which to reform the administration and impose his will on the bureaucracy, business, and the politicians. Given decades of Tammany misrule, two years was simply not enough time to show results. Low's rigorous honesty offended many vested interests that managed to coexist with Tammany, and his reform backers began to lose their enthusiasm. The reform impulse in New York has historically been both brief and vacillating.

Yet in his brief tenure, Low did achieve much. City franchises were renegotiated to raise income, and the dead wood of Tammany was ruthlessly pruned from the payroll. The entire city was reassessed, and the tax rates thereby reduced, although businesses had to pay more in actual taxes. Low also began a vast school construction program, authorized contracts for the Manhattan Bridge, and also accelerated design work for the subway system. He opened the first public baths on the East Side and sponsored tenement house reform. But despite his best efforts, the number of tenement dwellers increased by 500,000 from 1900 to 1910, surpassing the rise of 400,000 in the previous decade. In addition, Low worked hard to expand a program under which indigent New Yorkers were treated in voluntary hospitals with their bills paid by the city, thus initiating the humanitarian concern that led New York to build the world's greatest municipal hospital system. In all, Low's was an extremely progressive two-year term.

Given Low's substantial accomplishments, it was unbelievable that the major public issue of his tenure was the peripheral one of Sunday liquor sales. District Attorney Jerome's attempt to enforce closing laws ended in a failure that alienated the WASP and clerical adherents of Fusion. Even more important, when Police Commissioner Francis Greene continued that ineffective campaign into 1903, Low sacrificed the support of lower-class voters. Moreover, rigid police enforcement of the archaic peddler license requirements cost Low dearly in the increasingly powerful Jewish vote. The Fusion administration was rapidly moving toward political tragedy.

Low had begun a series of long-term innovations (for which he received no credit), but his short-term policies had alienated powerful blocs of voters. An uninspired speaker, Low could not articulate his concern for the common man yet was increasingly perceived as a traitor by his own class. Perhaps a four-year administration could have made both achievements and concerns obvious, but Low was mandated to stand for reelection in two years because of the very success of the reform movement he represented. When Boss Platt, who had received little patronage from the righteous Low, defected from the reform coalition, it became clear that 1903 would witness one of Tammany's periodic rebirths.

The organizer of a new Democratic coalition was Charles Francis Murphy (1858–1924), a former baseball catcher turned saloon keeper who presided over the Gas House district and ministered to the needs of his people from a lamppost on Second Avenue. Murphy, probably Tammany's greatest twentieth-century figure, displaced Louis Nixon as leader in 1902 and planned a strategy to restore respectability to the Democrats. Clearly, if they were to challenge Low, they needed a man of equal probity. Murphy found his man in George B. McClellan Jr. (1865–1940), son of the Civil War general and, at thirty-eight, a veteran of both Tammany politics and the House of Representatives. A victorious McClellan campaign would also allow Murphy to crush his opponents in Tammany and solidify the organization. To that end, Murphy willingly endorsed Fusion candidates for the posts of comptroller and president of the Board of Aldermen. McClellan was honest, but even better, he entertained hopes of running for national office. He was thus certain to attract independent voters, keep his eye off the details, and, according to the *Herald*, "take orders and he doesn't look it."

The campaign of 1903 was a clean campaign between two gentlemen, one seeking to maximize the organizational vote and the other seeking to recon-struct a factionalized reform coalition. In the end, reform was rejected be-cause it and Low appeared far too puritanical, whereas McClellan offered enlightened government and the right to drink freely. Murphy's "artful rais-ing of the partisan cry" was enough to win, and the organization had no need to even think of stuffing the ballot boxes. McClellan swamped Low by 314,782 to 252,086, and Platt proclaimed reform's epitaph: Low "came and went, and New York City is still the same old town."

McClellan's election in November 1903 signaled the start of two decades of Murphy rule in Tammany Hall. But despite the expectations of some Democrats, it did not mean that the "lid was off." Although McClellan provided vast patronage to the machine, he would not accept incompetents in high posts. He insisted, for example, on appointing his own men to the crucial posts of police, health, and street-cleaning commissioner. Jacob Riis called McClellan "the best organization mayor" New York ever had. Not only did he refurbish the machine, but he also instituted a city improvement commission to revitalize the entire city. A comprehensive traffic plan was adopted, and Police Commissioner William G. McAdoo saw that traffic ordinances were obeyed. A unified park scheme for the five boroughs was enacted, and approval was granted for the widening of streets, the public utilization of waterfront acreage, and the modernization of piers. From 1902 to 1907, the city spent $15 million on constructing nine Hudson River berths. In all, McClellan presided over accomplishments that not even Seth Low could fault.

All these improvements paled, however, before the grand achievement of McClellan's first administration, the opening of the subway system that had been under construction since 1900. Ever since the incorporation of New York's first elevated line in 1866, citizens had been offended by the noise and filth the high-rise trains created, and as early as February 1870, the Beach Pneumatic Transit Company had begun to dig a block-long subway beneath Broadway. Alfred Beach (1826–1896) was far ahead of his time—his stations included frescoed waiting rooms that featured a grand piano and fountains—but his initiative failed because of technological and political problems. One aspect of Beach's genius that survived, however, was a pneumatic mail system that for decades sped letters beneath the streets of Manhattan.

New York was not the only municipality to dream of underground travel. In 1863, London showed how it might be done. New York broke ground for its own subway system on March 24, 1900, and under the leadership of John McDonald and August Belmont II, work proceeded all during the Low administration. Some twelve thousand laborers worked long and hazardous ten-hour days at the magnificent wage of twenty cents an hour to build the underground tubes, with the excavated earth used to enlarge Governor's Island. Finally, on October 27, 1904, Mayor McClellan took the controls of an eight-car train and made a nine-mile, twenty-six-minute trip beneath Manhattan Island. On the first day, 110,000 citizens bought tickets to ride, and the first subway crimes were reported. By October 29, daily ridership had reached 350,000, the vanguard of future billions of fares.

Boss Murphy benignly watched his protégé's success. Perhaps the most astute leader in Tammany's long history, Murphy was honest and so limited himself to the "honest graft" to which his eminence entitled him. Modern investigators have discovered that his contracting firms performed jobs valued at $15 million for the city, but the work seems to have been well done. The boss lived in style but without ostentation; he never failed to serve his constituents. Murphy shared Tim Sullivan's credo, "There is no crime so mean as ingratitude in politics," and in 1905 he demonstrated the depth of his belief.

McClellan deserved renomination, and since the state had approved a revised mayoral term, he fully expected to serve another four years. But William Randolph Hearst, whose money had already won him a congressional seat, attempted to wrest the Democratic nomination from McClellan. When Murphy's control of the party denied Hearst the prize, the outraged publisher launched an independent candidacy. McClellan was all but ignored in the ensuing brawl, a campaign marked by bitter words and foul deeds on both sides. Murphy labeled Hearst a socialist who proposed municipal ownership of the expanding yet efficiently run subway system. Hearst counterattacked with personal libels: "Everybody works but Murphy, he only rakes in the dough." When the carnage ended, the organization had won, although some observers maintained that troublesome ballot boxes had been dumped into the Hudson River.

The mayor won by a mere 3,500 votes, thanks to Murphy fulfilling his obligations of loyalty. But McClellan was appalled by the activities carried out in his name and soon broke off his relationship with Murphy. Therefore when new appointments were announced on December 30, only two Tammany leaders were among them, and both were men personally committed to the mayor. Murphy's vendetta against Hearst had sentenced his party to a term in the political wilderness. And when the cynical boss forced the Democrats to nominate Hearst for governor in 1906, his breach with McClellan widened. Hearst lost, but McClellan allowed John Purroy Mitchel

(1879–1918) to investigate corruption in Tammany Hall. As a result of Mitchel's findings, a Republican governor removed three Democratic borough presidents from their positions. McClellan ignored both Murphy and the machine for the rest of his term.

From 1906 to 1909, McClellan pursued an independent course and effectively administered a thriving city. Business remained good, even though the tobacco industry had begun to desert Manhattan for the sunnier climate of the South. New York was the brewing center of the nation and had more breweries than Chicago, St. Louis, and Milwaukee combined; today no major brewery remains in the city. But new industries are always being born in New York. America's movie industry began in New York between 1905 and 1907. New manufacturing and shipping facilities were rising on the banks of Newtown Creek in Queens and added their taxes to the municipal treasury. Although McClellan's name is almost unknown to New Yorkers today, his administration was responsible for completing improvements to the harbor, beginning the municipal ferry service, and massively expanding the park and playground system. The last horsecars were removed from Fifth Avenue in 1907, in part because of pressure from the Fifth Avenue Association. By 1908, there were eighty-four miles of subway, and the track to Brooklyn's Borough Hall was opened. The outer boroughs were further integrated into Manhattan when both the Queensboro and Manhattan Bridges were completed in 1909. The city's water supply was ensured when contracts expanded the Croton reservoir system into the Catskill watershed. Not even the bank panic of October 1907 could impede the city's advance, for during the crisis, Mayor McClellan and his comptroller personally asked J. P. Morgan to arrange a $30 million loan to safeguard the city's credit and payrolls.

The greatest human drama of McClellan's tenure was not the mayor's conflict with Murphy; rather, it was the continuing immigration to New York. Huge though the city was, its resources were strained by millions of arriving immigrants. In 1903, the cost of steerage passage from Bremen, Germany, had been lowered to $33.50, and by 1907 Ellis Island recorded its all-time high immigration figure of 1.28 million. Significantly, it was in 1908 that Israel Zangwill wrote his popular play *The Melting Pot* to describe New York. The newcomers came primarily from Russia, central Europe, and Italy, but in number, Jews were dominant. By 1910, more than 1.1 million Jews were living in New York, and the city as a whole was 41 percent foreign-born. It seemed that all Jewish newcomers read Abraham Cahan's *Forward*, a newspaper first published in 1897, and every family intended to send their children—if not themselves—to the free City College. In 1905 the East Side's elementary school population was 95 percent Jewish, and an educational revolution was under way in the crowded classrooms. Although fifty thousand earlier Jewish immigrants had already moved to Brownsville in Brooklyn by 1905, their removal had little discernible effect on the streets of Manhattan's tenement district. In 1906, as McClellan began his second term, thirty-seven of the fifty-one New York blocks housing more than three thousand people were located on the Lower East Side. Jacob Riis estimated the population density of the area at 330,000 per square mile, and the housing codes were meaningless when faced with the enormity of the problem. To help cope with the abject poverty, the *New York Times* began to solicit aid for "neediest" cases during the holiday season of 1910.

It is true that many New Yorkers resented the Jewish immigrants. The riot that marred Rabbi Jacob Joseph's funeral in July 1902 was tangible proof of the scorn in which they were held by other, earlier arrivals. Still others believed that the Jews were prone to crime. McClellan's own police commissioner charged that 50 percent of all New York crime was committed by newly arrived Russian Jews but was forced into a public retraction by the outraged Jewish community. In any case, New York absorbed the new immigrants, and like the Irish, Italians, and Germans before them, the Jews became a valuable part of the greater city.

Viewed from any perspective, Mayor McClellan's New York was the most exciting and vital city in America. Although he chose to retire in 1909 to a life of scholarship at Princeton University, McClellan bequeathed to New York a style of integrity and accomplishment that Murphy intended to maintain. But to find such competence in Tammany Hall was not easy, and ultimately Murphy's eye of necessity wandered across the East River and fastened on Supreme Court Judge William Gaynor (1848–1913). Although Gaynor's electability was suspect because he was a lapsed Catholic, his many conflicts with Brooklyn's Democratic leadership had earned him a reputation for integrity and strength. Moreover, he was an intense worker who tried more cases per month and suffered fewer reversals than any other metropolitan area justice. On balance, he seemed like the ideal candidate to replace McClellan and once again frustrate Hearst's mayoral ambitions.

After hard negotiations, Gaynor accepted the 1909 Democratic nomination and agreed to head a slate of Murphy-named officials in the race. Early in the campaign, however, during a visit to Tammany Hall, the judge asserted his independence. Gaynor asked the assembled sachems the whereabouts of "the Tiger . . . which they say is going to swallow me up. If there is any swallowing up, it is not at all unlikely that I may be on the outside of the Tiger!" Although the race was complicated when Hearst ran an independent Fusion campaign, its result was predictable. Gaynor, with 250,678 votes, easily outdistanced Republican Otto Bannard and won about 100,000 votes more than Hearst. Tammany Hall was back in power, or at least so it seemed.

The machine's revival was aborted. Manhattan had a population of 2.33 million in 1910, but not even that huge number was enough to return the Tammany hacks. Although Gaynor won, the rest of Murphy's slate did not, and the new mayor did not intend to trade his reputation for integrity that of a spoilsman. He accepted Murphy's demands for patronage with a smile and a few kind words, but then he ignored them. Prickly independence was the hallmark of Gaynor's administration, a trait that Murphy should have expected from a mayor who daily walked three miles to his office and who told suffragettes that all persons aspire "to that thing which [they] are least fitted for."

Gaynor's accomplishments were so significant that of all New York's 4.8 million people, only Hearst and Tammany resented his success. Gaynor not only ignored Murphy's patronage expectations, but he also overhauled the city payroll; his purge of "no-shows" from the lists cost the organization more than four hundred positions. Gaynor worked out an agreement with the Fusion majority of the Board of Estimate, and together they reorganized the Bureau of Weights and Measures, demanded that city employees put in full eight-hour days, and launched the legislative initiatives that became the "Gaynor Charter" of 1911.

It seems likely that 1910 was the finest year of Gaynor's life; his prospects seemed so limitless that some observers believed that his career might extend to the White House itself. Then, on August 9, as the mayor boarded the SS *Kaiser Wilhelm* for a well-deserved vacation, he was shot by a disgruntled, recently discharged dockworker named James Gallagher. Instead of leaving for Europe, Gaynor spent the next three weeks in St. Mary's Hospital, Hoboken. Gaynor had always been testy and opinionated—Mayor McClellan believed he was "never normal"—but the assassination attempt changed him for the worse. The bullet could not be removed from his pharynx, and the mayor lived with pain and increasing irascibility. He fought with John Purroy Mitchel, president of the Board of Aldermen; lost his allies on the Board of Estimate; and generally lost interest in obtaining the best appointees. His intemperate behavior forced him to write three public letters of apology, and the last years of his administration were constantly in turmoil.

The mayor's instability was hardly conducive to easing the heated atmosphere of New York City in 1910. Workers, especially in those trades dominated by Jewish immigrants with militantly socialist backgrounds, were increasing their use of the strike to obtain greater economic benefits. In 1909, the "Shirtwaist" women had gone on strike led by Clara Lemlich, an epic struggle in which "70,000 Jews became 70,000 fighters," even though they lost. In 1910, the cloakmakers and the shirtmakers struck, a battle that ended only when Louis Brandeis negotiated a "protocol of peace" in August. As 1911 began, labor militants united to demand changes in the intolerable conditions of the sweatshop lofts.

At the Triangle Shirtwaist Company, for example, the women were billed for their needles, taxed for their lockers, and charged triple fines for spoilage. Nevertheless, Triangle, located on the top three floors of the ten-story Asch Building at 22 Washington Place, had successfully resisted all attempts to bring the union into its workrooms. No union could have prevented the Triangle disaster, though. Just before quitting time on March 25, a fire broke out, killing the elevator operator. Although the fire department quickly arrived, its ladders reached only to the sixth floor. Within minutes, the building was an inferno, and 146 workers, 125 of them girls, died. The greatest factory disaster in New York history, the Triangle tragedy was made more terrible when a buildings department ruling declared the Asch Building unsafe—two days after the fire. In court, however, no negligence was found, and the judge ordered an acquittal. The heritage of the Triangle was greater labor militancy and more state action. In Albany, the legislature responded to the appeals by Al Smith and Robert Wagner to produce fifty-six factory reform measures.

There is no doubt that the deaths in the Triangle fire intensified unionization across New York; in 1913, for example, Jewish building workers founded their first union. And in the massive clothing industry, which produced $1 billion worth of goods in 1914, the Amalgamated Clothing Workers Union (later the ILGWU) was established. New York was on its way to becoming the preeminent "union town" in the nation.

Beyond worker militancy and political strife, New York City experienced many physical changes. In 1901, Macy's opened on Thirty-fourth Street, and in 1902, the Flatiron Building was constructed. The New York Stock Exchange was occupied in 1903, and the *Times* moved into its Tower on Longacre Square. On January 1, 1908, the paper inaugurated the custom of dropping an illuminated ball to greet the New Year in what everyone now calls Times Square. Architectural gems such as Cass Gilbert's Beaux Arts

Custom House (1905) the New York Hippodrome (1905), Stanford White's Colony Club (1906), and the French Renaissance Plaza Hotel (1907) were dedicated while McClellan ruled the city. In 1908, Ernest Flagg's Singer Building—at 612 feet the tallest building in the world—celebrated its opening; in 1967 it became the tallest structure ever demolished.

Gaynor's accession only intensified the metropolitan mania to express economic preeminence in monumental architecture. In 1909, the Metropolitan Tower surpassed the Singer Building by forty-five feet. Then on September 8, 1910, the new Pennsylvania Railroad Station opened, a duplication of the baths of Emperor Caracalla. Also in 1910, the Long Island Railroad, ultimately the line of sometimes immobilized commuters, first entered Manhattan on newly electrified tracks. Not all the construction was privately sponsored. The city continued the modernization of its piers and in 1911 completed the Hellgate Channel to the East River to speed intracity commerce. Perhaps the most impressive statement of the city's domination of commerce and transport came with twin dedications in 1913. On February 3, the Grand Central Terminal on Forty-second Street was opened, and on April 24, President Woodrow Wilson turned on the eighty thousand bulbs that illuminated Cass Gilbert's (1859–1934) "Cathedral of Commerce," the 792–foot Woolworth Building. For almost twenty years, the Woolworth was the world's tallest building, and its managers carefully maintain Gilbert's Gothic ornamentation to this day. O. Henry's wry comment, "New York will be a great place if they ever finish it," seemed justified in these years.

But if buildings demonstrated New York's economic might, they could also indicate its intellectual stature. Long-established colleges, forced to leave the crowded streets of lower Manhattan, created educational enclaves of distinction elsewhere in the city. In 1895, New York University moved part of its faculty to University Heights in the Bronx; in 1897, Columbia moved to Morningside Heights; and in 1907, City College moved uptown to Convent Avenue. Joseph Pulitzer, perhaps partly inspired by Hearst's notoriety and the increasing prestige of the *Times*, decided to endow a school of journalism, which opened at Columbia's new campus in 1911.

In that same year, on May 23, President William Howard Taft and Mayor Gaynor presided over the opening of the New York Public Library. Constructed at a cost of $9 million on the site of the reservoir in Bryant Park, the massive Beaux Arts structure became home to the Astor, Tilden, and Lenox Foundation bequests to the city. More important to scholars was the fact that its reference resources, ably organized by John Shaw Billings (1838–1913), have made Forty-second Street a mecca for generations of scholars.

Only the reputation of such an institution could dwarf the glory of the J. P. Morgan Library (built in 1913) and the more modest resources of the Municipal Reference Library. Yet another cultural landmark was under construction in 1913. Henry Clay Frick's mansion at Fifth Avenue and Seventieth Street ultimately became one of New York's smallest but finest museums.

Mayor Gaynor presided over New York with increasing bile and intemperance. On one hand, he insisted that the police rigidly enforce the peddler license laws, a measure that alienated Manhattan's smallest entrepreneurs and that proved almost impossible to carry out. On the other hand, Gaynor prevented the police from moving without warrants to close prostitution or gambling houses; he even forbade the free use of billy clubs to control crowds. Perhaps the mayor knew his police's capabilities, however, for when confronted with a major challenge—the July 16, 1912, murder of gambler Herman Rosenthal—the department proved to be incompetent. Although the Rosenthal case launched two careers, those of the journalist Herbert Swope and the prosecutor Charles Whitman, it did Gaynor no political good. In fact, it probably destroyed the slim chance he had to head the Democratic national ticket in 1912. Despite his wounds, police scandal, and the enmity of Murphy's Tammany Hall, Gaynor was eager for another term in 1913. His ego led him to accept a reform coalition's nomination for the mayoralty, and he sailed for Europe to rest up for what he knew would be an arduous campaign. En route, on September 10, 1913, Gaynor died with Emerson's *Essays* on his lap. Emerson once wrote that reform is dangerous, for it "runs to egotism and bloated self-conceit." There was a hint of that in Gaynor's last message to New York: "No king, no clown shall rule this town, that day is gone forever."

The "clown" Gaynor referred to was Boss Murphy's handpicked candidate, Judge Edward McCall. A loyal party man, McCall normally would have been assured of election, but his candidacy was undermined by Murphy's immoderate use of Tammany Hall's political power. In November 1912, the Democratic Party had elected William Sulzer (1863–1941) to the state house by the biggest majority in New York history, a large proportion of that majority being supplied by Tammany. When Sulzer vowed his complete independence in his inaugural address, Murphy responded, "Like hell." And when the governor supported a direct primary law abhorrent to the machine and refused to appoint an organization regular to the State Highway Commission, the battle lines were drawn.

Under Murphy's direction, the Democratic legislature, led by Al Smith, rejected the primary law and counterattacked by authorizing an investigation into the financing of Sulzer's campaign. On August 13, 1913, almost coincident with McCall's nomination, the Democrats in Albany impeached their own governor on charges that he had perjured himself, submitted false financial statements, and diverted campaign funds into private stock speculations. Sulzer was tried and removed from office by October 17. Murphy had demonstrated his total command of the party, but his unprecedented display of naked power gave reformers in the city an opportunity to recover from Gaynor's death and once again elect a Fusion candidate. Murphy's eight years of patronage drought were extended to twelve as the Fusion coalesced to win 57 percent of the vote and a stunning, unexpected victory.

John Purroy Mitchel had been identified with reform ever since he led an investigation in 1907/8 resulting in the removal of several borough presidents. Elected president of the Board of Aldermen in Gaynor's 1909 victory, Mitchel cooperated closely with the mayor on major projects, and during the mayor's hospitalization he had been an effective acting chief executive. Since May 1913, Mitchel had served as collector of the port and had worked to master the bureaucracy and bring efficiency into traditionally lax customs operations. When the Fusion faction, now directed by Hearst, asked him to take Gaynor's place at the head of a reform ticket, Mitchel did not hesitate. With the support of President Wilson, Hearst, and Progressives of all types, Mitchel led his coalition to victory. Mitchel's platform was simplicity itself. "I want to make New York the best governed city in the world."

The greatest problem Mitchel had in governing the city was his own character; he was an elitist who constantly underestimated the importance of the machine in providing personal attention to the needs of New Yorkers. Instead, Mitchel believed that simply by naming efficient commissioners, among them several of his personal friends, he could rid the government of municipal patronage. Although the bureaucracy was hurt, it was never destroyed. Like his predecessor, Mitchel survived an assassination attempt, on April 17, 1914. He also successfully led the city through a short-term currency deficiency caused by the outbreak of World War I. Even though the state legislature ignored this crisis, Mitchel successfully negotiated an $80 million loan from the Morgan syndicate and placed the city on a "pay as you go" footing. The mayor's problem was that he could never convince the average citizen that this was a magnificent accomplishment: the ordinary person saw only fewer jobs and reduced public services. Mitchel won the approval of his friends from the upper classes but lacked empathy with workingmen. He was considered a "Manhattan mayor" unconcerned with the common folk.

Mitchel's creed was "Be right and speak out." He personally intervened to settle garment industry and transit strikes in 1916, but already he was entering political limbo. Murphy had regained the Board of Aldermen, the district attorney, and the sheriff's office in the elections of 1915, and Mitchel desperately needed to show the city he was more than a passing phenomenon. In July 1916, the mayor strongly supported a zoning plan that implemented the recommendations of the 1912 conference on city planning. New York soon adopted the first zoning code in the nation, one that mandated "setbacks" for skyscrapers and created the ziggurat form that characterized the next four decades of New York architecture.

Mitchel believed in economy and ruthlessly pruned the civil service lists while reducing taxes. He hoped to achieve major financial benefits by imposing the Gary plan, an educational reform that provided vocational training and made more efficient use of school facilities. In pursuit of this goal, Mitchel dismissed the head of the Board of Education, arrogantly ignored parents' objections, and vetoed most school construction projects. Although cities across the nation recognized the revolutionary nature of the Gary plan and adopted it widely, in New York City the mayor's political ineptness alienated many voters and ultimately destroyed the appeal of the innovations. To compound his difficulties, Mitchel, although he was himself a Catholic, decided to reduce public subsidies to privately administered religious charities. During those battles, he attacked religiously affiliated child care institutions and actually had the telephone of a Catholic priest tapped. By 1917, his Fusion coalition was shrinking, and he had lost the support of the Hearst papers. Mitchel's City Hall performance, even as he accepted Fusion's renomination on July 30, 1917, presaged a Democratic revival.

It had been twelve years since Tammany Hall enjoyed the patronage riches of New York City. Indeed, Murphy had been far more effective in influencing state government than in controlling his own city. Some party leaders called 1917 Murphy's "last chance" to prove his competence, and he rose to their challenge. To restore the normal Democratic majority against a weakened Fusion coalition, Murphy's eye fell on Brooklyn County Judge John Francis Hylan (1869–1936), a loyal Democrat, though many considered him rather dull witted. Murphy arranged a scenario in which Kings County Democrats forced Hylan "down his throat" at the party convention. To complete Murphy's coup, Hylan also won media support from the Hearst publications.

The unknown factor in the campaign was how voters would react to America's entry into World War I. Mitchel launched an independent campaign against "Hearst, Hylan, and the Hohenzollerns" while seeking to restore his middle-class base. Among the mayor's supporters were Presidents Taft, Roosevelt, and Wilson as well as New York Governor Charles Evans Hughes. But the result was inevitable. On November 6, Hylan (and Murphy) won an overwhelming victory, 313,956 votes to the mayor's 155,497. Not only was the "boy mayor" retired, but his upper-class supporters were shocked by the 145,332 votes cast for Morris Hillquit (1869–1933), the Socialist candidate. Mitchel, who had ardently supported Wilson's preparedness policy, decided to enlist in the air force, even though he was already thirty-eight. He died during a training flight on July 8, 1918, and his memory was honored when an aviation depot was given his name. Sadly, most New Yorkers believe that Long Island's Mitchel Field commemorated the career of bombing advocate General "Billy" Mitchell, rather than a former mayor of New York.

"Red Mike" Hylan was elected mayor in 1917, the year that America entered the war. In 1913, New York's trade had declined to only 58 percent of the nation's imports and 37 percent of its export trade, but the outbreak of World War I restored the losses. During the nineteen months of America's participation in the war, New York and Hoboken served as major ports of embarkation for the American Expeditionary Force. Even before April 1917, the demands on the port facilities had been overwhelming, but as men, munitions, and supplies of every description converged on the city, the situation became catastrophic. The local rail terminals could not handle the traffic, and trains were backed up as far as Pittsburgh. The harbor facilities, even including the 6 million square feet of the new Bush Terminal in Brooklyn, were so overtaxed that some ships were forced to sail without full loads in order to make wharf space available. Only the appointment of Irving T. Bush as chairman of the War Board of the Port of New York brought order out of chaos. By mid-1918, the port was operating more smoothly than it ever had, although tonnage going toward the port had increased owing to the widening and deepening of the Erie Canal in 1918. New York benefited from the wartime trade in money as well as commerce, replacing London as the center of international finance.

Perhaps the most impressive aspect of New York life during the war was the city's ability to avoid the animosities of the European conflict. Although Germans comprised 15 percent of the population, their lives and property were not subjected to ugly incidents like those occurring elsewhere in the nation, a fact for which Mayors Mitchel and Hylan deserve much credit. The city rallied as a unit to the war effort, and Hylan even dared to name

Hearst, whose newspapers had been pro-German in 1914, as an official greeter for returning soldiers.

The *New York Times* had been appalled when Hylan, "a man of marvelous mental density," was elected, and President Wilson wondered, "How is it possible for the greatest city in the world to place such a man in high office?" The answer, of course, was the organized power of Tammany. After 1917 and for the first time since 1906, Murphy could deal with a sympathetic partisan in City Hall. This did not mean dishonest government practice. No fewer than three investigating panels later agreed that Hylan was honest and that the city was well administered. Not even the destructive Wall Street explosion on September 16, 1920, a blast that killed thirty-three and was blamed on terrorists, could shake the stability of Hylan's administration.

Hylan pointed with pride to the opening of $30 million worth of municipal piers on Staten Island in 1919, the largest school construction/education budgets in city history, the elimination of police graft by Commissioner Richard Enright, and the construction of the Bronx Terminal Market. Above all else, Hylan maintained—as his campaign had promised to do—the five-cent subway fare. The mayor intended to construct a municipally owned transit system and named John Delaney to plan what became the Independent Subway System. In yet another transit innovation, the states of New York and New Jersey created the tax-exempt Port Authority on April 30, 1921, "to purchase, construct, lease, and/or operate terminals and transportation facilities" and to integrate all harbor activities. Modeled after London's Authority, the first such agency in America became one of the major forces in determining New York's future. The voters obviously perceived in Hylan an honesty of purpose that compensated for his lack of humor and uninspired rhetoric. Thus, on November 8, 1921, once again with the support of Murphy, Hearst, and the people, Hylan was reelected by a plurality of 417,000 votes. Problems of image notwithstanding, he became the first modern mayor to serve eight consecutive years and only the second since consolidation to win reelection.

Extraordinary municipal progress continued during Hylan's second term. A massive educational building program provided the city with 662 schools by 1925, an achievement lavishly praised by the *Daily News*, established in 1919. Pictures showed the mayor at the Regional Plan Association; he was there when automatic telephone dialing began in October 1922; and he became the first mayor heard over the facilities of WNYC Radio. Some of Hylan's ideas were too grandiose, and the subway to Staten Island that he authorized is still unbuilt. But this forgotten mayor endorsed projects such as the Triborough Bridge and a high school for the arts that were to return great benefit to the city.

In 1924, two "nonevents" occurred that helped determine New York City's future. The first of these incidents revolved around a "home rule" amendment that the voters had approved in November 1923. The Gaynor charter needed to be revised; "home rule" seemed to be the answer; and in 1924 the Board of Estimate was combined with the aldermen to form the Municipal Assembly. But this administrative "reform" accomplished nothing. Mayors fought just as much with the new body, and not for fifteen more years was a new city charter approved.

The second event that might have changed city history but did not was the convocation of the Democratic National Convention in Madison Square Garden. America's preeminent Democrat was New York Governor Al Smith (1873–1944), a politician groomed for national office by Charles Murphy. Many assumed that Smith would lead the ticket and focus his party's program on the needs of urban America. But then on April 30, 1924, death removed Murphy's sure hand from the political scene. State Senator James J. Walker (1881–1946) lamented, "The brains of Tammany lie in Calvary Cemetery." When the Democrats met on June 24, they lacked a directing authority, and the convention proved to be the greatest debacle in America's party history. A record 103 ballots were taken before the delegates, hopelessly divided between urban and rural constituencies, chose John W. Davis as their compromise nominee. Smith, Catholics, and urban America had been rebuffed, and not for another fifty-two did years a Democratic National Convention dare meet in New York City.

Others did come and marveled. When the great French architect Le Corbusier visited the city in 1920, he called it "a catastrophe, but it is a beautiful catastrophe." Manhattan, which Le Corbusier was referring to, reached the peak of its population in 1910 and had begun a slow decline from 2.3 million persons. Yet to visitors and to New Yorkers in the outer boroughs, it remained "the city." Manhattan was an amalgam of neighborhoods, encompassing the bohemian lifestyle of Greenwich Village, the staid residential enclaves of Murray Hill, and the exciting yet depressing streets of Harlem. Good housing was everywhere at a premium. In 1922, when revision of the state housing code permitted insurance companies to participate in housing projects, Metropolitan Life began a development in Queens. In Woodside, also in Queens, the garden apartments of the Steinway Company were built. Architects such as Otto Eidletz, August Heckscher, Adolph Zukor, and Louis

Horowitz added their visions of beauty to the urban skyline. In the 1920s, the Equitable and Strauss Buildings, the Paramount Theater, Gimbel's Department Store, and the McAlpin, Ambassador, and Waldorf-Astoria Hotels were constructed. In November 1925, a new Madison Square Garden on Eighth Avenue replaced the structure in which the Democrats met disaster. In sum, the vitality of New York during the Jazz Age was overwhelming, a vast contrast to its plodding, albeit efficient, mayor.

Within the sacred precincts of Tammany, changes became apparent after Murphy's death. The leadership had fallen to George W. Olvany (1873–1952), a lawyer who had previously directed only the Polar Bear Club at Coney Island. The state's most powerful Democrat was now Al Smith, who made no secret of his disdain for Hylan—the "imperfect demagogue"—and his principal supporter, Hearst. When the *Times* pointed out that the mayor had taken four vacations in the last six months of 1924, Smith decided to act. He joined Olvany and the new leader of Bronx County, Ed Flynn (1891–1953), to oppose Hylan. In the bitter primary battle of 1925, the three supported popular state Senator Jimmy Walker, an effective legislator whose bills had authorized public Sunday baseball, boxing, and movies.

Robert Moses later wrote that Walker "had genuine charm, not charisma," and later events proved this assessment to be true. However, the issue in 1925 was raw political power, and the party primary was a war of the Manhattan and Bronx machines against the outer boroughs. Walker won the September primary by 100,000 votes, thereby relegating Hylan to the sidelines. His November 3 victory over Republican Frank Waterman was almost anticlimactic. Walker, a loyal party man, took over as mayor, and his accession seemed to promise the continuation of good times for Tammany and the entire city.

Walker had a glittering personality, lots of show business pals, and an intuitive sense of public relations. But he had no knowledge of city government and no desire to learn. He was a dilettante with style, and it seems somehow fitting that he was the first mayor whose inauguration was broadcast live on the radio. Voters greeted his appointees for the police and health commissioners with universal approval; few complained that Tammany retained twenty of the twenty-five commissionerships. Moreover, Walker's excellent relations with the Municipal Assembly proved a welcome respite from the acrimony of Hylan's last years. Walker made his administrative responsibilities secondary to enjoying the wonders of his hometown.

Walker came to symbolize the Jazz Age in New York, a time of heavy drinking and rather loose private and public morals. Yet despite his habitual lateness, Walker did preside with flair over the ceremonial aspects of his office. He helped bury Rudolph Valentino, greeted channel swimmer Gertrude Ederle with a ticker-tape parade, and starred at the city's Tercentenary Celebration. City business was not entirely neglected, however. The mayor arbitrated a subway strike, improved the sanitation department, and encouraged the police department to continue gambling raids. But Walker was always happiest when he was in the public eye.

Official business intruded little on Walker's life. He took 149 days of vacation in his first thirty months in office, and often permitted men who hoped to do business with the city to pay his bills. Although New York had 7 million residents and a budget of $500 million, the mayor simply ignored his day-to-day responsibilities. Commissioners ran the city while Tammany Hall took care of patronage. In 1928 Walker named Grover Whalen (1886–1962) as New York's official greeter, to handle the ceremonial aspects of his office. The onerous weight of the mayoralty was thus totally lifted from his shoulders so that "our Jimmy" could fully devote himself to other pursuits, largely that of a dancer named Betty Compton.

In the vernacular of show business, 1928 was a year of mixed reviews for the "night mayor." Walker decided to leave his wife and took up residence with Betty Compton at the Ritz Carlton. Reporters tolerantly ignored the scandal, but Governor Smith, a strict Catholic, was appalled. Potentially as disruptive was a court decision on May 2 that increased the IRT's transit fare to seven cents. Walker, whose sense of political survival was always alert, ordered an immediate appeal. Later, when an IRT accident killed sixteen people in the Times Square Station, he used the tragedy and the fare hike to flay the transit operators. But Walker's attention always returned to Miss Compton, and he willfully ignored rumors of corruption. Even after the borough president of Queens was convicted of rigging sewer contracts, the mayor did nothing. Despite all the evil portents, Walker persisted in taking more vacations and having yet another drink.

The Great Depression began in 1929, but the year turned out a triumphant one for New York's mayor. In March, John F. Curry (1873–1957), a fine organizer and Walker's ally, replaced George Olvany as the grand sachem of Tammany Hall. On April 8, the Supreme Court denied the IRT its fare increase and even ordered it to pay the city an additional $6.3 million in overdue revenues. The electorate cheered the decision as a Walker coup and was also impressed when the mayor created the city's first Department of Hospitals. Walker's reelection chances suddenly seemed more secure, and as if to highlight his good fortune, a new Central Park casino opened in

May. Inside its gilded rooms. Walker was never presented with a bill. Both the mayor and the city were thoroughly enjoying themselves. Walker's only complaint was "I have not had as much fun as I get the credit or the blame for."

On July 18, the philanthropist August Heckscher led a group of public-spirited citizens who demanded that Walker accept renomination. The mayor honored the petition, and despite his loss of support from Smith and in the face of Republican charges of citywide corruption, Walker easily won the fall election by a margin of 865,000 votes. The only shadow on his victory was the collapse of the stock market on October 29, the crash that signaled the onset of the Depression. Blithely ignoring this catastrophe, Walker accepted a $15,000 raise in December. He was one of few New Yorkers who received a raise in the 1930s.

Aside from his larger salary, the decade did not begin well for Walker. In January 1930, he was warned to alter his lifestyle by no less a personage than Patrick Cardinal Hayes (1867–1938). In March, more than one hundred people were injured when Communists clashed with police in Union Square; a new police commissioner hastily had to be found. Moreover, U.S. Attorney Charles Tuttle had found massive incompetence or corruption in New York's magistrate's court system. As a result of Tuttle's charges, an investigation was launched in September by Judge Samuel Seabury (1873–1958). From Tammany's point of view, the Seabury probe meant danger. Corruption was soon discovered not only among the magistrates but also in the women's court and the police vice squad. The scandal grew even more ominous when eight Democratic district leaders refused to waive immunity and give testimony. The great Democratic machine was suddenly threatened with disaster.

Tammany fought back with an attempt at intimidation. Early in 1931, the city's corporation counsel refused to honor the salary vouchers for Seabury's staff of investigators, and only a court order forced a release of the money. It was becoming clear, however, that corruption in the magistrate's courts was so transparently manifest that the district attorney's office had failed to exercise its oversight function. When in March 1931 a prospective witness was murdered, Governor Franklin Roosevelt expanded Seabury's investigation to include the district attorney's office. By April 8, a general investigation of all city government was under way.

A picture of municipal incompetence on a gargantuan scale emerged when the "tin box" brigade, led by Sheriff Thomas Farley of Manhattan, was summoned to give testimony before Seabury. It was soon discovered, among other revelations, that the Board of Standards and Appeals had no standards; that city condemnation procedures cost the municipality millions; that the new Department of Hospitals was a bureaucratic nightmare; that the clerk of Queens Surrogates Court did not know his duties; that 90 percent of welfare went to Democrats; that George Olvany's law firm could "expedite" city contracts; that one witness could not remember where he borrowed $500,000; and on and on—the list seemed endless.

Nonetheless, Tammany leaders had no intention of waiving immunity. Why should they have to when, despite all these revelations, their machine swept the city elections of November 1931? But embarrassing questions now were being raised about the mayor's actions. Who had paid for his many vacations, and why? Why did Walker's personal financial agent refuse Seabury's invitation to return from Mexico and testify? What, if anything, had the mayor contributed when he participated in certain stock speculations? Finally, the long-anticipated confrontation between Mayor Walker and Judge Seabury took place on May 25–26, 1932.

Walker once said that every man must be "born, die, and testify" alone, and in sparring with Seabury the mayor was brilliantly evasive. On June 22, the governor ordered Walker to reply formally to Seabury's allegations. Walker did so only after his return from the Democratic National Convention in Chicago that nominated Franklin Roosevelt for the presidency. There the unrepentant mayor had voted for Al Smith and joined in Tammany's refusal to make Roosevelt's nomination unanimous. The governor, in turn, was less than pleased with Walker's response to Seabury. Therefore, as mandated by section 122 of the city charter, Roosevelt decided to hold public hearings on the Walker case. Once again, Walker confronted Seabury, but this time the investigators' questions were so cunningly prepared that a denial of one charge implied guilt in another area. After that session, Roosevelt had no option but to remove Walker. But before he could, "Our Jimmy" resigned on September 1, 1932. Walker blustered he would go to the voters in November for vindication, but he never did; he left shortly thereafter for exile in Europe. His departure signaled the end of the carefree Jazz Age in New York.

After suffering through the tenure of reform mayors, the Hylan-Walker years gave Tammany an opportunity to prove it could effectively administer New York. By 1932, however, the organization was thoroughly discredited, and the prosperity of the "roaring twenties" was replaced by welfare rolls approaching 900,000. Nevertheless, reform remained in eclipse, and the organization remained the single most potent force in New York politics.

Indeed, in the special election of November 1932, the machine swamped the hopes of the interim mayor, Joseph McKee (1889–1956), whose independent character made him anathema to professionals, and easily elected John J. O'Brien (1873–1951) to complete the final year of Walker's term. O'Brien's talents were perhaps best summarized by his often-quoted response when asked the identity of his new police commissioner. "I don't know," said the mayor of New York, "they haven't told me yet."

Although Tammany had experienced political disaster, the city's fundamental vitality could not be doubted. Depression had reduced the port's percentage of imports, but only to 50 percent of America's total. Despite the crash, membership on the stock exchange had expanded, and the assessed valuation of city real estate reached an all-time high in 1931. Although Manhattan remained the most valuable land on earth, even in an outer borough like Queens, land values soared 1,000 percent between 1905 and 1929. While the construction industry was temporarily depressed, previously begun projects were completed. In 1928, the Port Authority completed the Outerbridge Crossing to New Jersey, and in 1931 the Holland Tunnel and the George Washington Bridge opened. Old institutions such as Pulitzer's *World* would die (1931), but they were soon replaced. New landmark buildings soared upward. In 1930, Art Deco had its grandest monument when William Van Alen's seventy-seven-story Chrysler Building was occupied and, for a brief moment, reigned as the world's tallest building. It seemed that all New York needed—despite the Depression—was enlightened leadership to match its economic powers. But reform had frittered away several opportunities. Low, McClellan, Gaynor, and Mitchel all had proved to be less than inspiring. Tammany had brought prosperity, but its regime had culminated in scandal and cynicism. When would the world's greatest city have the leadership its eminence deserved?

8

The La Guardia Era

The hedonism and exuberance of Jimmy Walker perfectly suited the roaring spirit characteristic of the 1920s. In New York City, that glorious decade saw the traditional dominance of Tammany Hall reestablished after a long hiatus. Equally prevalent across the nation was a deep respect for business enterprise and corporate leadership. Then came the great market crash of 1929. Walker's failure was one of character that Tammany might someday overcome, but there could be no such quick fix for the reputation of the American business community. For half a century, the economy of both the nation and its biggest city had proceeded in an endless upward spiral, for which the American businessman took full credit. Americans had come to believe in the expertise, the acumen, and the style of business leadership just as much as Democrats had come to expect huge vote majorities from New York City. By 1930, however, both capitalism and Tammany Hall seemed to be tottering. As the impact of political scandal and economic catastrophe worked their way into New Yorkers' consciousness, it suddenly became apparent that calamity was now in control. Tammany Hall was unable to save Jimmy Walker, and formerly all-wise business leaders simply did not know what to do in the face of the market collapse.

The fifteenth census reported that the population of New York in 1930 was 6,930,416, and the assessed valuation of city properties in 1931 reached an all-time high of $19 billion. It was difficult to imagine that so vast a conglomerate of people and power could be threatened by financial collapse, especially since the city was well within its legal debt and taxation limits. Nevertheless, a sense of disaster pervaded Tammany, and its praise for the Walker administration seemed as hollow as President Herbert Hoover's platitudes about prosperity returning to America. As the deflation that characterized the early years of the Depression deepened, the city's ability to meet its obligations to its people became suspect.

In 1930/31, the harassed Walker administration had been forced to fire eleven thousand schoolteachers in a desperate attempt to balance its budget, but the benefits were fleeting. All municipal welfare funds had been spent, and private charity agencies, many of whose services had quietly been paid by the city treasury, proved incapable of providing much relief to the growing legions of unemployed New Yorkers. Governor Franklin D. Roosevelt was forced to convene a special legislative session to consider the twin issues of local relief costs and emergency food supplies. By 1932, a third of the city's manufacturing plants had closed, and up to 1.6 million New Yorkers were receiving some sort of relief; fully a quarter of the population was out of work. In such a situation, did it really matter if Jimmy Walker would be forced to resign? Never had the city of New York faced such an overwhelming economic crisis. And never had there been a better opportunity to make profound, even revolutionary, changes in American life.

If New Yorkers had anything to cheer about in these bleak years of the decade, it was the continued development of the cityscape. The Chrysler Building had been completed in April 1930, but even more impressive was the Empire State Building, which began construction on October 1, 1929. The structure proceeded upward despite complicated financial and union difficulties, and New Yorkers watched enthralled as the marvel grew, often at the rate of four stories in a single week. However, when its doors opened on May 1, 1931, there were few renters, and the Empire State Corporation teetered on the brink of bankruptcy for years. Less than a mile uptown, a new Waldorf-Astoria Hotel opened for business in October 1931, even as another gigantic project was being constructed. Midtown land slated to host an opera house had become available after the crash and was soon purchased by the Rockefellers. They soon announced that a business and entertainment center, ultimately covering 14.5 acres, would be constructed there. The project was Rockefeller Center, and constructing its fourteen massive buildings would be the work of a decade. In 1931, the project's workmen decided that they deserved a little Christmas celebration, so they decorated a small Christmas tree in the work site, beginning a tradition that continues today.

The nadir of the Depression in New York came in 1932, and the city approached bankruptcy as Walker's political troubles mounted. On July 22, the mayor told his 148,557 municipal employees that they must accept a cut in wages if the city was to survive. Already the city's debt of $1.9 billion was equal to that of all forty-eight states combined, and one-third of the city's budget was being used to service its obligations. Even as Walker was speaking, he was negotiating with a banking coalition that demanded a reduction of $40 million in the budget before it would make any more loans.

As events turned out, however, it was not Walker who implemented the harsh agreement, but his successor "Holy Joe" McKee. In the two months he governed following Walker's abdication, McKee carried out the painful job of slashing jobs and reducing salaries. His ruthlessness was one factor that allowed Tammany Hall to elect John O'Brien to complete Walker's term. O'Brien, a hack given to malapropisms, approached the crisis on a "business as usual" basis. Bankers were not convinced by rhetoric, however, and in 1933 they forced the city to accept another "bankers' agreement." In return for cash at high interest over a three-year period, the city limited real estate taxes, created a budget reserve, and made a serious effort to penalize those in tax arrears. New York also agreed to drop proposed new taxes on stocks, savings banks, and insurance companies. The agreement saved the city and protected Tammany's padded payrolls but also provided further evidence that the business/clubhouse alliance that had operated during the 1920s was still functioning. Did O'Brien, and constantly rising debt service, represent New York's future? Was it impossible for the nation's biggest city to have a leadership comparable to that of Franklin Roosevelt's, with his "hundred-day" domination of Congress? Responding to such demands, the old coalition of reformers and Republicans made plans to wrest control from the hated machine in the election of 1933.

The disgrace of Tammany and Walker rather than the Depression provided the backdrop for the reform campaign. The ideal reform candidate for mayor would have been the incorruptible Judge Seabury himself, but his eye was on the governorship, and he refused to run. His prestige gave him veto power over the reformers' selection, however, and he rejected such proposed candidates as Robert Moses (1888–1981) and General John F. O'Ryan. Ultimately, and perhaps inevitably, the reformers turned to the independent-minded candidate the Republicans had sacrificed to the Walker landslide of 1929. In that race, Fiorello La Guardia (1882–1947) had not carried a single assembly district despite his incessant charges that the Walker administration meant public larceny. But by 1933, La Guardia had been proved right.

La Guardia was available to run because he had been ousted from Congress during the 1932 Democratic landslide. Yet even defeat paid dividends, for La Guardia cooperated with Roosevelt's incoming New Dealers during the transition months. A La Guardia candidacy under the Fusion banner would ensure Roosevelt's neutrality in the campaign against Tammany. It was Adolf Berle who arranged a meeting between Seabury and La Guardia that resulted in a "meeting of minds" and the judge's approval.

On August 3, 1933, La Guardia received the Fusion nomination and began his campaign in a typically frenetic style. The Seabury revelations had so thoroughly discredited Tammany that the real contest was between Fusion and the Recovery Party led by Joseph McKee. La Guardia secured the increasingly influential Jewish bloc by accusing McKee of youthful anti-Semitism, a potent charge in the year that Hitler came to power. In November, the four-leaf clover ticket of Fusion was victorious, even though it received only 40 percent of the total vote. On January 1, 1934, in Seabury's office, La Guardia took his oath as mayor, and reform had the leader it deserved. A new era in city history was about to begin.

Fiorello H. La Guardia, the ninety-ninth mayor of New York, was born in Greenwich Village on December 11, 1882. Historians have called him an ethnic ticket all by himself, since he was the child of a Jewish mother and an Italian father, was raised in Arizona and Italy, and was an Episcopalian by faith. Moreover, while employed by the Consular Service from 1900 to 1906 and the Immigration Station at Ellis Island from 1907 to 1910, he had learned to speak half a dozen languages. As a young lawyer, La Guardia developed a hatred of Tammany and its corporate allies, and this loathing became his hallmark. He joined the Republican Party and in 1916 became the first Italian American ever elected to Congress. After a brief military career, he became president of the Board of Aldermen in 1919. There his independence alienated his own party regulars, although he effectively cooperated with Mayor Hylan. When the Republicans ignored him as a mayoral candidate in 1921, he again won a congressional seat and served brilliantly in Washington from 1922 to 1932. He learned where the levers of power were located and how they operated. No man had ever been more suited to the task of governing New York.

La Guardia took over a city in crisis and promised it only difficult times; there would be "no more free lunch" for New York, its employees, and its people. "Nonpartisan, nonpolitical local government" was his goal, and he believed that principles of good administration could overcome New York's heritage of corruption and the national depression. The mayor's immediate concerns were a budget $30 million in deficit, the 142,000 families on relief, and the fact that the city was mortgaged to the terms of the bankers' agreement. Only $39 million remained of the $70 million relief loan, and that would be gone by August 1934.

La Guardia wanted to dedicate his first hundred days to "clearing away the debris and repairing the ruins" left by Tammany misrule, but financial affairs took priority. It was immediately evident that only a tax increase could maintain the relief program. Therefore, the mayor's economy plan, proposed on January 2, contained as its centerpiece a major La Guardia concession. He dropped his lifelong opposition to a sales tax and proposed a 2 percent levy to finance the city's share of relief costs. When combined with a 3 percent utility tax, a gross profits tax of one-tenth of 1 percent, and modifications of the bankers' agreement, the "temporary" sales tax would keep the city solvent.

Major metropolitan tax programs must receive state legislative approval, and in Albany, the city's future looked uncertain. Democratic Governor Herbert Lehman (1878–1963) criticized the measure for leading to a mayoral "dictatorship," and it came close to defeat many times before he reluctantly signed it in April. After his one hundred days, La Guardia had a tax program, but as he wrote to Senator Robert Wagner, "I am so tired . . . at times I can hardly stand it." Nevertheless, with new taxes in place by the fall, La Guardia proceeded to balance his budget by breaking his campaign pledge of no reduction in civil service salaries. His economy measures included payless furloughs, but the job was done. Hundreds of municipal workers were abruptly terminated, not all of them Tammany drones. The harsh measures resulted in twenty years of financial stability for the city.

New York's economic recovery took years, but only days after taking office, the mayor had dramatically revealed his feelings about corruption and crime. His symbolic first act was to order the arrest of mobster Charles "Lucky" Luciano; the mayor's filmed physical attack on slot machines came later after the city won a legal injunction against federal acceptance of the gambling equipment. These were public relations spectacles, but more lasting was La Guardia's conviction that "to the victor belongs the responsibility of good government." He intended to purge city government of patronage hacks and named to his Fusion cabinet men free of political strings: their prime concern would be the proper management of their departments. The roster of his commissioners read like an honor roll of the most expert and capable New York public servants: Adolf Berle, Paul Blanchard, Edward Corsi, Sigismund S. Goldwater, Austin MacCormick, Robert Moses, John Rice, Louis Valentine, and Paul Windels.

Not only were these men whose dedication could not be doubted, but also their nonpolitical character eased the Democratic legislature's acceptance of La Guardia's financial program. In all, the city's "hundred days" saved its credit, laid the foundation for a balanced budget, and began a massive program of governmental reorganization. Moreover, Democratic fears that La Guardia would build a Fusion machine from his commissioners' expertise were soon dispelled. The mayor's intention was far more noble: he intended to create an electoral force based on the people's trust in him. La Guardia was sometimes a tyrant, an autocrat, a showman, and a clown, but he was always wooing his electorate. His strange love affair with the city lasted for twelve years and revolutionized both the form of urban government and the physical structure of New York.

La Guardia's administration endured tremendous problems in its first winter. It was so cold that armories had to be opened to the homeless lest they freeze to death. So much snow fell that the city was able to pay for its removal only by selling short-term city notes to the Teacher's Retirement Fund. Taxi drivers, waiters, and laundrymen all went on strike, and the 164 breadlines were hardly sufficient to feed the hungry. The WPA administrator for New York even accused La Guardia of not trying to move people from welfare to work relief, and a special committee on welfare, the first of many such investigations, had to be appointed.

Then the police commissioner decided that he could not work with La Guardia, and in September the harassed mayor named Chief Inspector Louis Valentine (1882–1946) as commissioner. With the mayor's full support, Valentine "got tough" with criminals and approved a "third degree" form of questioning. Above all else, he tolerated no police corruption. Valentine ousted 244 cops during his tenure, and angry patrolmen said he caused another 83 suicides. He set in motion one of the NYPD's periodic purges and actually slowed the upward surge of crime statistics.

Of all La Guardia's appointees, none figured more prominently in 1934 than Parks Commissioner Robert Moses (1888–1981). Moses, who had built the state's park system, began his thirty-four-year career as the remodeler of New York City by dismissing the five borough park boards and firing hundreds of workers. Beyond his talent, vigor, and administrative expertise, Moses had one additional virtue. Only he, of all La Guardia's men, dared yell back at him. La Guardia kept his parks commissioner even despite Roosevelt's dislike of him. By the end of 1934, sixty new parks had already been constructed, and the city was making plans to appeal to Washington for federal funds for similar projects. Before Moses completed his unique career, he supervised more than $20 billion of construction projects.

The single most vital factor in winning federal funding was La Guardia's budget achievements in the fall of 1934. After the mayor balanced the city budget, the federal government approved funds for a series of major construction projects that provided the foundation for New York's economic recovery. In welfare aid alone, New York received more than $1 billion between 1933 and 1939. La Guardia also received invaluable assistance from

Al Smith, who convinced Washington to take leases on the vacant floor space of the Empire State Building. The jobs and salaries brought to New York helped the city recover. But regarding Tammany, La Guardia had no mercy. The prime sufferers of La Guardia's purge of patronage jobs were Irish Democrats, and one historian estimates that only 5 percent of new government jobs under La Guardia returned to them. Far more favored, with 15 percent of the jobs, were Italians who had given Fiorello more than 60 percent of their votes and WASP reformers who had provided the crucial victory margin for Fusion. Most fortunate of all were the second- or third-generation descendants of the great Jewish migration. By the 1930s, more than half New York's doctors, lawyers, dentists, and teachers were Jewish, and this middle-class cadre saw La Guardia as the finest opportunity for good government in their lifetime. They rallied to La Guardia en masse, ignoring rumors that the mayor made both anti-Semitic and antiblack comments in private. Jews received even more government jobs than Italians did from La Guardia, and for a decade, they remained his most electorally loyal supporters.

One startling factor complicated the ethnic politics of the La Guardia years. The arrival of immigrant groups and their acculturation had long been a feature of New York life, but scholars suddenly discovered that the city's newest immigrants had arrived almost unnoticed, and they were black. The passage of restrictive quota laws in 1924 had briefly removed the question of foreign immigration from the consciousness of New York's politicians. But even then, the movement known as the Great Migration—which transferred the country's black farm population into its urban centers—had been under way for a decade. Indeed, in 1933 only Mayor O'Brien had wooed the black voters of Harlem, a neighborhood usually ignored but one he called "the garden spot of the world." In his usual bumbling fashion, O'Brien told unreceptive audiences, "My heart is as black as yours."

Yet suddenly and unexpectedly, La Guardia's New York was 5 percent black. Almost all this population was poor, and their future welfare became an important political consideration for the mayor. This concern was intensified in March 1935 when a sudden riot exploded in the streets of O'Brien's "garden." White shopkeepers had been threatened, and the black presence had to be discussed in the same way as had earlier questions of Irish, Italian, or Jewish immigration. The mayor's task force discovered enormous black resentment "against racial discrimination and poverty in the midst of plenty."

Although the La Guardia administration seemed surprised to discover that it had a racial issue on its hands, it should not have been. The history of blacks in New York began with black farmers tending crops in the bouweries of New Amsterdam, and the arrival of the first slaves was recorded in 1626. In the seventeenth-century city, both the Dutch and English had enacted slave codes to regulate the blacks who lived in Manhattan. Economic competition among the races and the abuse of blacks led to purported conspiracies in 1712 and 1741, and repression solved nothing. Yet the city also fostered a countervailing tendency toward tolerance. As early as 1750, blacks who met property requirements were entitled to vote, and additional blacks won their freedom during the Revolutionary era by serving in the Continental army. By the time the Constitution was adopted in 1787, 10 percent of the city population was black. although only a third was free. Slavery as a legal institution did not end in New York until 1827, but long before that year, Manhattan blacks had their own free schools and comprised a voting bloc important to municipal elections.

Until the 1820s, Tammany Hall identified with abolitionism, and it was only when Irish and German immigrants began to outnumber blacks that its antislavery commitment waned. European newcomers also took blacks' jobs. In 1830, 50 percent of Manhattan's servants were black, but by 1850, that number was reduced to 10 percent, with Irish serving maids becoming the new symbol of gentility. And as the Irish came to dominate the docks and cartage trades, the only accepted jobs for black men were as strikebreakers or scabs. In the face of continuing prejudice, fewer jobs, and political impotence, blacks began to drift away from New York, and by the time of the Civil War only 12,472 remained in the city.

The ratio of blacks in the city declined proportionately all during the nineteenth century even as their numbers grew slowly in real terms. The black community was slowly forced to migrate from the Five Points in the 1830s to "Little Africa" in the Village in the 1860s to the west midtown areas of the Tenderloin and San Juan Hill by 1900. Everywhere, prejudice followed them, and often they were the victims of police brutality. On August 15 and 16, 1900, for example, a knifing incident led to confrontations between blacks and white mobs, sometimes abetted by the police, that continued sporadically for a month. The first census of the new century showed that New York had 60,666 blacks, only 2 percent of the consolidated city's total population. But America's internal migration away from the rural South and toward the northern cities was beginning, and by 1910 New York's black population had risen to 91,709. The outbreak of World War I made the city even more attractive because jobs once again were available and for the first time in American history, a center of black hope was being created. It was called Harlem.

Harlem, founded in 1657, is probably the oldest true suburb of New York City. Only eight miles from City Hall, it first held the country homes of the gentry, and their horse races were held along Harlem Lane, later St. Nicholas Avenue. When elevated tracks reached the area in 1878–1881, it became accessible to downtowners fleeing Italian and Jewish immigrants. As a result, a building boom soon changed the bucolic face of Harlem into posh elegance. The area was now symbolized by the magnificent rows of townhouses commissioned by David King in 1891 and designed by architects like James Lord, Price and Luce, and McKim, Mead and White. The Irish populated the streets west of Eighth Avenue; a "little Italy" was growing east of Third Avenue; and a "little Russia" could be found below 125th Street between Fifth and Seventh Avenues; but Harlem proper remained the home of the elite.

Then in 1904/5, there occurred the inevitable bust after a speculative boom, and Harlem suddenly had a glut of housing that had to be let. Until this time, the black presence in Harlem had been restricted to the role of menials. But the riot of 1900, the massive dislocations caused by the construction of Pennsylvania Station, and the completion of the Lenox Avenue subway line suddenly coincided with the availability of uptown housing. The Afro-American Realty Company was organized to place blacks into the vacant apartments, and it mattered little how many tenants combined to pay a single rent. Within a decade, fifty thousand blacks had come to Harlem, and their downtown churches soon followed the northward exodus. Harlem, a black community with good housing, community churches, and a sense of growth became the natural mecca for migrating blacks.

By 1920, when more than 109,000 blacks lived in Manhattan, it was clear that the continuing influx of newcomers was overwhelming Harlem's resources. Real estate ownership remained in white hands, but repairs were inadequate and the area was already becoming a slum. High rents remained the rule, but the low-income jobs available to blacks made it impossible for all but a few to avoid overcrowding. With the increasing density of population, the pathology of ghetto life took hold. Vice and policy gambling, narcotics addiction, and juvenile delinquency were, in the 1920s, recognized as community issues. Harlem also had the worst rates of infant mortality and incidence of tuberculosis in New York.

Harlem had no effective political voice to plead its cause; its nominal representatives were white and uncaring. Flamboyant leaders such as Father

Divine, Marcus Garvey (1887–1940), and Sufi Abdul Hamid offered charisma rather than reform proposals, and even they still had to compete with more traditional political types such as Charles Anderson (1866–1938) for the allegiance of a community in chaos. Ultimately no one spoke effectively for Harlem. By 1930, more than 200,000 of the 327,706 blacks in New York City were packed into the two square miles of Harlem, but their potential power was dissipated by ignorance, lack of leadership, and poverty; half of Harlem's population was on relief as the Depression began.

Amazingly, out of the decay of the 1920s came the discovery of hope and pride through the discovery of the black past. The Harlem Renaissance set a literary standard of excellence. The white theater at least recognized blacks in plays such as *Green Pastures, The Emperor Jones*, and *Porgy and Bess*, and jazz and the blues were centered in Harlem. White visitors from downtown, led by Jimmy Walker himself, made certain cabarets nationally prominent. In 1934, two white businessmen purchased a failed burlesque house, refurbished it, booked Bessie Smith (1845–1937), and opened the Apollo Theater on 125th Street. Could La Guardia, who came from Italian East Harlem, relate to a community without leaders?

La Guardia almost immediately made a symbolic administrative gesture of great importance to blacks: he created the New York Housing Authority in 1934. Black areas had the fewest social services, the least amount of parkland, and the greatest concentration of crime and illiteracy in the city. Beyond this, a majority of New York's working blacks in the 1930s earned less than $1,000 yearly. If the city made it a policy to provide the most deprived with better housing, it would show a concern that not even the black elite of 139th Street's "Striver's Row" felt for the residents of Harlem. La Guardia tried but failed.

When La Guardia took office, there had not been a school constructed in Harlem for twenty-five years, despite all its population gains. It took another four years before a new school was built. In addition, despite the vast park construction undertaken by Robert Moses, only a single playground was opened in Central Harlem during this decade. Harlem River Houses, a project of 574 apartments at 151st Street, opened in 1937, but again, its higher rentals did not help the heart of the distressed black community. La Guardia attempted to placate black feelings with several high-level appointments; he named Hubert Delaney as tax commissioner, Myles Paige as a magistrate, and Jane Bolin as a judge. Gertrude Ayer became the first black woman principal in the school system. But these were only tokens.

Italians, on their way to becoming the city's single largest ethnic group, saw in the mayor the culmination of fifty years of progress. The "Little Flower" had won power by using the system. The Italian Americans' pride in La Guardia was intensified because of the terrible publicity they had endured due to the illegal activities of men such as "Lucky" Luciano (1896–1962), Thomas Luchese, Joseph Adonis, and Frank Costello (1891–1973). Their control over vice, gambling, and liquor was already fostering the legend of a superpowerful Italian crime syndicate. La Guardia abhorred these thugs and racketeers, and together with Commissioner Valentine and State Attorney Thomas Dewey (1902–1971), he forced many of them to flee. Law-abiding Italians cheered.

The schizophrenic nature of immigrant ambition was also evident in the Jewish community. There were Jewish gangsters—Arthur "Dutch Schultz" Flegenheimer and Meyer Lansky (1902–1983) are leading examples—but the Jewish community saw such men as pariahs and aberrations. Rather, their pride was the many City College graduates and the prominent role of Jewish commissioners and magistrates in the La Guardia administration. The Jewish tradition of intellectual excellence was augmented during the 1930s as émigrés from Nazi Germany flocked to New York.

A third major ethnic group became increasingly prominent during the La Guardia years. Archer Huntington had founded the Hispanic Society in 1904, and by La Guardia's administration that group was dominated by Puerto Ricans. In 1930, the number of Puerto Ricans in the East Harlem barrio around 125th Street had passed 45,000, and their neighborhood was even more miserable than that of Harlem. Battles between teenagers from Little Italy and the barrio were common during the 1930s, the arena often being Benjamin Franklin High School.

Clearly, one of La Guardia's greatest challenges was to encourage ethnic cooperation by establishing a sense of common purpose for the heterogeneous elements of New York's population. But La Guardia could not afford to focus on any single group, however powerful; instead, his concern was the salvation and rehabilitation of all of New York. To that end, he made countless trips to Washington to argue for the extension of New Deal programs to the city. Although he was assured of a sympathetic hearing from Roosevelt, Harry Hopkins, Harold Ickes, and Louis Johnson—none of whom wished the city to collapse—La Guardia constantly had to overcome their skepticism. The mayor's ability to do so is perhaps his single greatest achievement, for when he pledged to turn money into construction projects and jobs, La Guardia delivered.

One great metropolitan construction boom during the 1920s had ended with the builders either bankrupt or unwilling to start new projects in a depression-ridden city. Yet no single industry was as crucial to the economic recovery of New York as was construction. La Guardia, who had a love for buildings, engineers, and architects, understood that new construction depended on the availability of federal funding. The great community projects of previous years—New York Medical Center (1928), Riverside Church (1929), the Museum of Modern Art (1929), the Daily News Building (1930), Brooklyn College (1930), the Whitney Museum (1931), and the Museum of the City of New York (1932)—could no longer be financed by individuals or the city. The Independent Subway System was already in federal receivership, and the magnificent Knickerbocker Village housing development had been forced by the Depression to alter its financing and become a limited-dividend project. In 1934, the only building money available was that provided through the National Industrial Recovery Act, and La Guardia's task was to mobilize as much labor and cash as possible and use them to stimulate New York's recovery.

What New York needed were public works projects on an unprecedented scale, but their construction depended on federal largesse. The mayor fortunately had available—in the ten-volume Regional Survey (1929) brilliantly adapted by Robert Moses—a rough outline of needed community projects. La Guardia knew little about these blueprints, but he was the necessary catalyst for their implementation. Moreover, the mayor trusted Moses, kept him on despite Roosevelt's antipathy and Moses's disastrous defeat in the governor's race of 1934, and used his extraordinary productivity to loosen Washington's purse strings. Only La Guardia could have so successfully played the bureaucratic and personal game of obtaining federal funds. By 1936, La Guardia obtained for his city one-seventh of all WPA spending, and it was this that lifted New York out of the Depression.

None of La Guardia's achievements was greater than his building legacy. During his regime, the city built a comprehensive highway and mass transportation system as well as developing the most extensive public-housing program in the United States. In 1933, New York's harbor and waterfront were disaster areas; subway construction had halted; and the anchorages of the Triborough Bridge stood like tombstones in the East River. Yet in the next seven years, three major bridges (the Triborough, the Whitestone, and the Henry Hudson) and at least one hundred smaller ones were completed, as were fifty miles of intracity expressway. By 1940, there were more miles of nonintersecting highway in New York than in the next five largest American cities combined. In addition, a traffic tunnel under the East River tied

Queens to the midtown area. Twelve miles of track were added to the Independent Eighth-Avenue Subway, and the Sixth-Avenue line was completed by 1941; plans had already been made for the merger of all subways into a unified city rapid transit system. By 1939, La Guardia Airport was opened before a throng of 325,000 cheering people, and plans were well advanced for another field, Idlewild, which was constructed during World War II. The docks department constructed fourteen new piers and put superstructures on four others; suddenly, the city could easily accommodate mammoth ocean liners. Parks Commissioner Moses built 255 playgrounds, five thousand acres of new parks, and a dozen swimming pools. Using various financing schemes, La Guardia saw thirteen housing projects for seventeen thousand families open by 1941.

The construction ended by 1940 owing to several factors: the end of the New Deal, the start of the European war, and the fact that New York had reached its capital-spending limit. Indeed, La Guardia's 1940 budget contained only a symbolic one dollar for capital construction. But the physical revolution remained, and the achievement of these years is still evident in New York. As with Christopher Wren's London, if you seek La Guardia's greatness, you need only contemplate the city he loved and rebuilt.

"The Hat" also provided New York with a governmental reconstruction as great as its physical revival. Gaynor's city charter of 1911 had limited the authority of the executive while increasing the powers of the Board of Estimate and the borough presidents. Amendments approved in 1924, although limiting the state's control over New York City's "property, affairs, or government," had not altered that situation. La Guardia believed that only a strong mayor could control the city, but his first attempt to revise the charter through a commission headed by Al Smith collapsed in August 1934. La Guardia was undaunted, however, and after obtaining the necessary legislative approval, he appointed a nonpartisan commission that studied the issue for nineteen months. La Guardia himself testified before the commissioners with characteristic vigor.

The commission ultimately produced a charter that centralized more power in the hands of the mayor, created the City Council, authorized the creation of the office of deputy mayor and the City Planning Commission, and clearly established the responsibilities of the comptroller. "Home rule" for New York was strengthened, and in addition, a proportional representation system was established for election to the City Council. How great a "reform" this was is questionable, however, since it did not guarantee the selection of at least some representatives of the electoral minority. On November 3, 1936, while contributing to Roosevelt's landslide national victory, the city electorate also gave its approval to a forty-thousand-word document opposed by all the borough presidents and Tammany Hall. Effective on January 1, 1938, the new charter strengthened the mayor while preserving the autonomy of the Board of Estimate. In November 1937 the voters would decide whether they would entrust La Guardia with the opportunity to lead under the charter he had sponsored.

Never in New York history had Fusion been able to win reelection for its candidates against the entrenched power of Tammany and the disinterest of the voters. But never had Fusion been represented by such a dynamic figure, and never had an administration been able to boast of so many enormous alterations in the physical face of the city. What other reformer had ever been able to rely on the vote of Italians, Jews, most blacks, and also organized labor? Could anyone but La Guardia have held the allegiance of the anti-Fascist Jews and the rather pro-Fascist Italians?

Nonetheless, La Guardia repeatedly emphasized his political independence. Indeed, in his twelve years as mayor, he never endorsed a Republican for any state or federal office. Although the GOP resented his lack of partisan spirit and his meritocratic view of patronage, they had little choice but to renominate him in 1937. So too did the Fusion organization. The mayor's reelection was also endorsed by the American Labor Party, an organization created in 1936 so that liberal Democrats might support Roosevelt without voting for the Tammany ticket; that line provided the mayor with an astounding 482,000 votes in the election. Progressives, Socialists, and even Communists supported La Guardia in 1937. Democrats in fact attempted to identify La Guardia with Communist supporters he found it expedient to repudiate.

To run against this political phenomenon, the Democrats chose Jeremiah Mahoney, a man who probably deserved a better fate. Mahoney charged that the mayor had broken his word on sales taxes and that he was maneuvering to obtain a cabinet position. However, when La Guardia presided over the opening of the West Side Highway on October 12, 1937, less than a month before the election, the campaign was effectively over. Fusion won more than 60 percent of the vote. La Guardia amassed 1,344,690 votes and held a plurality of 454,000. His candidates controlled fifteen of the sixteen Board of Estimate votes as well. Tammany barely held control of the incoming City Council. The election of 1937 was a triumph of ability and personality almost unprecedented in the history of New York.

La Guardia was now a national figure. His administration continued to build with the aid of federal money, and slow economic recovery made possible other projects financed by the city. In 1938 alone, the Bronx High School of Science was opened; Jacob Riis Park was made available to millions of bathers; and a master plan for future construction was published. Expansion of the subway system continued; port trade was definitely on the upswing; and the Civil Service continued to be reformed. So evident was the progress that newly elected comptroller Joseph McGoldrick was able to issue $375 million in revenue notes at interest rates as low as 1.35 percent. The pleased mayor not only declared the bankers' agreement at an end but also approved pay raises for city workers, an action that effectively undermined five years of economizing. After years of depression wages, the political reality of worker pressures could not be denied. Besides, argued La Guardia, the 1939 property tax rate was only $2.82 per $100, hardly excessive when compared with the tremendous physical improvement of the city.

One vignette is instructive. A Latin American diplomat touring the city was awed by all the construction under way. At each stop, he asked who let the contracts, and the mayor answered "I did." By the end of the day, candor overcame tact, and the diplomat remarked, "Ah, La Guardia, you must be a very rich man." But the fact was that La Guardia still lived in his East Harlem neighborhood, still cooked Italian meals for his friends, and lived on his salary. Not even his opponents accused him of personal dishonesty, although many believed he would willingly serve a national constituency.

La Guardia's second term initiated an administrative revolution within the city government. Under the new charter, the first deputy mayor was appointed. However, because La Guardia was psychologically incapable of delegating authority, the "job came swiftly down to handling some of the mail and sitting for the mayor in the Board of Estimate." Not for another three decades did the office reach its potential. More immediate in its impact on city government was reform of the Civil Service structure. By 1939, 74.3 percent of all employees had to take competitive examinations to obtain city jobs, a gain of 20 percent in five years. The merit system imposed by La Guardia guaranteed better-qualified workers and made a career in municipal service extremely attractive. From 1933 to 1939, the number of applications for Civil Service jobs rose by 3,884 percent, enhancing government performance for the New York citizenry.

Better economic conditions also became apparent as the city slowly recovered from the Depression. After a temporary downturn in 1938, economic statistics advanced steadily during the La Guardia years. By 1939, for example, the city handled 23.4 percent of the United States' wholesale trade, compared with its 7.6 percent of retail trade. New York exported 40 percent of all America's goods in 1940, a percentage that increased as the global war intensified.

The international eminence of New York was heightened when it welcomed the World's Fair of 1939. Completion of the Triborough Bridge, the Midtown Tunnel, and their connecting highway systems made central Queens accessible to millions of travelers. When the city obtained the right to honor the 150th anniversary of George Washington's inauguration with a World's Fair, Parks Commissioner Moses insisted that Flushing Meadow in Queens be the site, or he would oppose the project. Naturally he had his way. Two years and $591 million later, Moses had transformed the Corona dumping grounds, home to a ninety-foot mountain of ash and river rats the size of dogs, into an elegant fair site extending over 1,216 acres.

The last of La Guardia's great services to New York also took place in 1940: he realized an administrator's dream by consolidating the subways and elevated lines into a unified, municipally owned transit system. Experience had shown that the Independent Subway constructed by La Guardia could never be self-supporting at a fare of five cents. Moreover, the private companies that operated the once profitable BMT and IRT systems were bankrupt and totally dependent on city subsidies. In 1938, New York asked the state to approve an exemption from debt limitations so that it might purchase the bankrupt companies, combine service with the Independent line, and create a self-supporting system. Authorization was granted, and in June 1940, the three systems were unified at a cost of $326 million. The city suddenly was running a thirteen-hundred-mile system valued at $1.5 billion and doing it profitably; the merger produced an operating profit of $28 million in its first year. Soon, however, union cooperation waned, and as costs rose, praise for La Guardia's foresight faded as well. The unified systems became a deficit operation, an albatross to burden all future city budgets. One cosmetic benefit for New York came with transit consolidation. The removal of surface elevated lines that duplicated subterranean routes eased the flow of traffic, increased property values, and improved many New York vistas. The Civic Center-Cadman Plaza redevelopment near Brooklyn's Borough Hall is perhaps the best example of this welcome offshoot of subway unification.

La Guardia's reelection in 1941 should have been far easier than it actually was. Eight years of Fusion rule had fundamentally altered the city, but the office itself—often described as the second most difficult job in America—had somewhat soured the mayor. Always an imperious boss, La Guardia had become increasingly intolerant of failure, delay, and opposition; personal conflicts often erupted between "the Hat" and his staff. He seemed to recognize that he would never hold national office but willingly accepted service on the Canadian-American Defense Board and as Roosevelt's coordinator of Civilian Defense. As America moved closer to war against the Axis powers he despised, La Guardia seemed almost to have lost his desire to govern the city.

Nevertheless, as he stood for reelection in 1941, La Guardia proudly displayed an endorsement from Roosevelt. A June Gallup Poll showing 59 percent voter support before his intemperate personal attack on popular Democratic Governor Herbert Lehman alienated many of La Guardia's natural liberal constituents. La Guardia berated Lehman for always endorsing Democrats and used some hard language to describe such unenlightened thinking. Moreover, he refused to apologize, saying only that his choicest epithets were intended to describe political bosses, not Lehman. The mayor's stubbornness gave Democrat William O'Dwyer (1890–1964) of Brooklyn, an adept campaigner with great personal charisma, an issue that allowed him to cut deeply into La Guardia's lead.

In the November balloting, the mayor trailed his Fusion ticket and won reelection by only 132,000 votes. Although victory made the Little Flower the first twelve-year mayor since Richard Varick (1789–1801), it also indicated that the rigors of mastering the metropolis might ultimately be too great for even this leader. Democrats argued that La Guardia was only a part-time mayor, and since New Deal construction had halted and animosity was in the air, the question of what La Guardia could achieve in his third term was much debated. That issue became moot, however, only a month after his reelection. Pearl Harbor made it certain that the mayor and his city would become a vital part of the national effort to win the war. The great era of achievement was over.

Governing the city of New York during wartime was neither glamorous nor easy. The lights of Broadway were dimmed and La Guardia's star seemed to set with them. In February 1942, La Guardia resigned his position as head of the Civil Defense Agency, a job in which he had not been able to obtain many results, and he made no discernible attempt to refocus his attention on the city. After Pearl Harbor, the mayor placed security guards on all bridges and tunnels as well as in many factories. He interned some two hundred Japanese Americans on Ellis Island and did his best to cope with a loss of city labor to private industry and the U.S. Army. In reality, La Guardia wanted to serve America in another war and believed that it was his destiny to lead men against Fascism. One of the greatest disappointments of his life was that the call never came. La Guardia was restricted to a civilian's role, and he was allowed only to make propaganda broadcasts.

In May 1942, La Guardia and his family moved into the Executive Mansion refurbished for them by Robert Moses. Gracie Mansion had been constructed in 1804 by a Scottish merchant, and later it housed the Museum of the City of New York. The federal-style mansion now became the symbolic power center for the city, and it was from there that La Guardia and his successors dealt with crises. For example, on the night of August 3, 1943, Harlem once more exploded in a spasm of looting. Sparked by high rents, wartime discrimination, and economic deprivation, the riot resulted in five deaths and hundreds of arrests. La Guardia pledged reforms, and a rent control law was adopted, but nothing fundamental was changed. The mayor and his family happily lived out the rest of his term less than two miles from Harlem, a cesspool of misery, whose continued decay challenged the peace of the city La Guardia governed.

La Guardia always understood that New York set the tone for urban life in the United States; if he always seemed to be in the forefront of events, it was because the city itself was the focus of national and even international attention. In May 1945 La Guardia announced his retirement, fully aware of his enormous achievements. New York had been placed on a firm financial basis by Fusion. Even with the plethora of physical additions to the city, its bonded debt in June 1946 amounted to only $2.194 billion, and this total represented a reduction of $500 million since 1941. Construction had halted during the war, but blueprints existed to complete the massive plan of the 1930s, and Commissioner Moses would remain present to see that the projects were built. Wartime employment gains had ended the relief problem, but the welfare department stood ready to assist indigent New Yorkers; it would soon again be dispensing millions in aid. A hundred thousand city workers were content under the generous pension plans that La Guardia had approved, and his initiatives led to the creation in 1947 of a health insurance plan that had a nationwide impact.

In the area of race relations, La Guardia's administration had enacted housing and fair employment laws that prohibited discriminatory practices, and did so well in advance of any national initiatives. Moreover, his reelections proved that Fusion need not be temporary. Havemeyer, Low, and Mitchel all had failed to be reelected, but in La Guardia's three terms, New York became more governable than it had been in decades. His legacy was a happier, more livable, more prosperous city.

On October 21, 1945, a Manhattan ceremony changed Sixth Avenue into the Avenue of the Americas. Although city natives refused then and now to use the new name, it was true that New York's true constituency had become the world community. Probably the change in name was also part of a strategy that New York adopted to win a great prize, to provide a home for the newly created United Nations. Although the initial meeting of the world body had been held in London, by the end of 1945 the Bronx campus of Hunter College had been designated as the organization's temporary headquarters. Internationally famous planners opposed putting the United Nations in an existing city, but the lure of New York was undeniable. If the city could provide a permanent home, there was little doubt the UN would choose to remain here. In 1946, while formal sessions were being held at Lake Success (Nassau County) and in Flushing Meadow Park, a mayor's committee ultimately arrived at a consensus; a permanent home would be offered to the United Nations in eastern Manhattan on Turtle Bay. A seventeen-acre development site organized by William Zeckendorf (1905–1976) was purchased by the Rockefeller interests and donated to New York. The UN accepted the proposed site on December 11, 1946. Plans were drawn, in part by Wallace Harrison (1895–1981) who had helped create Rockefeller Center, and by the end of 1947 the glass-curtained, forty-five-story Secretariat began its climb toward the sky. La Guardia, who had headed the Relief and Recovery Agency of the UN during 1946, certainly was thrilled. He had always believed the city was a symbol of hope for the millions who came here: now it could play a similar role for all humankind. The mayor never saw the structure completed, however, for he died of pancreatic cancer on September 29, 1947. Nevertheless, he must have known that he and the United Nations together had helped make New York the "world's capital city."

9

The Long Slide

With the end of the global conflict in 1945, the city of New York seemingly had every reason to be confident of its future prosperity. Since consolidation, its population had virtually doubled. The census of 1950 counted a city of 7,891,957 people, larger in population than forty-five of the forty-eight United States and far surpassing in size many of the original members of the United Nations. The manufacturing vitality of New York, honed to a fine edge by the trauma of war, was unsurpassed anywhere in the country. A magnificent harbor made it America's commercial capital, and 40 percent of the country's freight traffic passed through the city each year. Each year its transit system carried the equivalent of the world's population. New York was truly a world city, even though the newest statistics showed that it was becoming more American; in 1948 only 30 percent of its population were foreign born, versus a 1910 figure of 41 percent.

The immediate challenge faced by the city as it welcomed back America's armies and accepted thousands of the world's refugees was a severe housing shortage. From 1946 to 1956, unprecedented numbers of public-housing rental apartment units were constructed. The first were temporary wartime-style Quonset-hut apartments in sites such as Canarsie Beach Park, the East Bronx, and Queens. Even more significant for America's future, however, was the desire of young married couples to buy homes in the suburbs. In the counties surrounding New York, tract housing—whose model was Levittown in Nassau County—proliferated. Of necessity, the Long Island Railroad adopted as its symbol a harried commuter called Dashing Dan, and a symbiotic relationship between the suburbs and the central core city was soon established. Nassau County alone received more home mortgage loans from the Federal Veterans Administration than all of New York City.

Within only a few years, 400,000 commuters entered the city daily to take advantage of its seemingly inexhaustible supply of job opportunities. In 1947, for example, New York City held 37,870 of the nation's 240,881 manufacturing establishments. Among these were a clear majority of all apparel factories. Clothing had been New York's greatest industry since before the Civil War and provided jobs to more workers than did the autos of Detroit or the steel of Pittsburgh. With a manufacturing base this powerful, the city's finances were secure, even though much of its working population now resided outside its geographical boundaries.

The postwar era was thus a time of population flux and physical alteration in New York City. Perhaps nothing illustrated the change so graphically as did the city's battle with the automobile. As Detroit began once again to manufacture cars for consumers, the city discovered to its chagrin that it had lost control of its own streets. A surge of postwar buying and the increasing numbers of commuters made traffic control a nightmare that even today is unsolved. It was estimated that if the autos entering New York each day were put end to end, they would span the nation. In 1946, the famous double-deck buses of Fifth Avenue were phased out, and in November the Forty-second Street crosstown trolley made its last trip. All trolley service, even in the outer boroughs, ended by April 7, 1957.

In May 1945, Fiorello La Guardia announced his intention to leave office. Thus the first item on the political agenda was selecting the man who would serve as New York's hundredth mayor. After twelve years in the opposition, Tammany Hall desperately needed to field a winning ticket. The candidate it selected to make the mayoral race was almost a prototype New Yorker. William O'Dwyer had immigrated to New York from Ireland in 1910, arriving with only $25 in his pocket and a desire to succeed. He worked at a variety of menial jobs until he obtained his citizenship in 1916 and immediately thereafter became a policeman, the almost mythic road of Irish advancement. But his aspirations were higher than those of a patrolman, and he soon entered Fordham Law School; he also participated in Democratic politics at the precinct level. By 1939, as the crusading district attorney for Brooklyn, O'Dwyer won most of the credit for the effective prosecution of the infamous Murder Incorporated. In 1941, he ran and was defeated in the mayoral race, but he gave La Guardia a far closer race than expected. During the war, O'Dwyer was chief of the Allied Control Commission in Italy and left the army with the rank of brigadier general. While In Italy, he won an almost unanimous reelection as district attorney. In 1945, he was clearly Tammany Hall's best hope of returning to power.

The Republicans offered Jonah Goldstein, a former Democrat and once himself a member of Tammany. In a weird reversal of history, the Democrats accused Goldstein of being "boss nominated." Moreover, they mocked La Guardia's chosen successor, Newbold Morris (1902–1966), the candidate of the No Deal Party, as an unwanted legacy of the past. Both his opponents claimed that O'Dwyer's official record really was less than met the eye, with Morris claiming that O'Dwyer had left Brooklyn a "rotten mess." But there was never any doubt about the outcome of the election. On November 4, Bill O'Dwyer became New York's one hundredth mayor and the darling of Tammany Hall.

O'Dwyer's career had always been based on loyalty to Tammany, but the new mayor was hardly a typical hack. Often described as a leader who knew the city better than any other elected mayor, O'Dwyer recognized that his major task would be to oversee and control New York's transition to a peacetime economy. Accordingly, he decided that the housing needs of the returning servicemen and women should take immediate priority and that the wartime rent controls drawn up in 1943 should be expanded. Although often controversial and repeatedly amended over the decades, these regulations still remain in force. The unrelenting crusades of the real estate industry to dismantle the system provided renting New Yorkers with a convenient caste to despise, the landlords. New York has always been largely a rental market; in 1948, for example, 76 percent of its residents lived in apartments. Thus it is hardly surprising that the rent control system institutionalized by the mayor became the most sacred of sacred cows.

Bill O'Dwyer proved to be remarkably in tune with, and adaptable to, the changing human face of the city he governed. As with all modern incumbents of the mayor's office, the perennial problem of finance dogged his administration. O'Dwyer accused Albany of "shortchanging" the city and created the Analysis Section in the Bureau of the Budget to prove his case. Among his many administrative initiatives were the Traffic and Smoke Control Bureaus created to deal with environmental problems and the reorganization and purported improvement of the welfare department.

Reconstruction of the city government became easier after November 1947, when the voters approved the abolition of proportional representation on the City Council. This vote was fundamentally due to the onset of the cold war. As the public grew fearful that the strength of the American Labor party, combined with the vote of other Leftists, might give legitimate representation to a Communist, voters decided that councilmen henceforth would have to command majorities, a mandate that enhanced not only the dominant position of the Democrats but also the power of the mayor. Another of

O'Dwyer's early successes was a vigorous campaign against a smallpox scare; in 1947, almost 6.35 million persons were vaccinated by the reconstructed health department.

Perhaps no single administrative action was more important to the city's future than the creation of the Division of Labor Relations. It was inevitable that the city's labor force should demand catch-up pay increases once the necessity for patriotic sacrifice was ended. When a May 1946 strike by tugboat workers severely curtailed the commerce of the port and caused fuel shortages, O'Dwyer first issued a mayoral declaration of emergency and then helped mediate the dispute. His intervention established a precedent for executive participation in labor disputes with city employees that subsequent mayors have since attempted to repudiate.

All of New York's mayors simply had to deal with the growing militancy of labor, even if it was represented by leaders such as "Red" Mike Quill (1906–1966) of the Transport Workers Union (TWU). Since the city did not wish to deal with so-called Communist unions, the Condon-Wadlin Act was passed by the legislature in 1947 for the purpose of outlawing strikes by government employees. The statute's provisions, including loss of jobs, were so severe, however, that no politician has ever been able to invoke the full force of the law. Nevertheless, whether or not the city recognized the TWU, it was unthinkable that any mayor could allow a transit strike. The subways and buses of New York carried 8 million riders daily, and so in 1948 it was mandatory that a wage settlement with the unhappy transit workers be negotiated. Its cost was the nickel fare that had lasted since 1904. On July 1, 1948, the cost of a subway ride rose to a dime, the first of many subsequent increases. Moreover, the city in 1949 accepted the principle of collective bargaining with its employees, thereby inaugurating a new era of power for the army of 180,000 city employees.

High on the municipal agenda was the celebration of the Golden Anniversary of Greater New York in 1948. At the age of fifty, the city encompassed 320.26 square miles with 5,719 miles of street and 578 miles of waterfront. Its 80 high schools and 569 grammar schools served a million pupils. In density of population, New York was five hundred times the national average, but no one seemed aware of it. People preferred talking about the power of New York's economy: a fifth of all American wholesale transactions took place within its boundaries.

As part of the Golden Anniversary festivities, Idlewild International Airport was dedicated on July 1, 1948; by 1960, activity on its new runways allowed it to surpass La Guardia as the major entry point to the city. In

1949, the long-awaited Brooklyn Battery Tunnel opened to relieve the traffic congestion, and President Harry Truman arrived to dedicate the cornerstone of United Nations Plaza. Even the shortage of housing seemed to be alleviated in 1949 when Manhattan's vast Stuyvesant Town housing project, funded by Metropolitan Life Insurance, began renting. Urban planners also were pleased when federal urban renewal funds for slum clearance won congressional approval. In all, O'Dwyer and his administration were well positioned for the reelection campaign. All the voters recognized that the difficult transition years had not been without problems, but most agreed that O'Dwyer had done a creditable job.

The mayor, however, constantly delayed the announcement that he was again a candidate. Rumors began to be heard that he had allowed his town to become too "wide open" and that scandals were about to surface. There were claims that fewer than one thousand policemen were on patrol some days and that the "mob" had too much political influence. Indeed, there was little doubt that among the most influential men in Tammany Hall was Frank Costello, the "prime minister" of American organized crime. Tammany apologists argued that the mayor was equally on good terms with the new archbishop of New York, Francis Cardinal Spellman (1887–1967), and that neither mobster nor churchman had any political control over the city's decision-making process. Nevertheless, the rumor was that O'Dwyer had secret ties to organized crime that could be proved by an inmate of Sing Sing Prison. As if to confirm this charge, it was not until after that prisoner had died in the electric chair that the mayor finally decided to offer himself again to the public. Once O'Dwyer decided to run, he became the instant favorite, and the Democrats easily won.

The scope of the Democratic victory in 1949 was overwhelming. Not only did O'Dwyer win 59 percent of the vote, but also the Democrats won all the borough presidencies (Robert F. Wagner Jr. [1910–1991] was elected in Manhattan) and twenty-four of the twenty-five council seats. Once again, O'Dwyer's main victim was Newbold Morris, who ran as the Republican-Liberal-Fusion nominee and denounced the administration for "plunder and corruption." One fascinating aspect of the race was the relatively strong showing of Socialist Victor Marcantonio (1902–1954), who demanded a return to the five-cent subway fare and mandated rent rollbacks, lower utility rates, and an end to police brutality against black and Hispanic New Yorkers. He also claimed that "you could fill Central Park with the . . . labor unions Bill O'Dwyer has tried to smash." Nobody seemed to listen to either Morris or Marcantonio.

Yet hardly had the election dust settled when vague charges suddenly took on substance. A series of well-documented exposés in the *Brooklyn Eagle* charged that an alliance of policemen and judges was protecting four thousand bookies in return for annual payoffs of more than $1 million. Although the evidence was overwhelming, O'Dwyer refused to accept it, insisting that the charges were a press vendetta. He defended the NYPD even after an accused policeman committed suicide. The evidence of corruption was clear, nonetheless, and so overwhelmingly hostile was the public's reaction that in January 1950, the mayor fled to Florida because of "nervous prostration."

O'Dwyer began to cast about for release from the griddle that New York suddenly had become. The flame became even hotter when more than 110 police resigned in the face of an investigation that the mayor had termed a "witch-hunt." Corruption was hardly new to the New York police, but never since the Tweed days had a mayor seemed so obtuse. Finally, Bronx boss Ed Flynn arranged a deal in which O'Dwyer resigned on August 31, 1950, to accept appointment as Harry Truman's ambassador to Mexico. "There he would be safe from the petty annoyance of transportation problems, dirty sidewalks, snowstorms, a recalcitrant district attorney digging up scandals about corruption in the Police Department, and racketeers always showing up to be photographed at important functions of Tammany Hall."

But O'Dwyer's sudden flight did not remove his name from newspaper headlines. After bookmaker Harry Gross told of contributing $20,000 to the former mayor's reelection fund, O'Dwyer was subpoenaed to testify before the Kefauver committee investigating organized crime. This famous committee also questioned Frank Costello, who admitted he knew ten of the sixteen Tammany leaders "well," and "maybe they got a little confidence in me." Then on March 19 and 20, 1951, O'Dwyer testified. He ultimately admitted his awareness of police department corruption and acquaintanceship with various mobsters, and he confessed that he had also once visited Costello's apartment. But he denied receiving any illegal contributions and ever afterward was able to assert, "I have never been charged with a crime, let alone convicted." But the final report of the Kefauver committee was damning. O'Dwyer's actions, the committee asserted, "often seemed to result favorably for men suspected of being high up in rackets." Moreover, "his failure to follow up evidence of organized crime . . . contributed to the growth of . . . gangsterism in New York City." No hard evidence of malfeasance was provided, however, and Bill O'Dwyer remained ambassador until he resigned in 1952 and established a law practice in Mexico City.

Automatically on O'Dwyer's resignation, the president of the City Council, Vincent Impellitteri (1900–1987), took office under the charter until a special election could be held in November 1950. Impellitteri was a Sicilian-born New Yorker who had an excellent reputation as a successful prosecutor and an "unbossable" lawyer. Although nominally a Democrat, he was determined to be elected as an independent candidate in the Fusion tradition. Proclaiming his freedom from Tammany influences, Impellitteri entered the mayoral race as the nominee of the Experience Party. Perhaps the most interesting feature of this brief campaign was that it marked the debut in municipal politics of the new boss of Tammany Hall.

Carmine DeSapio (1908–) had actually been Manhattan's Democratic leader since 1949, but O'Dwyer's easy reelection had not brought him to prominence. Now he selected Ferdinand Pecora to run against "Impy" and Republican Edward Corsi. Not surprisingly, the campaign often resembled a balance sheet accounting of which of the three candidates was the best Italian. Appeals to this voting bloc were important, for by 1950 Italian Americans comprised the single greatest element in New York's electorate. No candidate could claim all the Italian voters, however, and the key to Impellitteri's 225,000–vote plurality was the word *independent*. The voters seemed alienated by the continuation of corruption and the seamy politics of the Tammany clubhouse. It was impossible to argue—even though it was true—that DeSapio as leader was systematically purging his party of its ties to Costello; rather, he was making the democracy "saintly." But few, even among Democrats, believed that in November 1950, and it was not surprising that New Yorkers instead elected Impellitteri.

Vincent Impellitteri was the "best-dressed, best-rested" mayor to govern New York since Jimmy Walker, but his three years in office proved insufficient time for him to compile a substantial record. In fact, his tenure severely disappointed reformers because he failed to use the power of his office. As an independent, he lacked a firm party base and was thus at a disadvantage when dealing with a Board of Estimate and City Council more mindful of DeSapio than the mayor. Impellitteri's few initiatives were ignored, and the mayor often made political blunders. For example, in 1952, he submitted New York's largest budget, $1.336 billion. To finance it, the sales tax was increased to 3 percent, and a long-range financial plan to prevent deficits was presented to Albany. The proper legislative preparation had not been done, however, and in February 1953 state officials rejected the proposal because the city was taxing itself into "economic paralysis." Like O'Dwyer before him, Impellitteri tried to convince Albany that New York City received proportionately far less in local aid than it contributed in taxes, but the legislature ignored his analysis.

"Impy" did make good appointments, however, and like all mayors since La Guardia, one of his best was Robert Moses. Moses was selected to head the Slum Clearance Committee which would use federal urban-renewal appropriations to build largely middle-class housing. Under this program, Moses pushed through the construction of cooperatively owned developments at Morningside Gardens and Corlears Hook. Since the projects resulted in the removal of site residents who could not afford the new housing, the mayor took the heat. Its political gains were few, since credit for the housing increases went to Moses. The mayor's reputation was also slightly tarnished when an investigation of waterfront corruption implicated one of his oldest friends. Finally, to complete his discomfiture, transit fares had to be increased to fifteen cents in July 1953. The mayor's critics said he was indifferent to the increase, since he spent most of his time on vacation. In all, Impellitteri's performance proved less than his promise, and his mayoralty was only an interlude in Tammany's reign.

Regardless of who was mayor, the glamour and allure of New York City continued to attract new immigrants. The census reported the city's 1950 population as 7,891,957, with Italians comprising the single greatest ethnic component. The Immigration Act of 1952 provided the lowest quota ever for Italians, fewer than six thousand annually, so their continued influence depended on natural increases. An amazing 56 percent of all New York residents still were either foreign born or first-generation Americans. In a city that continually boasted of its opportunities, economic mobility continued to be stagnant among the 10 percent of the population that was black. Most blacks remained segregated in ghettos, and even middle-class blacks were stigmatized by color. For example, they were tacitly excluded from renting apartments in projects such as Stuyvesant Town.

The most rapidly increasing ethnic group in New York was the Puerto Rican community, which in the early 1950s numbered 325,000. There had been sizable numbers in Manhattan since the time of the Spanish-American War, and barrios had been established adjacent to the Brooklyn Navy Yard and in parts of East Harlem by the 1920s. In the 1930s, many Puerto Ricans settled in Washington Heights, and the South Bronx assimilated the influx of the war years. But few New Yorkers were ready for the vast migration that began at the end of World War II. More than a million immigrants fled the collapsed agricultural economy of Puerto Rico between 1945 and 1960. As the island government launched Operation Bootstrap for its economic revitalization, thousands of unemployed or underemployed Americans left Puerto Rico for the mainland and America's traditional city of opportunity. Not only were these newcomers citizens of the United States, but also they were the first immigrants to arrive in New York by plane.

O'Dwyer had recognized their growing numbers and had ordered his welfare commission to examine the problems that Puerto Ricans would face in adapting to an urban environment. A 1949 report discovered that 98 percent of Puerto Ricans came to New York for better economic conditions, but because of a lack of education, the language barrier, and discrimination, most failed to achieve success. By 1952, as an estimated 1,135 Puerto Ricans were arriving weekly in New York, they already constituted the most rapidly increasing segment of the welfare rolls. By 1953, Puerto Rican New Yorkers comprised 5 percent of the city and increasingly sought a sense of community; in 1959, for example, the first Puerto Rican Day parade was held.

But Puerto Ricans were not the only Caribbean migrants in the 1950s. Refugees from dictatorships or revolutions were constantly fleeing to New York, and the numbers of Haitians and Cubans in the population grew quickly. In addition, thousands of Hungarians were admitted to the United States as displaced persons after the abortive revolution late in 1956. By some estimates, a total of 2 million persons arrived in New York during this decade, and many stayed to make new lives for themselves. The city made strenuous efforts to house and care for these new arrivals but fell ever further behind. It is interesting, however, that the enormous influx of the 1950s did not substantially alter the total central city population because the continuing middle-class move toward suburbia drained residents from the city at an almost equal rate. In time, the increasing percentage of minority residents in New York that resulted from these dual migrations became the most explosive issue facing the city's political leadership.

But that future crisis was inconceivable in 1953. The immediate concern then was the mayoral race in which Tammany once again hoped to return to power. Democrats recognized that simply to assert that they had purged themselves of mobster influence and corruption was not enough; they needed a "superclean" candidate to defeat the lackluster Impellitteri. The longtime chief of Bronx politics was Ed Flynn, a realist who recognized DeSapio's internal party achievements. Moreover, DeSapio was "the first Tammany man since Murphy I can sit with and not have to talk out of the side of my mouth." So in early 1953, the two reigning bosses selected as their candidate the young borough president of Manhattan, Robert F. Wagner Jr. Wagner had one of the most revered names in New York politics and also had proved himself an effective administrator. Perhaps more important, he believed in party regularity. Although Ed Flynn died in August 1953, making DeSapio supreme in Tammany, the joint effort of the Manhattan and Bronx machines routed Impellitteri in the Democratic primary race and secured the nomination for Wagner.

When "Impy's" forces failed to collect enough independent signatures to qualify the Experience Party for the November ballot, the race effectively ended. There remained for the Democrats only the formalities of dispatching the Republican and Liberal candidates and bringing the remaining outer borough dissenters under DeSapio's rule. On November 3, Wagner was elected mayor, a position he held with some distinction for the next twelve years. A triumphant DeSapio acted magnanimously even toward Impellitteri, who had regularly refused patronage to Tammany: he allowed Wagner to appoint "Impy" a judge of special sessions.

The incoming Wagner slate had been elected on the slogan "Promise means performance," and no one could doubt that Wagner certainly had promised. The administration was committed to providing more policemen, improving civil service performance, protecting and expanding civil rights, constructing more and better public housing for every class of citizen, cleaning up the dilapidated waterfront, eliminating and replacing 170 "firetrap" schools, and embarking on "a genuine pattern of collective bargaining" with its municipal unions. The means by which all this would be accomplished was the city's economy, which remained the greatest single marketplace of the nation. In 1954, New York still had forty thousand manufacturing firms, and its 104,000 retail outlets sold $10 billion worth of goods annually. Its great port handled 40 percent of the total value of America's water trade, and twelve railroads and 750 trucking firms served its needs. More impressive still was the fact that its airports serviced 37 percent of all domestic flights. Almost half a million commuters entered Manhattan daily to ply their various trades, and business was even better now that the war in Korea had finally been settled.

Wagner capitalized on the optimism of these prosperous years. He was politically adroit in making above-average appointments while remaining on excellent terms with the DeSapio machine. Not only was there continued labor peace, but also the city managed to provide substantial new services for its residents. For example, the first of the city's public community colleges was created in 1955. The ubiquitous Robert Moses was kept on to push through the redevelopment of the Columbus Circle area, and the renovation of Manhattan's brownstone housing slowly marched up the West Side of Manhattan. Committed to providing additional housing, the mayor used his full political weight to support the passage of the state's Mitchell-Lama legislation which would provide moderate-rent apartments for middle-income families. Today, more than 100,000 New Yorkers live in those units, although the rents are no longer very low.

Wagner's first administration was also a time of optimistic expectations in race relations. Everyone was proud that a black politician, Hulan Jack (1906–1986), had replaced the mayor as Manhattan's borough president in 1953. Most New Yorkers were confident that this presaged the incorporation of blacks into the political system. So many ethnic groups had previously been successfully assimilated that there seemed no reason to doubt the full societal acceptance of blacks. Indeed, there was more concern about youth gangs and their battles than about the larger issue of successful integration. On the national scene, the Supreme Court's 1954 decision in *Brown v. Board of Education* declaring that "separate but equal" schooling was unconstitutional was hailed by liberal New York, and locally Wagner's appointment of his Commission on Intergroup Relations won universal praise.

In all, the mid-1950s appear as a time of lost innocence. The political system seemingly embraced all groups while the economy appeared impervious to ordinary forces of decay. The constant renewal of the city continued when the Third Avenue Elevated Line, the oldest in Manhattan, was demolished, and daylight flooded once dark streets. New York's greatest problem seemed its inability to pick up trash, and Wagner launched an "anti-Litter Bug" campaign to encourage cleanliness. It came as no surprise, therefore, that he was renominated and in 1957 won an almost million-vote victory over the weak Republican opposition.

Often derided as a dull and uninteresting decade, the 1950s in New York were highlighted by a construction boom that once again transformed the cityscape. High-rise apartments and slum clearance projects were going up virtually overnight, and major architectural projects long under development were now rapidly brought to completion. Architectural historians may decide that the new corporate style had its origins in the glass walls of the UN Secretariat, for suddenly the format was being adapted for office buildings such as the Lever House (1952) constructed by Skidmore, Owings, Merrill. The stone and brick of an earlier age was now superseded by metal and glass constructs that dramatically altered and often enhanced the streets of New York. Glass walls and open ground spaces added a quality of airiness to Manhattan's traditionally constricted spaces. Perhaps the greatest single achievement of the decade was the thirty-eight-floor Seagram Building (1958) designed by Mies van der Rohe with the interior by Philip Johnson. Dramatically set back from the whiteness that predominates along Park Avenue, this bronze and glass tower lures pedestrians into its piazza. Indeed, this building set such a high standard that major zoning changes were enacted by 1961 in an effort to duplicate its enhancing effect on urban space. Unfortunately, the quality of the Seagram Building was rarely matched in the following decade.

The construction undertaken in New York was massive. From 1947 to 1963, more than 58 million square feet of office space were added to the city, a total greater than that built in the next largest twenty-two cities combined. Among the most prominent additions to the skyline were the Chase Manhattan, Time-Life, and Equitable Buildings, each of which included pedestrian plazas. By 1959, the city's assessed valuation soared past $32 billion, $22.5 billion of it fully taxable. In 1956, moreover, the $35 million, nine-acre Coliseum was opened to the public, a structure intended to solidify Manhattan's claim to be the "world's exposition capital." Among the public facilities added to New York's infrastructure was a third tube on the interstate Lincoln Tunnel (1957), while ground was broken to construct a major arts complex at Lincoln Center. In 1960, President Dwight Eisenhower chose New York to host another World's Fair in the expectation that the city could repeat its triumph of 1939/40.

But as sometimes happens in a seemingly healthy organism, a cancer was slowly growing inside. The disease grew even as the population of the city rose to 7,781,984 persons in 1960. The underlying reality of the 1950s was an alteration in the city's economic fabric so fundamental that it would no longer be able to fulfill all the dreams of its residents. For almost a century, the basic strength of its economy had been its manufacturing sector, with the small factory its most typical business establishment. It was in these many smaller enterprises that the immigrant waves of the past had traditionally found employment. The wages they earned, though often meager, provided millions with the means for their first steps toward dignity and independence and inspired them to higher goals, if not for themselves, then for their children. Similarly, the immigrants of the 1950s were expected to conquer not only their poverty but also the unique burdens of racial and linguistic discrimination.

Perhaps all this might have been possible if the lowest rung of the job ladder had not been suddenly narrowed. During Eisenhower's presidency, from 1953 to 1961, the national economy experienced three recessions, and their cumulative effect on New York's manufacturing employment was substantial. Even in the surviving factories, an accelerating trend toward automation demanded more educated and skillful workers while reducing the number of workers needed to maintain production. Finally, as evidenced by the enormous surge of office space construction, New York's white-collar needs were increasing as the urban economy became more service oriented at the expense of manufacturing.

Economists and social science researchers were quick to discover these trends and to speculate on their impact on New York's prospects. In 1959, a detailed report on the future of the three-state metropolitan region was issued by a team led by Raymond Vernon. While forecasting general growth for the entire region, the report predicted a troubled future for urban communities, and especially for New York City, within the tristate area. Studies indicated that both public facilities and private enterprise were suffering from obsolescence: factory procedures, housing, transit systems, streets, and schools had simply not been able to keep pace with changing needs. Vernon was certain that New York City's "position as the nation's business and financial capital seems virtually unassailable for the next few decades" but predicted that future growth in jobs and commerce would be largely outside its boundaries. As if to underscore this conclusion, from 1958 to 1964, metropolitan factory employment reportedly fell by 87,000 jobs. Although it was widely criticized for undue pessimism, the Vernon study has held up remarkably well.

Not to be outdone by the economists, political scientists completed three major studies of New York's government by the start of Wagner's second term: the Committee on Management (1950–1953), a temporary State Commission (1953–1956), and the Joint City-State Fiscal Committee (1955–1956). Each of the studies found serious inadequacies in the city's political and fiscal situation. Their suggestions for reforms were largely ignored by Mayor Wagner, who believed he had mastered the techniques of city government. An administrative structure that tolerated many layers of overlapping authority was thus allowed to perpetuate itself without interference, and inevitably corruption appeared. In 1959 alone there were scandals in the market department, in city fuel oil purchases, and in the office of the Manhattan borough president.

In February 1960, only a month after this last affair led to the indictment of Hulan Jack, a fourth study of the city was published. The New York State "Little Hoover Commission," led by Otto Nelson, charged that the government of New York City was inherently ineffective owing to one-party predominance, a weak mayor's office, a hack-ridden Board of Education, and a rubber-stamp City Council, the "weakest but highest paid" in America. The Nelson committee attacked Wagner personally for compounding these governmental inadequacies by his inaction: the mayor apparently has "no appetite, willingness, or capacity to initiate or carry out . . . substantial changes" as suggested by previous studies.

Nevertheless, the Nelson panel did propose a series of specific reforms such as increasing the cash flow, staggering the collection of real estate taxes, and adjusting the debt service. Had these reforms been implemented, they would have served the city well. Indeed, they might have spared New York the national humiliation it experienced in the 1970s. However, the Nelson commission's too-general allegations of mismanagement and corruption enabled the Democrats to excoriate the entire report as a "partisan political document" funded by the Republican legislature. Wagner, Comptroller Lawrence Gerosa, and Council President Abe Stark united to reject the commission's conclusions. As was the case with the Vernon commission, nothing of substance changed.

All intimations of economic decline and governmental disorder notwithstanding, the Wagner years represented the last good times for New York for twenty years. They also became the last hurrah for Tammany Hall. Although the immensely popular Eisenhower twice carried New York State in his two presidential elections, DeSapio remained successful by nominating and electing the Democrat Averell Harriman (1891–1986) as governor in 1954. DeSapio even served as New York's secretary of state and so had as much patronage to distribute on the state level as he did in the city. Although his appointments were given to capable but loyal party men, his reputation as a manipulator remained strong. DeSapio's very success as party manager made him increasingly prominent, and whether due to vanity or his desire to overcome the "boss" label, he began to seek the political spotlight for himself. In 1958 he overcame liberal opposition to impose his own candidate, District Attorney Frank Hogan (1902–1974), on the Democratic State Convention. The losers inevitably raised the old cry of "bossism," and DeSapio's dark-glassed image (he had an eye disorder) seemed to give it substance. Then, when both Hogan and Harriman were defeated, his regime was suddenly shaken. Not only had DeSapio become so visible as to become an issue himself, but he also had committed the unpardonable sin of backing losers.

DeSapio's once sure touch deserted him during the presidential campaign of 1960 when he only belatedly joined the John F. Kennedy bandwagon. When Kennedy won, he decided to chastise DeSapio by awarding patronage not through Tammany but instead through Mayor Wagner. Thus was the stage prepared for perhaps the most outrageous of all the amazing mayoral campaigns in New York's history. The Republicans, anxious to run against a mayor widely perceived as weak, vacillating, and machine dominated, would not be allowed to do so. Instead, Wagner openly broke with his mentor, announced his support for a different borough president in Manhattan, and denounced as "bossism" the political record he himself had constructed over eight years. It was 1961, a year for miracles, and just as a New York Yankee was shattering Babe Ruth's "unbeatable" home run record, so Robert F. Wagner set out to destroy the myth of the invincible Tammany machine.

In September, even before Roger Maris hit his sixty-first home run, the mayor crushed DeSapio's candidate and won the Democratic primary; he immediately therefore became the odds-on favorite for reelection. A despondent DeSapio was forced to back an independent candidacy by Comptroller Gerosa in November. Almost no one paid any attention to Gerosa's claim that the "real issue is whether the city is to become solvent or go bankrupt"; everyone knew that the only issue was DeSapio. On November 7, Wagner won 1,237,421 votes to trounce Republican Louis Lefkowitz; Gerosa got only 13 percent of the total vote. DeSapio's humiliation was not yet ended. He had concentrated so completely on the citywide campaign that he had neglected his own position. In Greenwich Village, a group of liberal insurgents led by James Lannigan and Edward Koch (1924–) ousted him as district leader. Wagner had not just abolished "bossism"; the boss himself had fallen. Never again would a Tammany chief dominate New York.

The demise of Tammany was not immediately apparent, of course. The leader who replaced DeSapio, Edward Costikyan, was the first Protestant leader of Tammany Hall since Boss Tweed. His prickly independence made it difficult for him to work with Wagner, however, and critics of the mayor, who were legion, soon were asserting that bossism had only relocated to City Hall. After his reelection, Wagner demanded resignations from four hundred city workers identified with DeSapio. Wagner let it be known that he intended to lead both the city and party, citing charter revisions approved by the voters in 1961 to prove that the people wanted strong leadership. In September 1962, a select panel was appointed to review all judicial nominees and to remove the courts from politics. Yet despite the rhetoric, nothing really changed. It was a bitter Costikyan who summed up Wagner's style as mayor: "Create no potential opponents, eliminate those who appear, take care of yourself, and never make a decision until it can't be avoided."

Nevertheless, the third Wagner administration began in the glow of political independence and good economic times, even if both were partly illusory. The city's population had never been bigger. Internal improvements such as the Throgs Neck Bridge (1961), a second deck for the George Washington Bridge (1962), and the Verrazano Bridge (1964) across the Narrows tied the city even closer to its suburbs. Under the surface, though, forces were growing that gradually undermined the city's self-sufficiency. From the early 1960s to the present day, New York has endured a succession of debilitating budget crises. In 1960, the city received more than $150 million in federal grants, but even that enormous sum was inadequate to provide all the services that New Yorkers needed. Wagner had to negotiate a special infusion of state aid from Governor Nelson Rockefeller (1908–1979) before he could balance his budget. As the mayor began his third term, a quarter of his money came from state and federal sources, and in the next two decades the proportion of city expenses purchased with subsidies continued to grow. But all these transfusions provided only temporary help. By May 1963, as part of a general revenue-raising package, the City Council reluctantly approved an increase in the sales tax. The outcry was loud but short lived. Even though the city has never used all its potential taxing authority, its beleaguered residents are already the most heavily taxed Americans. By the time Wagner left office, the city's budget had reached $3.4 billion and was still rising rapidly.

The question of race relations assumed even greater importance. Inevitably, reductions of city services would have the greatest impact on already struggling minority populations. It was Mayor Wagner who was forced to confront the racial revolution that stemmed from the 1954 Supreme Court decision integrating the schools. But how was this to be implemented in New York, where the minority population was clustered into ghettos? Wagner's administration had made housing discrimination illegal—in theory if not in practice—and thousands of units of urban renewal apartments available to all New Yorkers were constructed. The Mitchell-Lama housing program offered middle-class housing to thousands, and in the 1950s, New York City constructed more housing project units than did the rest of the nation. Still the demand grew. In 1960, the Housing and Redevelopment Board was established to coordinate the construction. In the West Side renewal area, the mayor argued, any minority residents displaced by construction would have the "right of return" to one of the projected 2,500 units. The high rents, however, made it difficult for many displaced minority families to do so. Despite good intentions, much of New York's educational system and housing remained de facto segregated.

As part of the city's effort to deal with the depressed economic status of its minority groups, a major educational innovation was announced in 1961. The City University of New York was created to provide a free college education to any qualified New Yorker. The consolidated institution would guarantee to all students the opportunity to advance as far as their talents allowed. The leavening effect of education, it was argued, would ultimately raise both the income levels and the status of the city's minorities. In addition, during 1962 Wagner increased the antidiscriminatory powers of his Commission on Human Relations and created the Rent and Rehabilitation Administration to deal with specific complaints by the poor. The optimism that these efforts would be successful seems almost utopian today.

The situation of most minority groups remained dismal. In 1960, for example, blacks comprised 13 percent of the city population but received 45 percent of welfare payments. Even more depressing was the discovery that Puerto Ricans, who had arrived with such high hopes and who then constituted 8 percent of the city, received 30 percent of public assistance. There seemed few places on the success ladder for minorities. Equally troubling was the increase in animosity evident when middle-class white residents spoke scornfully of a "welfare class." Slum conditions spread when public housing was neglected; crime statistics soared as joblessness grew among the unskilled; and neighborhood communities in New York moved farther apart.

In April 1964, when another World's Fair opened in Flushing Meadows-Corona Park, disgruntled black leaders threatened to bring their cause to national prominence with a "stall-in" on the roads leading to the fair. It did not happen, but clearly only a single misstep could have precipitated violent confrontation. Later that year, during a July heat wave, a policeman shot and killed a black boy, and four days of sporadic violence erupted in Harlem. Before it ended, there were fires, 140 injuries, and one death. Harlem provided the first harbinger of the "long, hot summers" to come, but this omen was ignored. A troubled racial future was also indicated in the striking but unpublicized fact that during the Wagner era, 800,000 white residents left New York for the suburbs. They were replaced in the city by various minorities with lesser skills who did not qualify for jobs but required a greater amount of public service than did the exiting whites.

To deal with the myriad urban crises confronting the city and the nation, the cliché of the 1960s held that "strong executive leadership" was imperative. On the national scene, President Kennedy labored to invigorate a reluctant Congress, and on the local level, mayors like Bob Wagner tried their best to imitate his example. A major revision of the city charter had been approved by the voters in 1961, and when it took effect on January 1, 1963, the mayor suddenly had unprecedented budgetary authority. He alone was given the right to estimate revenues and also to determine the level of debt that the city could afford for its capital construction program. In its first year of operation, the mayor overestimated general fund revenues by $68.4 million. Of equal importance for the city's fiscal future, on April 3, 1964, Governor Rockefeller approved an amendment to the Local Finance Law permitting mayors to include current expense items in their capital construction budgets. Thus were put into place two of the mechanisms that led to the fiscal disaster of the 1970s.

Toward the end of Wagner's third term, commentators understood that race and finance were the most important long-term issues facing New York City. Beyond cosmetic announcements and short-term provision, little effective action in these areas was undertaken by a mayor both famed and blamed for his "dedicated inactivity." Wagner found it far more politic to emphasize the continuing strengths of the metropolitan economy than to respond to the discovery of slow hemorrhage. In 1963, the city still was home to 33,000 manufacturing establishments employing 927,000 workers, a total surpassed by only five of the fifty states. Its clothing factories created 28 percent of the total apparel value for the nation, and its many small print shops and publishing houses handled 19 percent of America's printing business. New York's retail trade surpassed that of forty-three of the fifty states, and the city maintained its traditional position as the nation's leading wholesale market.

With statistics like these, it was easy to ignore facts showing that the port's total share of national cargo handling had dropped by 10 percent in the previous decade, that the local job market had grown only 1.6 percent from 1958 to 1963 against a national average of 11 percent, and that 227 manufacturing firms had left the city during Wagner's third term. Nor was it incumbent on the administration to explain why with more teachers instructing fewer pupils and with more police on the streets, the city was plagued by badly educated, truant children and rising crime statistics. If the public perceived any threat, it probably was in the area of racial tension, most apparent in a series of battles to achieve more integrated schools that were waged in 1964/65. Since these disturbed public serenity, Wagner professed great concern, but his answer was merely soothing words and a new superintendent of schools who promised increased institutional sensitivity to minority concerns.

Few noticed that the greatest casualty of the Wagner years was the Democratic machine. After the mayor's rout of DeSapio in 1961, the last boss's return to power was frustrated first by Greenwich Village reform groups and later by legal battles. No universally accepted leader succeeded DeSapio in ruling Manhattan. The mayor selected officials on a merit basis, and each long-term appointment cut further into the sinews of the machine. In 1964, Charles Buckley (1890–1967), boss of the Bronx since the death of Ed Flynn, also was defeated by a reform Democrat; his death three years later removed another tie to the past.

Although perceived as an ineffectual, vacillating mayor, Wagner proved a veritable tiger when it came to dispatching his political foes. During his third term, he purged the Democratic Party of its machine-oriented politicians, organization men capable of delivering the vote. They were easy prey now, for the ethnic groups they represented were exactly those who were relocating to the suburbs. Like a row of dominoes, they collapsed before Wagner's onslaught. It is one of the great ironies of city history that even as the mayor destroyed the remnants of the Tammany machine, the legislative apportionment law that had for fifty years underrepresented the city in Albany was being declared unconstitutional. The gains that a unified city delegation elected by machine vote might have won for the financially troubled city would never be forthcoming. The areas of New York that most benefited from reapportionment were the suburbs. The end result of Wagner's twelve years in office was a Democratic Party sadly lacking in organizational leadership when the mayor announced he would not stand for a fourth term in 1965.

Wagner's timing was, as usual, correct. His personality was hardly compatible with the temper of a year when diverse protest movements seemed high on the public agenda. Causes as disparate as women's rights, consumerism, student activism, black power and anti-Vietnam protests all would have to be confronted by a strong mayor. Across the nation, new young leaders were attempting to don the mantle of the assassinated president. It was a time when a rather shell-shocked public hoped and perhaps even believed that one man might still make a difference.

Manhattan Republicans believed they could exploit the Democrats' disarray and use the public's psychological malaise to return to power. The young paladin whom they chose to lead them was John Vliet Lindsay (1921–), a forty-four-year-old graduate of Yale Law School, who since 1958 had represented in Congress the "Silk Stocking" district of East Side Manhattan. Lindsay's appeal was summed up in his campaign advertising: "He is fresh and everyone else is tired." Pledging to master the city's problems, Lindsay won not only both the Republican and the Liberal nominations but also the unanimous backing of the press. The *Times* looked forward to "renewal" for the city, and the *Herald Tribune* found in Lindsay a "capacity to inspire"; he offered the vision of a city physically and spiritually transformed. The press warned that if the electorate rejected Lindsay, it meant a return to "backroom government," a signal that the city was a "haven for mediocrity" which they equated with the sedate Democratic nominee, Comptroller Abraham Beame (1906–). All these advantages might have meant nothing had not Lindsay also benefited from the third-party candidacy of conservative columnist William F. Buckley (1925–). In November 1965 the 341,226 votes that Buckley won from potential Beame voters provided the Liberal Republican Lindsay with a narrow margin of victory. It now remained to be seen if the man and the times had met.

Immediately after Lindsay's election on November 9, the infamous "blackout" of the northeast power grid struck. Some areas of the city had no electricity for up to fifteen hours; not unexpectedly, nine months later there was a minor baby boom. Although the power outage was inconvenient, it was temporary, though perhaps it symbolized the general plight of New York. The city was increasingly the victim of outside forces it could not control. Even more figuratively, it might be asserted that there was a blackout of effective thinking about the city in the 1960s, a failure of political will that led to its humiliation in the 1970s.

Simply to read the newspapers and magazines of these years is a sobering experience. Writer after writer accurately identified the nature and the causes of the looming urban crisis. In *Commentary* Nathan Glazer asked, "Is New York City Ungovernable?" and wondered whether the city's main problem might not be bigness itself. The *Herald Tribune* in 1965 ran an extended analysis of the city's problems and concluded that "New York is the greatest city in the world, and everything is wrong with it." Almost all writers agreed that the city was living beyond its means and that financial reforms were necessary, During the Wagner-Lindsay interregnum, yet another Temporary Commission on City Finances concluded that "sooner rather than later [New York] will find itself unable to meet current charges" owing to its widening budgetary gaps.

Closely tied to the financial mess was the dawning recognition that a virtually permanent welfare class of minorities was taking shape in New York. Many welfare recipients were unemployables who lacked the technical skills to serve modern business and whose raw muscle power was not useful in the shifting economy. Most of the welfare class, however, consisted of women and young children. Politicians united to ignore or to offer platitudes about this issue rather than to face up to its serious implications. Indeed, when Buckley's eccentric campaign proposed alternatives to the constantly rising welfare rolls, opposing politicians and the press labeled him a crypto-racist. It was far easier to cite the victory of Puerto Rican migrant Herman Badillo (1929–) as borough president of the Bronx to prove that New York's minority population would be successfully integrated. In any case, the future of New York became Lindsay's problem on New Year's Day.

On January 1, 1966, a beautiful sixty-one-degree day in early winter, the future turned bleak. At 5:00 a.m. that morning, 33,000 public transport workers led by Mike Quill, whose union had always talked tough but had never struck the city, shut down the world's largest transit system. The resulting twelve-day strike has been described as the "greatest catastrophe since the Great Depression," a disaster in both economic and psychological terms. The economic effects of the walkout were devastating, of course, with business losses totaling $800 million, lost wages reaching $25 million daily, and ripple effects spreading across the nation.

Even more destructive, however, was the damage done to Lindsay's "can-do" image as he attempted ineffectively to cope with the calamity. He did the expected things, like walking to work, but he flailed about wildly searching for solutions. He denounced the "power brokers" of New York—coyly adding that "they know who they are"—as the real culprits behind the strike. On January 4, Lindsay allowed Quill to be jailed for leading the walkout. "Red Mike" loved it and called on the judge to "drop dead in his black robes"; he even scornfully refused to pronounce the mayor's name correctly. Harried and desperate, Lindsay ultimately approved a settlement twice as large as the TWU had originally requested. Not only did he accept a contract the city could ill afford, but he also earned no support from labor for doing so. The other municipal unions perceived his political tentativeness and subsequently whipsawed the reform mayor into granting each of them settlements far larger than they had obtained from the easygoing Bob Wagner. It seemed, after all, that New York's glamorous new mayor was a politician just like all the others, though perhaps less gifted with tact and strength. Lindsay attempted to recoup administratively. In January 1966, he created by executive order the massive Transportation Administration to rebuild the defective system. He also attempted to replace the extraordinary Robert Moses as head of the Triborough Bridge Authority. But the powerful Moses shrugged aside Lindsay's challenge as efficiently as he had warded off all such attacks in the past.

Lindsay's "on-the-job training" did not end with his inept performance in transit affairs. His early denunciation of the "power brokers" was not forgotten by the New York establishment that had supported his election. When the mayor chided businessmen for not contributing enough time or money to help the city, it was interpreted as another gratuitous slap at his natural constituency and as an indication of his political paranoia. By March, Lindsay had alienated major elements of the coalition that had elected him (bankers, businessmen, and members of the New York Bar Association and Century Club), and it was many months before they forgave him.

If this was not enough, Lindsay then decided to challenge the single most visible bureaucracy in his city, the New York Police Department. In a move to appease both the liberal and ghetto critics of the department, the mayor suggested that a civilian review board be established to assess and control police performance. In a city where 150,000 felonies were committed each year, the public at large perceived this suggestion as a way to tie the hands of the police and to coddle criminals, especially those from minority groups. When Lindsay appointed a new police commissioner whose task was to implement the proposal and "reform" the department, the poor man was virtually destroyed by the entrenched police establishment and driven from the city.

To cap a generally dismal initiation period, Lindsay also isolated himself from political support by feuding with Republican Governor Nelson Rockefeller. Both men were liberal politicians with presidential aspirations, and their one-upmanship battles continued for several years. On the local front, moreover, Lindsay treated Democratic City Council President Frank O'Connor with studied contempt, even though O'Connor at least understood how the city operated. Wagner, whose maligned performance in office suddenly seemed admirable, was quick to point out the gaps between Lindsay's rhetoric and his accomplishments, and he predicted a fiasco. As early as June 1966, *Fortune* magazine echoed that judgment in an article entitled "This Lindsay Takes on That City," which lamented the confrontational attitude of New York's new leader. At a time when the city was running out of time, the mayor was mired in a series of battles that accomplished little and ignored the slow deterioration of the metropolis.

In July 1966, yet another commission, this one led by Earl Schwulst, reported, to no one's surprise, that New York's basic problem was a lack of money. "The city at present borrows for everything it possibly can, including some truly current expenses which the state permits it to fund." The result was enormous debt service charges and excessively high taxes. The report did acknowledge that the city provided "unusual and costly" services such as the municipal hospital system, high employee pensions, and CUNY, but it insisted that additional revenues were needed to support them. Lindsay naturally was aware of the conclusions long before they were published, and he blithely responded that "the situation in New York is always desperate." In a fireside chat to his city, he conceded that taxes would have to rise, but he never altered his systematic use of the bogus deficit-financing techniques he had inherited.

The immediate budgetary issue was solved on July 1, 1966, when after a protracted struggle with the legislature, an income tax for city residents and a commuter tax were instituted. Great as the new revenues were, however, they still did not balance the books. To run the subways, another transit fare increase, to twenty cents, was enacted, and that autumn additional bond issues were floated to fund a budget suddenly above $4.5 billion. The budget had doubled in ten years, and projections said it would double again by 1974; actually, it would be far greater.

John Lindsay never gained control of his budgets. He accepted the ramshackle system, the poor managers, and the questionable financial practices that had begun under Wagner and, by ignoring the fundamental problems, compounded them. It was not all his fault; the banks, the legislature, the governor, and the people also were to blame. But the task of leadership was his responsibility, and in that regard, he failed.

Lindsay's inability to come to grips with the financial question had long-term effects. In the short run, the mayor achieved the dream of every politician: he dominated the headlines. Sometimes the stories were disastrous, as when the voters in November 1966 defeated his Police Review Board by almost two to one, and sometimes they were triumphant, as when the mayor negotiated $30 million in Model City aid from the federal government in 1967, but always it was Lindsay who "got the ink." He created the Public Development Corporation to relocate firms to New York and to halt the slow ooze of jobs to the suburbs. The Human Resources Administration combined welfare, manpower, and antipoverty programs under one commissioner. In 1968, three of the planned superagencies to restructure the city's administration were operating. Others were stillborn or, like transportation, were defeated. One clear problem was the mayor's inability to retain able commissioners: fourteen quit during the first two years of his administration. One effective bureaucrat was Thomas Hoving of the Parks Department who shared the same flair for headline grabbing as did his boss. In sum, after its rocky start, the Lindsay administration settled down to maintaining the system rather than mastering it.

Lindsay's greatest success was in race relations, as he managed to keep New York's streets "cool" during the many discontents of the late 1960s. It had been shocking to discover in 1966 that in New York's schools, whites were now the minority and that the system was essentially segregated. The fears and traumas thus released led to the "Great School War" of late 1968 when blacks contended with Jewish-dominated teacher organizations for control of the educational process. Lindsay ultimately moved the city into a decentralized educational system that lasted into the 1980s.

In the greater arena of racial protest, Lindsay had more success. Violent protests led by the Students for a Democratic Society racked Columbia University, and anti-Vietnam demonstrators often filled the streets, but the race issue was muted. Probably only Lindsay's leadership spared New York the trauma of riot that devastated cities such as Detroit, Newark, and Washington. Although welfare rolls soared beyond 800,000, the attendant costs were minor compared with those of the race war that some commentators had expected. It was not a payoff that prevented this in New York; it was the almost heroic figure of a mayor in shirt sleeves walking the ghetto streets and really caring. It was Lindsay's finest hour.

As New York reached the end of the troubled 1960s, there was little public recognition that the city was undergoing fundamental economic and social changes. Probably on a subconscious level, everyone recognized the danger but tended to focus on headline happenings rather than underlying realities. Besides, how could New York City be in trouble? It still was larger than 67 of the 122 members of the United Nations, and its mayor supervised the second largest budget in the nation. Lindsay often spoke of having the "second-toughest job" in America, and many suspected he longed to try on the first for size, especially when he used his membership on the Kerner Commission in 1968 to become the spokesman for urban America. There was no doubt that New York City in 1968 was still strong, but each day its finances worsened, its restive minorities grew more sullen, its institutional fabric weakened, and its resilient spirit eroded just a bit more. A time of testing was approaching when many would question whether New York could survive the 1970s.

10

Disaster and Rebirth

During the turbulent 1960s, the urban crisis took tangible form in the mind of the American nation. The violence in Detroit, Newark, and Washington resulted in scores of deaths; ethnic immigration to urban centers continued to exacerbate racial tensions; the increasing gap between city revenues and services they were meant to support haunted the nation's mayors; and thousands of jobs were lost from the urbanized East to the warmer climate of the Sunbelt. Taken together, these facts brought the reality of urban transformation to the center of the national stage.

In no other American city were the contradictions between the dreams of urban residents and their troubled reality so apparent as in New York. Mayor John Lindsay won his first election by a narrow plurality not because he was a Republican—the very idea was laughable given the voting record of New Yorkers—but because citizens believed he represented their best chance to solve their city's problems. Exemplifying New York's dilemma was an article appearing in *Fortune* magazine shortly before Lindsay's election, entitled "A City Destroying Itself." Then, early in his first month of office, as New York clawed its way out of the debris of the transit catastrophe, *U.S. News & World Report* asked, "Does New York City Have a Future?" (January 24, 1966). Besides the twelve days of the transit strike, Lindsay's first-year experiences included a twenty-five-day newspaper blackout, a thirty-three-day dock strike, and a seventy-five-day hiatus of shipping deliveries. It was a year of unending racial conflict featuring battles over educational priorities, police-minority relations, and a welfare system whose expenditures had doubled in five years. As if these afflictions were not enough, the city was suffering the effects of a five-year drought which forced restaurants to stop serving water with dinner. Finally, the rate of serious felonies tripled in the 1960s, and "crime in the streets" became a preoccupation of city residents. By 1968, many New Yorkers agreed with the despairing comment by one of Lindsay's trusted commissioners: "The city has begun to die."

Yet despite all the difficulties, New York's social fabric held firm, and the city again proved its toughness. While urban centers across America were convulsed by racial conflict, New York remained relatively unscarred. Lindsay personally deserves much credit for maintaining the peace. The mayor also served with distinction on Lyndon Johnson's National Advisory Commission on Civil Disorders. In March 1968, he was instrumental in proposing to the nation an urban bill of rights, calling for "a cooperative attack on the problems that beset the underprivileged." But the project was ignored in a Washington obsessed with Vietnam.

Lindsay's New York still benefited from a powerful economy that provided decent jobs for working-class residents. In fact, the city's 1969 unemployment figures were lower than those of any other major American city except Dallas. In the spring of 1969, the mayor submitted an operating expense budget of $6.1 billion, a figure that had tripled in only a decade, but no one was shocked. The *Times*, a staunch Lindsay supporter, considered it a budget of "wisdom and equity" and informed readers that the administration consistently applied city resources with skill and discretion.

Yet to Lindsay's critics—and they were legion—praise from the *Times* rang hollow. Some charged that he had purchased racial calm only by offering New York's minorities the most generous welfare benefits available anywhere in the nation. Others held him guilty of mindlessly expanding the public payroll to offset the decline in private job creation. Almost all his detractors agreed that the mayor had cravenly agreed to extortionate labor settlements with militant city workers so as to avoid a repetition of the calamity of January 1966. Civil Service salary gains were compounded by increased pension obligations: in 1966 police officers were granted full pay pensions after thirty-five years of service, and firefighters received equal treatment the next year. Sanitation workers won twenty-year half-pay pensions in 1967, as did transit workers. In 1968, employee unions at the Board of Education, City University, and elsewhere quickly joined the parade, and New York even agreed to "sweeten" some contracts by paying a larger percentage of pension costs. How, asked Lindsay's opponents, could New York hope to pay these bills in the future when its high taxes were causing business and white flight? As New York became the "land of taxes," the "money providers" were leaving the boroughs, and the demands for city resources were constantly increasing. With a welfare population about to reach 1 million persons, caution was wise. Yet despite all the storm warnings, the city persevered in its policies, and its mayor walked tall.

In retrospect, the election year of 1969 represents a watershed in New York history as the last good economic year the city would enjoy for a decade. Employment reached the astronomical figure of 3.884 million, establishing a municipal record that may very well never be broken. But beyond job statistics, the city experienced a memorable series of emotional highs and lows. The year began with a collective ego trip when on January 12, an underrated but confident New York Jets football team led by Joe Namath beat the mighty Baltimore Colts and gave New York its first Super Bowl victory. The celebrations were hardly concluded when a sudden February snowstorm turned the economic hub of the nation into a frozen wasteland. Manhattan was rapidly plowed out, but the streets of the outer boroughs were ignored for up to a week. City Hall's seeming indifference to their plight left many citizens furious with the mayor. The mayor who argued that New York City must lead the nation to an urban renaissance suddenly was "only a politician" who could not even keep the streets cleared.

Then the mayor faced deep political trouble in his party; Republican regulars perceived him as loyal only to minority voters and the "beautiful people" of the East Side of Manhattan. Republicans believed that Lindsay had abandoned traditional party principles and "given away" the city. Among Democrats, the seemingly endless series of strikes and confrontations marking Lindsay's first term encouraged a plethora of candidates eager to oppose him. It came as no surprise to knowledgeable observers when Lindsay was routed in July's Republican primary by a respected conservative state senator named John Marchi. Less predictable but still not unexpected was a fierce five-way Democratic dogfight to choose his opponent. Victory went to Mario Procaccino, an almost unknown and somewhat inept clubhouse politician, who assumed that his nomination meant the restoration of normal Democratic control. But despite his repudiation and dire prospects, Lindsay refused to quit the race. After obtaining the nomination of the Liberal Party, Lindsay also managed to have his name listed on the ballot as an Independent. Both Marchi (Republican-Conservative) and Procaccino (Democratic-Nonpartisan) also held two ballot lines, but during the heated campaign they competed viciously for essentially the same groups of conservative and ethnic voters. Neither attracted support from the minority poor or Manhattan-based liberals, the staples of Lindsay's power. Moreover, it is a tested truism that mayors of New York City are not elected by calling for vigorous economy. Lindsay pledged to maintain programs that supported the least successful residents of the city until they could become productive citizens and join in the American dream. In the end, his Fusion-Liberal coalition of 1965 had just enough power to coalesce one last time, and in November 1969 Lindsay was returned to City Hall with only 42 percent of the vote.

Many pundits asserted that Lindsay's triumph by plurality was a political wonder, but real New Yorkers knew that a far greater miracle had taken place a month before the election. In October 1969, the perennially hapless New York Mets had won the World Series. Many believed that the euphoria of seeing a last-place team become a champion was Lindsay's greatest asset in the hectic last days of the campaign. Although that argument is not quantifiable, an analysis of the 1969 vote leaves no doubt that Lindsay's victory was due to declining party influence in New York, a process that had been apparent since the Wagner administration. Democrats, more than 70 percent of all registered voters, had refused to unite behind their official candidate. The remnants of their once-vaunted organization could not deliver a reliable vote for the party slate. Regularity had collapsed; Democratic totals were the lowest since the O'Brien disaster of 1933, and the Republican vote hit a forty-year low. Citizen indifference was as responsible for Lindsay's second term as were his real accomplishments or the Mets' victory. The continued decline of party loyalty was reinforced on August 10, 1971, when the mayor announced that he was leaving the Republican Party and becoming a Democrat. The Republicans were glad to see him go, and Democrats welcomed his defection with ambivalence.

One fact was certain: New York remained unchallenged as America's largest city. The census of 1970 showed that the city had reached its peak population level of 7,894,862, but that growth had slowed to only 1.5 percent in the 1960s. A precipitous fall was to be the demographic reality of the next decade. During his second term, Lindsay worked hard to obtain administrative control of the monstrous corporation called New York City. There were always two aspects to his mayoralty, the job itself and the far more glamorous role as spokesman for urban America. The mayor proved to be a more capable administrator than expected and continued his grand scheme of consolidating the many city agencies into ten superunits. Albany cooperated by authorizing the Metropolitan Transit Association in 1969 to deal with subway, bus, and commuter problems. Nevertheless, Lindsay's administrative record was mixed; city agencies never effectively spent even the monies they received. For example, it took ten bureaucracies seventy-one separate steps to purchase a single sanitation truck. Decision-making was slow, and in 1969 the city failed to spend the $65 million received from the federal Model Cities program. In fiscal 1970, the city lost $16 million in state education aid because it had not yet dispersed previous funds. Such administrative failures became rarer in the course of Lindsay's second term, but they were never completely eliminated.

In eight years, Lindsay never came close to solving the city's perennial housing crisis. In 1965, he had pledged that 160,000 low- and moderate-income housing units would be built by 1970, but private builders simply refused to construct housing except for the well-to-do. Using state and federal support, the city attempted, but failed, to fill the gap. Only 34,167 units were begun over a five-year-period, 8,920 of which were low-income apartments. During the same time, 200,000 existing units in sound buildings were either abandoned by their owners or fell prey to fire or vandalism. Arson for insurance profit emerged as one of the most prevalent crimes in the city; the early 1970s saw fire transform the South Bronx into a national symbol of urban decay. The city already owned 189 housing projects that its Housing Commission called generally well run and less crime ridden than other areas of the city. Critics mocked that assertion. Not even the presence of extensive city projects could compensate for the continued attrition of residential stock.

To control the situation, the administration tried zoning changes, the introduction of "scatter site" projects, and the integration of retail and recreational facilities into new construction. But nothing seemed to arrest the decay and depletion of housing units. Between 1970 and 1975, the South Bronx alone lost 16 percent of all its housing (43,000 apartments) as four square blocks were lost weekly to physical decay and fires. An accelerated exodus from the devastation was the inevitable result. Some white Bronxites fled northward into Westchester County. Others moved east into the massive development of Co-op City, which began to fill its thirty-five apartment towers in December 1969. And significant segments of the white, black, and Hispanic middle classes simply decided to leave New York.

The movement toward suburbia, long a national phenomenon, had a great impact in New York. Census statistics showed that nearly all the growth in urban America during the 1960s took place not in center cities but in suburban enclaves. The commuter's lifestyle was pioneered by New York and its bedroom communities, whether located in nineteenth-century Brooklyn Heights or twentieth-century Manhasset or Mahopac. But in the early 1970s, a ruinous new trend became apparent. Not only were city residents fleeing, but they appeared to be carrying their jobs with them. Whereas the number of commuters from Westchester to Manhattan had risen by 50 percent since 1950, the percentage of New Yorkers traveling northward to jobs had risen an amazing 500 percent in the same twenty years. By 1971, 115,000 Westchester residents came south to the city each day, but an almost identical number of city residents headed north.

In 1970, the city still was home to 125 headquarters operations among the nation's Fortune 500 companies, but in that year alone, six other corporations decided to leave Manhattan. Discontent with the atmosphere of New York—its crime, its dirt, its taxes—seemed common in executive suites. A corporate exodus reduced headquarters operations to a mere ninety-four by 1975, and the process drained jobs from the city economy. After a corporate relocation to Connecticut, Westchester, or New Jersey, 80 to 100 percent of all executives retained their positions, as opposed to only 10 to 25 percent of lower-level workers. Perhaps the most publicized departure was that of the football New York Giants, a city institution that decided in 1972 it preferred Hackensack, New Jersey, to a cramped Bronx stadium. The Brooklyn Dodgers and the New York Giants baseball teams had gone to California in 1958, and now the beloved football Giants had fled to a swamp in Jersey. Perhaps corporate America knew something?

Undoubtedly, a major reason for the hemorrhage of corporate executives was the attractiveness of suburban living, as opposed to the unceasing hustle and perceived dangers of the city. But there were objective reasons as well. The cost of doing business in Manhattan constantly increased; in 1970, transit fares rose again, and the sales tax increased to 7 percent. Although city employment was at an all-time high, the quality of the work force was perceived to have deteriorated along with the school system. Business was loath to bear the unending burden of 1 million welfare clients. Even though the city's operating budget was in excess of $6.6 billion, the delivery of city services seemed increasingly irregular, and the creation of superagencies had not improved the situation. From a human perspective, crime and the fear of violence had become a pervasive reality of city life. Leadership by the mayor had so far averted major racial violence in New York, but a riot at the Tombs prison in October 1970 indicated that this trauma was never far below the surface of city life. Lindsay himself termed the Tombs hostage situation his most difficult moment. In all, the corporations leaving the city had valid arguments for their flight.

Lindsay's second term became a constant struggle to provide his city with the services it demanded and required if it was to preserve its dominant position. Yet the mayor was forced to wage his battle with revenues that increased only slowly. New expedients such as off-track betting added millions to the city's coffers, but accelerating costs rapidly outstripped such marginal gains. Between 1961 and 1975, the city's debt almost tripled while the cost of debt service rose beyond 500 percent. National forces beyond the city's control—the mechanization of farms, immigration by air, and the appeal of suburbia—facilitated the exchange of 1.6 million whites for an equal number of minority residents between 1950 and 1970. This vast migration altered the ethnic character of the city and forced it to spend far more than expected on welfare and health programs. Whether Lindsay's Manhattan-centered tunnel vision compounded the difficulties he inherited is debatable. But that he presided over the transformation of New York was clear.

Assessments of Lindsay's two terms differ widely, but certainly he ranks as one of the master builders of modern New York. His accomplishments in construction rankled Robert Moses, one of Lindsay's harshest critics, who was quoted as saying, "If you elect a matinee idol as mayor, you get a musical comedy administration." Lindsay was deeply interested in urban planning and courageously insisted that the special needs and desires of local groups be considered when designing municipal projects. Partly as a response, the city had almost 10,000 block associations by 1975. The Urban Design Group was created within the City Planning Commission and conscientiously consulted sixty-two community boards before completing scores of police and fire stations, playgrounds, pools, and libraries. Under Lindsay, the city became involved in Lyndon Johnson's Model Cities and constructed the first residential units to emerge from that program. A new master plan of development had been promulgated in 1969, and special offices to plan and develop midtown and lower Manhattan, Jamaica (Queens), downtown Brooklyn, Staten Island, and Fordham Road (Bronx) were organized to develop projects. As a result of "incentive zoning" initiated under Lindsay, seventeen skyscrapers were added to the skyline of New York during 1970 alone.

The climax of this extraordinary construction boom occurred in 1972 when the 110–story "Twin Towers" of the World Trade Center, a project launched in 1966 by the Port Authority, finally opened. Designed by Minoru Yamasaki and Emery Roth Associates, these 209–foot squares contained more than 9 million square feet of office space and were expected to spur a major revitalization of lower Manhattan. In time, they became the center of the port's international trading community and disproved claims that they were unrentable. Advocates of the WTC megastructure emphasized its sheer size and magnificent engineering: the buildings had their own zip code, consumed enough electricity to light Schenectady, and hosted fifty thousand workers and eighty thousand visitors each day. Although condemned by some architectural critics as "General Motors Gothic" featuring soaring lobbies of "pure schmaltz," the public readily accepted the structures. They rapidly became a fixture of downtown activity and an integral part of the world's most famous skyline. A decade later, when the trade complex contained six buildings, the earth excavated for the project was used to create 23.5 acres of new landfill for Battery Park City.

As the Lindsay years drew to a close, there was little public or private recognition that New York was about to be traumatized by a fiscal nightmare. For almost twenty years, the city had provided the widest possible spectrum of services to its citizens, and the bills were about to come due. As Lindsay concluded his eight years as mayor, his valedictory remarks gave no hint of crisis. Listing gains in seventeen separate areas, the mayor claimed that he was leaving office with New York "in the best shape it has ever been." In an interview with the editors of the *New York Times*, Lindsay cited substantial gains in worker productivity, accountability, and improved management techniques. Exchanging his seat in the House of Representatives for the mayoralty had afforded him the "best eight years of my life." Lindsay clearly believed in his litany of accomplishments. He was a gifted leader blind to the long-range impact of his fiscal profligacy. His career is remarkable testimony to the lack of technical skill possessed by many modern politicians.

A more realistic accounting must begin with the fact that New York never recovered from the recession of 1969. Job erosion and white flight continued to bleed the city, and in Lindsay's second term, a staggering quarter million jobs vanished. The *Annual Survey of Manufacturing* in 1973 still found New York above the national average in worker-added value, but the percentage of manufacturing workers in the city was now below 5 percent. Even progress had its price, for many lost positions were due to the construction boom of which the city was so proud: the World Trade Center alone was responsible for the virtual decimation of Manhattan's small print trade. Because of inflation, revenue continued to rise while Lindsay was mayor, but the cost of providing social services to a growing percentage of the population was outstripping gains by 9 percent each year. Despite this gap, Lindsay added new commitments to the budget. For example, open admission at the City University for all high school graduates began in 1970, a full five years before originally planned.

Lindsay worked closely with Comptroller Abraham Beame, and together they announced annually that the city had again balanced its budget. These yearly proclamations ultimately were seen as acts in a long-running farce.

"Inventive accounting" was the order of the day, and a precarious stability was achieved only by issuing ever greater amounts of short-term debt. Between 1965 and 1973, the size of the operating budget quadrupled; contractual pay increases for a municipal labor force of 300,000 far surpassed the cost of living; and obligatory pension benefits trebled in size while remaining largely unfunded. Outstanding debt rose beyond $8 billion. Facts such as these were ignored in Lindsay's summation, and they were also disregarded by most New Yorkers. Overlooking the city's changed population, capital flight, and an increasing agenda of required services, everyone assumed that the good times would last forever.

Perhaps most remarkably, the dismal fiscal facts were equally ignored by the man soon to be Lindsay's successor, Comptroller Abraham Beame. During June 1973, the two worked together to craft an expense budget for 1973/74. The document that emerged from those deliberations helped elect Beame, but unfortunately, it relied on budgetary gimmicks fashioned to obscure the city's fiscal plight. Among its innovations were the placement of $564 million of operating expenses in the capital budget; a rollover of $308 million in 1971 notes, almost draining the "rainy day fund"; and simply inventing $100 million in "special" revenues to be uncovered by the comptroller. After all the deception, the budget still contained an official deficit of $211 million, which the two smiling leaders expected the Albany legislature to close. Two years later, as the city struggled to survive its insolvency, Beame claimed that Lindsay left him with a $1.5 billion budget gap. In 1973, the last summer of fiscal "business as usual," he had willfully ignored the existence of the chasm. As comptroller, Beame surely understood the dangers of excessive short-term borrowing. Nevertheless, he certified that city revenues met expenditures for each of the last four Lindsay budgets. Accepting the Democratic nomination that fall, he ran for mayor as the man who "knows the buck!"

To most commentators, Abraham Beame was a tragic figure who played a pathetic role in the great New York fiscal crisis. Yet from another perspective, he represented the marvelous opportunities New York traditionally offers to the "storm tossed" of the world. Beame's family were immigrants from Poland, and his father worked as a paper cutter. Maturing in the socialistic tumult of the Lower East Side, young Abe attended rousing meetings of the faithful before deciding that education and politics provided a more promising road to success in America. A graduate of City College, Beame worked faithfully for Brooklyn's Democratic machine for decades. In the 1960s he served as comptroller and lost the 1965 mayoral contest to

Lindsay. Finally, in 1973 Beame's persistence was rewarded. Loyal and competent, he also was the first Jew elected to lead the city of New York. Beame's critics believed him to be a clubhouse hack without abilities or ideas, but New Yorkers expected miraculous transformations. Hadn't the amazing Mets won another National League pennant that fall? Surely Beame would bring the city constructive leadership.

In any case, the normal Democratic tide again crushed Republican candidate John Marchi, and on November 6, 1973, Abe Beame attained the crowning achievement of his career: being elected New York's 104th mayor. Then in December 1973, as Beame prepared to take his oath, a long section of the West Side Highway collapsed under the weight of a repair truck loaded with asphalt. The rain of concrete closing a major city artery was the first harbinger of the disasters about to inundate the city of New York.

Beame assumed office in January 1974, a year of economic stagflation marked by the resignation of President Richard Nixon. American society was in crisis, and New York's economy was particularly vulnerable, since it had not yet recovered from the recession of 1969/70. The economic tide was running against a city that still earned 10 percent of all the money made in America and was home to ninety-six of the Fortune 500 corporations. New York, with six of the ten largest American banks, four of the top six insurance corporations, 90 percent of the most prosperous advertising agencies, and one-third of the nation's most prestigious law firms, was about to undergo its bleakest moments. It was a city with 28,000 restaurants, 1,000 foreign corporations, 500 galleries, a similar number of Off and Off-Off Broadway theaters, 61 museums, and 30 major department stores. It was totally beyond the power of reason to imagine the collapse of such an amalgamation of power and talent.

Not all these institutions and businesses collapsed, of course, but their host city did. New York spent more than twice as much per capita on its people than did any other city. With a population greater than that of Sweden and a budget virtually equal to that of India, the city provided more for its citizens in education, medical care, and social services than did most nations. The operating expenses for these programs were often shifted into long-term budgetary accounts, and by 1975 about half the capital budget was being used to finance current expenditures. New York's leaders simply were spending more money each year than the city was taking in, and they were hiding shortfalls by creative accounting; revenue anticipation notes were issued yearly to bridge the gap. As debt accumulated during the early 1970s, the city was regularly unable to repay its outstanding notes in June, at the end of its fiscal year. For about a decade, it simply rolled over its debt, borrowing even more to pay current expenses and the accumulating interest on its previous notes. The practice was inherently destructive, but so long as no one complained and the banks were willing to accept city IOUs, the system worked magnificently. After all, more debt for the city meant more business for the banks themselves. Even when New York marketed 30 percent of all the short-term paper sold in the nation, no one appeared unduly concerned. A short-term city debt of $4.5 billion clearly did not seem to bother Abe Beame as he settled in for what he confidently believed would be the greatest four years of his life.

By May 1974, the wages of fiscal sin began to appear. New York State monitors declared that the city was in an "unprecedented fiscal crisis," and Governor Malcolm Wilson, running hard for reelection, responded by approving a special measure authorizing the city to borrow even more. During the past decade, the expense budget of New York had tripled: its total debt exceeded $13 billion, and the 1975/76 estimate for debt service alone was more than $2.3 billion. In July, City Comptroller Harrison Goldin was forced to pay interest charges of 8.586 percent in order to market one-year city notes, and New York's long-term bonds yielded investors an unprecedented 7.9 percent. Goldin's annual report in November 1974 contained the dire warning that unless the city reduced its borrowing, the comptroller's office might not be able to market future bonds. On November 8, the mayor joined the chorus by conceding that his budget for fiscal 1975, which had gone into effect only months earlier, was already $430 million in the red. Beame disclosed that several thousand municipal employees would have to be fired in phased stages. By December, the beleaguered city had to pay an "outrageous" interest rate of 9.479 percent to obtain a $8.5 billion short-term loan; the city's October offering had been ignored by all investors. Compounding the sense of crisis, the Albany-funded Urban Development Corporation (UDC) collapsed in February 1975, bringing the state's credit rating into question as well.

As the financial disasters piled up, Beame enjoyed a final political success; he played a key role in the party maneuvering that made Hugh Carey (1919–) the Democratic nominee for governor of the Empire State. A former member of the House of Representatives from Brooklyn, Carey was elected in November 1974, in large part by an outpouring of New York City votes. In return, Carey would save the city he loved! For several years, his compassion for the city and his political deftness were the city's main—occasionally only—protection.

When he assumed office, Carey was forced to deal with the threat to state credit posed by the UDC's default. He did so quickly and effectively. The drama in Albany had the disquieting effect of focusing investors' concerns southward, where an infinitely worse fiscal disaster appeared imminent. As precise information on New York City became available, a horrified investment community not only withdrew its support but scrambled to save itself. Beame had failed to deal with fiscal reality, and so Hugh Carey, almost by default, was left as New York's primary defender.

On February 27, 1975, lawyers for a banking syndicate considering upcoming city bond issues—suddenly made more wary because of the UDC's default—asked to examine the municipal books. They professed shock at the irregularities and shortfalls they discovered, even though the banks they represented had overlooked such accounting practices in happier days. Once the report became public, the city failed to obtain any purchasers for its pending notes. Moreover, the value of outstanding New York bonds plummeted to two-thirds of face value. Standard and Poor's acted with indecent speed and suspended its comically high A credit rating for the city. In April, City Hall had no money to meet its obligations, and only a state-supplied emergency loan of $400 million kept the city solvent.

Governor Carey had produced the first of a series of monthly salvage operations. Beame's contribution to this first crisis was to reiterate his faith in New York and cancel the phased layoffs he had ordered a year earlier. His speeches became meandering searches for guilty parties. He did not seem to know whether the culprit was Washington, Albany, the banks, the unions, Lindsay, or God, but he was certain it was not Abe Beame. On May 29, he berated the newspapers for creating an "atmosphere of doubt and uncertainty" by reporting the bad fiscal news. Often, with the touching faith of a child, Beame would assert that "the crisis is behind us." Rarely had a political man been so out of touch with reality. In truth, the affairs of New York City were in the process of being taken away from Beame, and for the rest of his term he remained a figurehead mayor.

The key institutions that shepherded New York through its extended crisis were created by Governor Carey and the state legislature: they were the Municipal Assistance Corporation (MAC), irreverently known as Big Mac, and the Emergency Financial Control Board (EFCB). President Gerald Ford announced in May that the nation's largest city could expect no special aid from Washington. During that month, it was an advance of revenue-sharing funds from Albany—this time a transfusion of $200 million—that allowed the city to pay current expenses. Nevertheless, City University was temporarily closed, and its faculty, along with other municipal workers, were, for a short time, not paid as New York tottered on the edge of formal bankruptcy.

No relief was in sight, for the public bond market now completely spurned all New York City offerings, just as millions of dollars of municipal obligations were coming due. Albany, not City Hall, was the arena for late-night meetings and intricate maneuvering as deadlines for payment approached. Not until early in the morning of June 10 did the legislature agree to create the Municipal Assistance Corporation, an agency expressly designed to alleviate the immediate cash flow crisis by refinancing New York's short-term debt. Big Mac would also oversee the city's long-range borrowing policies. To back the new bonds with cash instead of promises, the money raised by city sales and stock transfer taxes was specifically earmarked for Big Mac. New York State asserted its "moral obligation" to protect investors who purchased MAC bonds against default, and a billion-dollar reserve fund was established in Albany to back this promise. Despite unrelenting protests from Beame, both current city revenues and control over New York City's fiscal future now resided in a state-created body. "Home rule" temporarily ceased as state, city, bank, and union officials worked desperately to save New York City.

Mayor Beame was displaced and ignored. In the terrible weeks that followed, he defiantly asserted that municipal workers would never endure a wage freeze, then he imposed one. After claiming that a budget ceiling was impossible, he agreed to one. His old and dear friend, the first deputy mayor, was sacrificed to the state's new fiscal watchdogs. Transit fares increased to half a dollar, CUNY suffered harsh cuts, and city services were reduced everywhere. The city was informed that it must adopt new accounting procedures and gradually excise operating costs from its capital budget. Many workers suddenly realized that budget cuts meant lost jobs. Police officers responded viciously, distributing pamphlets urging tourists not to travel to "fear city" and not to walk the streets after 6:00 p.m. It was not the department's finest hour. Not to be outdone, the sanitation workers staged a wild-cat strike, allowing 58,000 tons of garbage to accumulate on the streets, and firefighters protested with a "sick-in." By July 25, even the City Council, a kind of long-running joke, roused itself from lethargy. Recognizing the gravity of the crisis, it decided to raise the round-trip fare on the Staten Island Ferry from ten cents to a quarter. At such times, it seemed as if the city was only one step from anarchy or madness.

Big Mac sold $1 billion of new bonds in June to prevent default, but its constant friction with Beame appeared to doom a second sale. Pressure from all quarters collapsed City Hall's opposition, and on August 6 the mayor agreed to a three-year budgetary plan with absolute spending ceilings. Within weeks, Big Mac was able to market another $960 million and maintain the city's solvency. The August package was possible only because of another advance from Governor Carey and the timely participation of several city employee pension funds. MAC's chief financial negotiator, Felix Rohatyn (1928–), simply termed it the "monthly miracle." Almost immediately the divine intervention ended, however, as accountants studying the city ledgers discovered that the looming budget deficit for 1975/76 was $2.8 billion to $3.3 billion rather than Beame's illusory figure of $641 million. It became increasingly obvious that the mayor lacked the political will to make harsh political decisions and even seemed to oppose reform. Investors shied away from investing in more MAC bonds, and it appeared certain that New York would soon default.

Governor Carey now openly intervened, bypassing Beame completely and convincing the legislature to take a final "gamble," one last "major effort to save a city and secure a state." On the evening of September 9, Albany agreed on a $2.3 billion aid bill, placing harsh financial curbs on the city and granting control of all its monetary decisions to the state-appointed Emergency Financial Control Board (EFCB) whose chairman was the governor. As of November 1, all city revenues belonged to the board, which would disperse them for three years in accordance with an overall financial plan. A special state deputy controller for New York City would be named to monitor the city's compliance. The existing municipal wage freeze was incorporated into state law, and all new city contracts became subject to EFCB approval. Only the harshest measures, affirmed Carey, could save the city, the state, and the nation itself from "inestimable harm for an indefinite time." Although Mayor Beame was a member of the EFCB, the governor completely dominated its proceedings. The control board's legislation completed the process of metamorphosing New York's mayor into a figurehead.

During the chaos in New York and despite the devastating effect its collapse would have on national and world commerce, there was an almost surrealistic unconcern in Washington. Treasury Secretary William Simon suggested that a New York City default would cause only "moderate and relatively short-lived disruption," and President Ford seemed to have no interest in the proceedings. On October 2, the unending crisis caused Moody's Investor Service to downgrade all New York State and New York City securities, as well as to withdraw its ratings of other state agency bonds. Analysts estimated that a hundred banks across the nation might fail if New

York defaulted, and across the nation, other states and cities were experiencing the ripple effects of the crisis; they were being forced to pay higher interest rates in order to market their own securities.

A delegation of fifteen mayors visited President Ford to warn him of a "domino effect" should the "Big Apple" fail. West German Chancellor Helmut Schmidt remarked that the crisis was even disturbing financial centers such as Zurich and Frankfurt. Vice President Nelson Rockefeller, who as governor of New York had approved much of the shoddy financing, now argued that the mere possibility of default was causing the value of the dollar to decline on international exchanges. On October 18, "Rocky" bolted from Republican ranks and became the first administration official to support a direct federal aid or loan guarantee program for New York.

Instead of abating, the crisis intensified in October. On October 17, the city's cash needs totaled $477 million, but it had only $34 million in all its current accounts. New York was only fifty-three minutes from defaulting on its obligations that afternoon until an eleventh-hour infusion of cash borrowed from teacher pension funds completed yet another complex financial package. Offices stayed open late into the evening so that the city could redeem $453.1 million of its notes as they were presented. MAC Chairman Felix Rohatyn lamented that "the dikes are crumbling and we are running out of fingers." Carey cabled President Ford begging that he recognize New York as "part of the country."

The EFCB gave final approval to a three-year city austerity plan on October 20, ordering Beame to further reduce capital-spending projections for that period. Congress, realistically but reluctantly, moved to consider the city's plight but halted when the president, on October 29, vowed to veto any federal "bailout." Ford suggested that Congress merely adjust existing bankruptcy statutes to facilitate an "orderly reorganization" of city obligations after its default. He used the occasion to criticize specifically the high wages and pensions of municipal workers, CUNY, the eighteen-unit hospital system, and ineligible recipients on city welfare rolls. The President's unyielding National Press Club address led the *Daily News* to headline its next edition, "Ford to City, Drop Dead." Carey predicted the city would lapse into bankruptcy by December 1 and bitterly remarked that "it isn't fair when the President . . . kicks the people of . . . New York in the groin." In October 1975, for perhaps the first time in two centuries, the city on the Hudson was clearly an underdog.

Many Washington conservatives embraced Ford's "no bailout" position, but the weight of informed opinion and fiscal probity clearly indicated that federal action was required. On November 1, the Joint Economic Committee of Congress declared that a default by New York would immediately add 300,000 workers to the jobless rolls and reduce America's real GDP by a full percentage point. Three separate polls taken after Ford's speech all disagreed with his hard line: respondents believed the entire nation, not just the city, would suffer the impact. Since 29,000 workers had been dismissed by October 31 and millions of subway riders were paying higher fares, no one could legitimately argue that the city was not trying to reform. Gradually, the administration eased its intransigence, and on November 26, Ford asked Congress to consider granting $2.3 billion in direct federal loan guarantees to New York on a "seasonable basis." Harsh repayment conditions were exacted; there would be "no cost" to taxpayers because all outstanding loans from one year had to be repaid before new monies would become available. Indeed, the U.S. Treasury made millions on the loans.

Several additional state measures orchestrated by Governor Carey preceded the final federal turnabout. On November 14, the legislature passed a controversial debt moratorium procedure that enabled the city to postpone for three years repaying the principal on $1.6 billion of its short-term notes. Bondholders were offered the option of receiving ten-year, 8 percent Big Mac bonds or holding their existing notes at 6 percent. In either case, they would not be permitted to regain their principal. In strict financial terms, this was default, although no one admitted it. Carey's second great achievement was to put in place a $200 million tax package on the eve of Ford's November 26 address. The legislative measure was the capstone of an elaborate $6.6 billion, three-year financing program that drew on the resources of the city's pension systems. Gubernatorial pressure combined with self-interest finally brought New York's banks into the rescue operations. Manhattan's largest financial institutions agreed to extend the maturity dates of their notes and to accept a lower rate of interest. The final and now inevitable step was taken on December 9, when Ford signed Congress's seasonal loan guarantee program for New York City. After months of crisis, the city's solvency was assured. All that remained was to implement the budget cuts and endure the suffering.

The fiscal crisis abated temporarily in December 1975 after a state court decision upheld the moratorium imposed on bond redemptions. After another year of appeals, lawyers for the Flushing National Bank convinced the New York Court of Appeals in 1977 that the legislative action was unconstitutional, and the city scrambled to find another billion dollars. After the trauma of 1975, such an operation appeared relatively simple because, as

Mayor Beame chuckled, "We looked in every pocket." More debilitating was the long-range deterioration of the urban economy. From December 1974 to December 1975, New York lost another 143,000 jobs, and important political leaders argued publicly that city default was preferable to inflicting continued sacrifice on the citizenry. Their counsel was ignored.

A few slivers of hope glittered amid the debris of the rescue operation. Statistics showed that in 1974 the long-neglected Port of New York had handled more long tons of cargo than in any year since 1941. Containerization facilities were rapidly being completed, and the vast harbor that for so long had guaranteed Manhattan's prosperity slowly revived; it remained America's busiest port, with approximately six hundred ship clearings per month. Despite the constant economic attrition, the city in 1975 still had 172,000 taxpaying business enterprises. The resilience of city people even in the face of reduced services was amazing. Thousands of block associations maintained their community spirit, and latent pride began to resuscitate areas as disparate as Little Italy and Soho in Manhattan, Belmont in the Bronx, Long Island City and Astoria in Queens, and Park Slope in Brooklyn. Adversity appeared to have triggered an appreciation of the past, creating a preservationist spirit that created dozens of special historical districts. And finally, amid the canyons of downtown Manhattan, the office space glut of the early 1970s showed signs of ending, and plans for new construction began to be discussed. In small but important ways, the beleaguered city demonstrated that its vitality had not been destroyed.

After two years of unceasing misery, the growing psychological revival was capped by the national Bicentennial in 1976. Celebrations were held across the United States, but the one image that remains indelibly imprinted in the American memory is the parade of "tall ships" through New York Harbor and up the Hudson River. The beauty of New York's modern skyline behind acres of sails brought home to all citizens the city's enduring historical importance. In August, this spirit was again in evidence as the city played host to the Democratic National Convention. Twenty thousand delegates and visitors were almost overwhelmed with affection as they nominated Jimmy Carter for the presidency. Suddenly city prospects looked brighter, since Beame was one of the first politicians on Carter's bandwagon. Having survived two years of trauma, even tourists had returned to Manhattan; in 1976 they constituted the city's second largest industry, with 834 conventions held there. And in a city that was determinedly small town about its sports teams, the New York Yankees returned to their newly renovated stadium and promptly won a pennant. On many levels, New York's turnabout had begun.

Early in 1977, Big Mac bond issues were selling at a premium, and the brief emergency created by the invalidation of the bond moratorium was over. Jimmy Carter had been elected to the White House; optimism was in the political air; and anything seemed possible. Therefore, in March 1977, Abe Beame announced during his State of the City speech that he, as a "dynamic" leader, had decided to run for another term. The mayor felt entitled to reelection, since he had made the "tough decisions" that saved New York. The incredulity that this statement evoked is difficult to recreate, since even the most obtuse voter recognized that all those "tough" decisions had been forced on a protesting mayor. Beame pressed forward, however, and in April the EFCB approved his proposed $13.9 billion budget. The size of the budget was striking, as were its pre-crisis assumptions. Beame proposed higher municipal salaries, more capital construction, and an end to reduced services while promising to hold property taxes level for the next five years. Despite Beame's bravado, there was nonetheless a veritable stampede of Democrats rushing to oppose him. Because the mayor maintained the support of the remaining borough machine vote, it was possible he might win in a crowded primary field.

Probably no one was as shocked by Beame's decision as was Hugh Carey, and he moved decisively to prevent a farcical renomination. Not only did Carey openly endorse another candidate (Mario Cuomo [1932–]), but he also decreed that the Democratic primary be delayed until September. By then, he was certain, the long-delayed SEC investigation into the causes of New York City's crisis would have been published. The report actually appeared in August and severely criticized city officials for not informing investors of the reality of municipal securities. Beame's campaign was outraged at the timing of the report and cried sabotage. The mayor himself admitted that he had lied about financial matters, but only in the best interest of the city. Beame argued that because everyone in authority had perpetuated the illusion of solvency, no one really was guilty of fraud. The voters—aware that they were being ruled from Albany, were paying higher transit fares and CUNY tuition, and were receiving fewer services for more dollars—disagreed.

After a marvelously complex political season, the citizens of New York turned for leadership to the official nominee of the Democratic party. The victor was neither Abe Beame nor Mario Cuomo but instead Edward Irving Koch, a Reform Democrat who boasted of being a "capital punishment liberal." Koch won the party nomination with a no-nonsense, abrasive, confrontational style that the voters found immensely attractive. Even before his election, Koch demonstrated a singular independence of thought. During Jimmy Carter's telegenic excursion to view the devastated South Bronx, he handed the president a letter protesting administration policy toward Israel.

Victorious in a four-way race against Conservative, Liberal, and Republican candidates, Koch declared he intended to be a three-term mayor and restore both prosperity and social idealism to New York. His inaugural address voiced the faith of millions when he asserted that "New York is unique in the history of human kindness." The mayor also argued that "New York is not a problem. New York is a stroke of genius. From its earliest days this city has been a lifeboat for the homeless, a leader for the hungry, a living library for the intellectually starved, a refuge not only for the oppressed but also for the creative." Koch confessed a few municipal stumbles in the past, "but our mistakes have been those of the heart." He pledged to be tough enough to sustain the recovery process.

Recovery was indeed in the air by 1978. Labor statistics indicated that after eight years of decline, New York had not experienced a decrease in manufacturing jobs in 1977. Perhaps the hemorrhage of jobs, after having drained almost 650,000 positions since 1969, had finally been cauterized. During the remainder of the decade, there were slight gains in employment each year, although they were largely confined to service industries. Cost-of-living indexes proved that the city was no longer the most expensive place to live in the United States; indeed, it had dropped out of the top ten. Moreover, the massive influx of minorities ceased, at least temporarily. Welfare rolls were reduced to 907,126 in June 1977, owing to more effective management of the system. The standing inventory of surplus office space had finally been leased, and a building boom seemed imminent.

Symbolic of the new optimism was the gala opening of the City Corp Building on Lexington Avenue just as Koch took office. Hugh Stebbins's 915–foot tower was designed to be a functioning element of its neighborhood around the clock, and it became a commercial if not a critical success. Similar headquarters structures for ATT and IBM were also planned. Although the Citizens Budget Committee alerted Koch that budget problems still loomed, the mayor clearly preferred to remember that more than one hundred Manhattan real estate sites were worth more than $10 million each.

Despite a brightening prognosis, the Koch administration's first priority remained money. A campaign to secure extended federal loan guarantees was waged and won in Washington. Participants in the rescue operation of 1975 all had vehemently insisted that a one-time infusion of federal support would be sufficient to save New York, but they all had lied. Although the city successfully repaid all federal seasonal support, adding $12 million in interest payments, its cash flow problems necessitated the continuation of Washington's backing to soothe the nerves of a skittish investment community. With a Democratic president in power, the case was easier to argue, and Jimmy Carter soon traveled to Manhattan to sign legislation extending the loan guarantee program until 1982. As he initialed the bill, Carter praised the resilience and spirit of a city that had reigned as the nation's "Big Apple for more than two centuries."

Koch, who often displayed a tendency to euphoria, was already claiming that New York was experiencing a renaissance. No fewer than sixteen Nobel Prize winners called New York home, and he cited their presence as proof of the city's continued cultural dominance. Elated by fiscal success, Koch temporarily forgot that he was elected to put things right in the city, not recreate business as usual. Welfare rolls were at their lowest since 1969, but they still contained 907,126 clients. In June, a contract negotiated with a coalition of city workers provided only a 4 percent pay raise, a meager one indeed considering growing inflation, but the mayor failed to obtain promised union "give backs." Claiming that productivity gains would flow from higher wages was more typical of past wishful thinking than present reality. Critics of Koch's cave-in conveniently forgot that union investments and worker sacrifices were fundamentally important to saving the city. Perhaps it was too much to expect that either the unions or the mayor they supported could avoid a mutually congratulatory pact. Far more difficult to justify was the sweet "catch-up" contract the mayor agreed to in 1980.

Improving economic conditions increased the city's revenues in 1978 and 1979, and the retirement of short-term debt continued. In July 1979, the city began its fiscal year with a planned budget of only $12.8 billion, an increase of merely 7 percent since 1975. Fiscal monitors for Albany and the General Accounting Office (GAO) in Washington constantly demanded budgetary restrictions so that 1982 might arrive with spending balanced according to Generally Accepted Accounting Principles. A Planning Commission report conceded that New York in the future would be smaller, but as a new decade began, it was proving to be immensely attractive to foreign-based corporations seeking secure havens for their money. The city's agony had reduced its number of headquarters operations to only eighty of the Fortune 500, but the corporate gap was being filled by foreign corporations and banks taking advantage of the weak American dollar. Moreover, domestic corporations suddenly discovered that business expenses were actually cheaper in New York, and shippers found that improved harbor facilities meant more expeditious handling of greater cargo volume. In July 1979, for the first time in four years, a consortium of banks agreed to market $600 million in city revenue anticipation notes without any participation by pension funds. It was a tentative step toward monetary responsibility. Budgets remained spare, and additional money to rebuild a crumbling infrastructure was lacking for several more years, but New York again was back in the fiscal game.

By early 1980, it was obvious that a corner had been turned. Not even a rerun of the subway strike scenario that so damaged Lindsay could halt the revival. Mayor Koch endured an eleven-day stoppage in April 1980 with strength and good humor. His query "How'm I doin'?" was heard in every borough, and the public answer seemed to be "Fine." As new construction proliferated, no fewer than five major hotels opened to cope with the flood of tourists and business visitors that had risen each year since 1975. Prices for a night's accommodations passed $100, but delegates such as those at the Democratic National Convention of 1980 did not seem to mind. The theater was selling more tickets than ever at prices up to $40, and opera goers could choose between two companies challenging each other across the completed Lincoln Center. The number of welfare recipients continued to decline, and the resident magicians at Big Mac announced the refinancing of all remaining short-term debt. The city's life signs were again highly positive.

Citizens' attitudes, too, reflected fundamental changes. They accepted that a future New York would be smaller and have fewer schools, hospitals, and corporations than in the past. Although some marginal gains in factory jobs were reported at the end of the 1970s, the city could never regain its manufacturing primacy. In the past, manufacturing jobs fueled New York's greatness and had always been available to its aspiring poor. For the 1980s and beyond, however, the city shifted into a service-oriented economy requiring better-educated workers. Modern job skills demand better schools, and so the delivery of education services became a dominant public concern. The only major source of blue-collar jobs was the obligation of the city to refurbish its crumbling infrastructure. Billions of dollars were spent to rehabilitate roads, bridges, sewers, waste recycling, waterfront improvements, and industrial park projects. By 1981, a building boomlet returned new office space construction to 1975 levels, and 8.504 million square feet of office space were completed by 1982. The critical weakness was that this office space demanded efficient workers that New York did not yet have in great supply.

Office construction and the reappearance of large-scale projects, despite the "stagflation" of 1980/81, promised future prosperity. Vast residential complexes at Waterside on the East River and Battery Park on the Hudson were under way as was a new convention center on the West Side of Manhattan. Zoning changes were enacted to shunt new construction away from the overbuilt confines of midtown toward the Upper West Side of Manhattan and to the outer boroughs. An industrial park opened in the blighted South Bronx, and a complex program of $7 billion in mass transit renovation was finally in place. The despised subway system, for all its smell and graffiti, remained one of the city's greatest potential strengths by efficiently delivering labor to jobs; in 1982, however, ridership fell below a billion for the first time since 1917. It was undeniable that even despite the long manufacturing slide, Manhattan remained the apparel center of the nation, and 140,000 legal workers—there were thousands of underpaid illegal garment workers—daily created union-label goods.

The census of 1980 revealed that 3,298,400 persons held jobs in New York and that the city retained 11,321 manufacturing establishments providing 280,000 jobs. Despite all its travails, the New York Metropolitan Area still ranks as the largest manufacturing center of the United States to the present day. And in another echo of its past, the census provided graphic evidence that New York was a city of diverse ethnic groups. The city could still boast that it contained more Jews than Tel Aviv, more Irish than Dublin, and more Italians than Florence. But the official figures also documented a tale of severe shrinkage from its former domination. Manufacturing decay, middle-class flight to suburbia, and generalized concern about rising violence combined to reduce New York's total population to 7,071,030, with minorities making up almost half that number. There were 1,723,124 blacks and 1,405,957 Hispanic residents in the city, and many suspected that thousands had not been counted. That multitude included enormous numbers of talented entrepreneurs and hard workers, but the two largest minority groups also included the citizens making the greatest demands on city social services, hospital facilities, and welfare.

The social amalgamation of minority groups had been impeded by lingering racial animosity and housing patterns, and undoubtedly the political establishment had prevented them from attaining power to the extent that their numbers seemed to demand. But the Democratic mayoral primary in 1977 featured candidates from both the black and Puerto Rican communities, and there was wide expectation that the ethnic succession amply demonstrated by the city's past would finally embrace these groups as well. In the meantime, community leaders predicted that their time had finally arrived.

Mayor Ed Koch had been elected with the votes of many blacks and

Hispanics, but his first term had been so dominated by the fiscal crisis that his reputation as a Greenwich Village liberal sensitive to the expectations of minorities had suffered. Koch saw himself as breaking with "business as usual" politics, even though he had been elected with the support of the political bosses of the outer boroughs. Modern-day "bosses" in the Bronx and Brooklyn had provided his victory margin over Mario Cuomo in 1977. Considering himself to be a reformer, Koch abhorred governing via patronage and agonized when pressed to reduce the level of city services. When he was forced to do so in his first term, the services most affected by budgetary stringency were exactly those most open to blacks and Hispanics.

Tightened government hiring meant that there were fewer job slots in the Civil Service, and city employment was ruthlessly slashed from 332,298 in 1975 to only 245,618 in June 1978. CUNY, the traditional pathway to education and a middle-class life, had pared its registration by 70,000, a reduction that disproportionately affected minority students. When the mayor in 1979 decided to close Sydenham Hospital, a facility that served a minority population but did so badly, the surrounding community reacted with such anger that violence was only narrowly averted. The Sydenham decision caused the resignations of Koch's black and Hispanic deputy mayors, and the mayor himself wrote that it "caused the most damage in my relationship with blacks." Minority populations were also most affected by the inevitable rise in transit fares to seventy-five cents, an increase that took effect in July 1981. Although fares were no longer the mayor's responsibility, the gap of misunderstanding widened between him and black constituencies. In time, this misunderstanding became distrust, and Koch would end his career with little black support.

The primary theme of Koch's first term was the need to regain control of the city's finances. Pruning costs and controlling spending were repeated mantras, and the budget was allowed to increase by only 60 percent of the inflation rate. With money in short supply, many of Koch's early initiatives were symbolic gestures. Some cost no money at all. Because he had been outraged at Mayor Beame's last-minute appointments of judges, a traditional way to reward faithful friends and party stalwarts, Koch instituted a procedure in which new judicial selections were screened by a legal panel before being presented to the mayor. The institutionalization of this "merit" system was important to Koch, and he considered it "probably the most salutary and lasting" of his political accomplishments. During 1978, Koch's fourth executive order ended discrimination based on sexual orientation in the awarding of city contracts and housing. During the 1977 campaign, Koch had been deeply wounded by rumors that he was homosexual, and his administrative action seemed a fitting response in keeping with the tolerance necessary for life in New York. Later, during his third term, the mayor signed legislation prohibiting such discrimination in the private sector as well.

Administrative reform was also used by the mayor to show New Yorkers that all levels of the city shared in the pain of fiscal austerity. Political circumstances and his own inclination permitted Koch to reduce the number of deputy mayors from seven to three. He proclaimed that recapturing the "public school, transportation and hospital systems from the unions and special-interest groups" was his primary concern, and he moved aggressively in those areas. The new school chancellor, Frank Macchiarola, an effective choice who held the position for five years, succeeded in making *dropout* a term of opprobrium. Catering to middle-class concerns became a powerful unifier as the city slowly fought its way back to fiscal integrity.

The payoff was tangible by 1981. In January, Koch's budget proposal called for the expansion of previously reduced city services. In February, the city sold $100 million in short-term notes at less than 8.5 percent interest, its first entry into the bond market since 1974. The sale was backed by future tax revenues, an income source more predictable since the city had reformed its dubious accounting practices. In the spring, the comptroller's office marketed twenty-year "investment-grade" bonds for the first time since the financial crisis began. Finally, the mayor was able to announce that the 1981 fiscal year had ended on June 30 with a true budgetary surplus according to Generally Accepted Accounting Principles. It was true that inflation was responsible for some of the increased tax revenue, but the administration could legitimately boast that it had tamed the budget monster a full year in advance of the state mandate. The acerbic and ebullient Ed Koch had, with the invaluable backing of Big Mac and the Emergency Financial Control Board, made the "rotten apple" palatable once more.

In 1981, Koch announced for renomination as a hard-nosed miracle worker who had saved New York. Opposition to his accomplishments seemed incomprehensible, especially since the new budget proposals pledged to hire more police officers, firefighters, and teachers to rebuild the curtailed services. On September 22, the mayor achieved an unprecedented coup, winning nomination from both the Democratic and the Republican organizations. Suddenly the choice of everyone, Edward Irving Koch, the underdog candidate of 1977, was triumphantly reelected on November 3, 1981. His victory was sweet recognition of his leadership in dire circumstances, but it also represented a growing consensus in the electorate that party was less important than performance. Political loyalty had been in decline for a generation, and by 1981 there was hardly a "boss" to be found in either party. The virtual coronation of Koch, a candidate of competence who had "promised God" he would serve for three terms, seems in retrospect part of an ongoing process reducing the relevance of party affiliation. Middle-class voters appeared universally appreciative of the harsh procedures that had restored budgetary balance to the profligate city. Minority voters voted for Koch because they had no alternative but to trust in his fundamental political philosophy. The city as a whole congratulated itself on accomplishing an impossible task in record time. New Yorkers now could legitimately anticipate full restoration of their prosperity and influence.

If the era of fiscal impoverishment can be said to have had a silver lining, it was that it restored New York's competitive edge even as the nation entered a decade of enormous growth. The high cost of doing business in New York had become outrageous in the early 1970s, and dozens of major corporations had left the city. But tax cuts and an improved climate for investment made New York viable once again for corporate America. Moreover, the success of Reagan Republicanism on the national scene made the 1980s a time of almost unrestricted opportunity for true believers in capitalist America. The rebirth of America's metropolis allowed it to benefit inordinately from what has been called the "greed decade." Fiscal disaster and loss of city sovereignty had been overcome, and the city was again ready to lead the nation forward.

11

Contemporary New York

New York has always been notorious for its impermanence: it is envied and scorned for simultaneously being in both disintegration and re-newal. Under Ed Koch, the city appeared at least politically unified as it faced the challenges of the 1980s. Census figures showed that it had lost more than 820,000 residents during the traumas of the previous decade, but its population of 7,071,030 was still twice that of Chicago, the perennial second city. A few world cities were now more populous; many were larger in area; still others were more scenic, certainly more sedate and safe; but none represented the spirit of its society as well as New York did. Wall Street remained the epicenter of American capitalism, a true icon of the most success-driven society on the planet.

New York listed 202 commercial banks, eighty-two savings institutions, and hundreds of brokerage firms servicing the world's investors. The gross city product exceeded $100 billion in 1980. Its dilapidated but still excep-tional port handled more than 50 million long tons of cargo annually. As New York entered a new decade, its retail sales rose by 20 percent, surpassing $24 billion for the first time. Perhaps most impressive was the fact that the city—afflicted by a manufacturing decline that had erased more than 600,000 jobs since 1969—had retooled its economy so that half its service industries were engaged in providing information, a key predictive element for prosperity in the postindustrial age. The city seemed poised to dominate the emerging cybernetic world just as it had presided over the fabrication stage of economic development.

In addition, the city remained the national center of both culture and education, with sixty-five museums and historical societies and more than fifteen hundred galleries and twenty-nine universities and colleges. Broadway theater was about to embark on its most prosperous era. The rest of the country and the world might justly ponder how a population of only 3.1 percent of Americans, packed on a mere tenth of 1 percent of the national domain, could so dominate the spirit of the age.

*

In explaining the gestalt of the contemporary age, historians find it hard to define or overestimate the change in American political thought that occurred after the election of Ronald Reagan in November, 1980. A one-time liberal Democrat transformed by political expediency into a conservative Republican, Reagan embodied the hopes and frustrations of a generation of Americans who believed that the nation had somehow lost its moral compass. The new president benignly presided over the psychological dismantling of federal governmental power, encouraging Congress to cut taxes and reduce national spending on social programs such as housing and welfare. Reagan firmly believed that Washington's excessive expenditure in those areas undercut the self-reliance that had always characterized Americans. At the same time, he reoriented America's budgetary priorities toward military strength and recommitted the nation to a confrontation with the "evil empire" of the Soviet Union. Accordingly, during his two terms the national debt tripled, even as the commitment of the United States to civil liberties and social welfare programs lessened.

While history's verdict on his administration is pending, there can be little doubt that Reagan's emphasis on individual accomplishment and smaller government represented values congenial to most Americans. Moreover, his uncompromising prosecution of a new cold war did hasten the demise of the Soviet Union. But domestically, Reagan was no friend to cities and always seemed willing to exclude the poorest and most alienated groups of people from government programs. Naturally, his reputation in the nation's greatest city was never very high.

New York's budgetary reliance on federal and state aid programs had been escalating since 1961, and systematic reductions in funding aid during the 1980s caused substantial suffering in a recovering city. By 1981, when 21.7 percent of the city's residents earned an income below the national poverty level, the city's multi-unit hospital system and the viability of hundreds of thousands of housing units depended on subsidies from the federal government. As partial federal financing for the many "welfare state" programs traditionally provided by the nation's most liberal city progressively declined, each city budget of this decade became a battlefield. Service agencies warred to obtain their "rightful" share of ever shrinking funds, and successive mayors struggled to provide constituents with programs to which they felt "entitled." Juggling precarious resources to bring services to a needy population defined each mayor's yearly performance.

Edward I. Koch won a second term in 1981 with the endorsement of both major parties because he was the "savior" of New York. Elected by a huge majority on a platform that promised to expand public services within a budget of $14.8 billion, Koch quickly realized that the city faced a future of austerity instead of the growth he had blithely pledged. Moreover, the city's social problems were hardly disappearing. Violence became a public fixation as crime continued to rise with the proliferation of the drug culture, and in 1981 alone, more than eighteen hundred murders were committed within the city's boundaries.

As if these were not enough, the national economy appeared to be slipping into recession. On the positive side, the city's unimaginably high short-term debt load had been virtually eliminated by MAC's rigor and Koch's management; fiscal year 1981 ended in June 1982 with a second successive surplus in the city coffers. Before that, however, the mayor had been forced to admit, on January 16, 1982, that only the "dramatic" cuts proposed in his new budget would maintain the city's solvency. The interplay of these competing economic factors in Koch's mind is uncertain, but such complexities led him into the greatest error of his career. Less than three months into a second term he had pledged to complete, he announced his candidacy for the Democratic nomination as governor of New York State.

One abiding truth of American politics is that attaining the mayoralty of New York is a politically final position. With great bravado, a previous incumbent had placed the presidency below the opportunity to occupy City Hall, but it was no secret that both LaGuardia and Lindsay had dreamed of the presidency. During the nineteenth century, only John Hoffman, backed by the power of the Ring, and DeWitt Clinton, advanced to Albany's state house. History itself seems aligned against mayoral ambition, and it seems foolish to linger over Koch's fruitless quest to attain happiness on State Street. During his ill-advised campaign, the mayor needlessly insulted upstate voters who lived in a "sterile" atmosphere, and he was outdebated and outmaneuvered by Mario Cuomo, a candidate he had handily defeated in 1977 when they competed in the city. In the September primary, Koch suffered a humiliating defeat when voters everywhere decided to "Keep the mayor mayor." A chastened Koch returned to Gracie Mansion lamenting a "decision born of equal parts of hubris and chutzpah." Never again during his remaining six years in office did Koch publicly aspire to higher office.

Koch turned to applying his political skills to wringing the most possible aid for New York from reluctant legislators in Albany and parsimonious bureaucrats in Washington. The 1980s were years of increasing financial demands on city resources, forcing the mayor to become a successful beggar.

As the circumstances required, Koch emphasized either the escalating needs of the city or the dire consequences of ignoring its plight. Homelessness, AIDS care, drug intervention, child support, environmental safety, and a bevy of other pressing needs were always on his agenda. Demonstrating the competence of his administration to use aid from other levels of government, Koch was able to retire New York's federal loans in 1985, long before the city was mandated to do so. Yet by mid-decade, despite improving national economic data, the proportion of city residents with incomes below national poverty levels had not been reduced. In fact, it continued to rise, soaring from 15 percent in 1975 to 23.9 percent a decade later. Two increases in poverty grant allowances did not reverse the trend. Even as Koch performed his annual budget miracle of attaining balance, even as he refilled payroll positions lost in the fiscal crisis, there existed the unacknowledged, uneasy perception that the city was becoming both poorer and bleaker. For example, in 1985, the leading cause of death for New Yorkers aged twenty to twenty-four was homicide and for those aged twenty-five to forty-four, it was AIDS.

But the irrepressible Koch refused to concede any shortcomings in either his programs or in the citizens of his city. His personal mantra, "How'm I doin'?" infected the population with his own optimism, and he soon overcame any resentment lingering from his abortive defection to Albany. His reputation as a guru of growth was enhanced in 1985, by chance an election year, as the effects of a Manhattan construction boom became apparent. Philip Johnson's AT&T Building (1984) was judged a success, and the World Financial Center at Battery Park City began to take shape. The latter project also provided housing units for a cross section of Manhattan's apartment dwellers.

Critics of the mayor charged that he had entered into an unseemly alliance with building and real estate interests, permitting sweetheart deals with preferred businesses. As both jobs and construction sites spread into the outer boroughs, such carping was muted, for the municipal economy was clearly strengthening. The annual budget continued to rise, but among its benefits was more money to hire additional police officers, firefighters, teachers, and transportation workers. Seventeen million visitors spent $2.4 billion in New York in 1985. Gradually, the trauma of city bankruptcy receded into memory.

Presiding over the turnaround with his customary arrogance, Koch published *Mayor: An Autobiography* in 1984, a self-serving memoir candidly assessing contemporary political figures who had helped or hindered the renaissance of New York. His one-sided retelling of the fiscal crisis was devoured by the public and resented by some politicians. Koch remained in excellent political shape as he prepared to run for a third term, which, if won, would fulfill his promise to the Almighty.

The winning coalition Koch created in 1985 was based on middle-class support and also included a large number of liberal reformers and conservative ethnic voters. His city, "Mine, all mine," had overcome great adversity and been restored to relative prosperity. Accordingly, Koch's political endorsements crossed racial lines; he enjoyed substantial backing in both the West Indian and the Hispanic communities. Koch insisted that he had done much to help blacks as well, pointing with pride to his appointment of Benjamin Ward as the first African American police commissioner in the city's history (1984–1989). Even after the turmoil of two terms, Koch's position remained strong, and he won 78 percent of the vote in November. A triumphant mayor seemed poised to not only enjoy his third term but perhaps also achieve the unprecedented feat of winning a fourth.

On January 9, 1986, Donald Manes (1934–1986), the borough president of Queens and county Democratic leader, was found bleeding in a car on Grand Central Parkway from what turned out to be self-inflicted knife wounds. Manes, one of the most powerful politicians in the city, had been Koch's personal choice as successor if his gubernatorial bid in 1982 had ended differently. As Manes recuperated at home from the bizarre incident, investigative reporters slowly lifted the lid on a vast network of bribery and influence peddling that had transformed city contracting into a "municipal marketplace." Gradually it became clear that the political leaders who had backed Koch in 1977 and who had remained his allies ever since, had used the mayor's popularity as cover for looting the city. As the investigations mushroomed, Manes succeeded in a second attempt to take his own life.

During 1986/87, a raft of municipal officials, primarily from the outer boroughs but many who had claimed close ties to the mayor, were indicted, pled guilty, or were tried on various corruption charges. No hint of personal dishonesty from the scandals stained Koch, but he was reduced to apologizing for former friends, reluctantly conceding his failure of oversight, and combating the growing perception that he was a lame duck. Because his two terms had been relatively free of scandals, Koch had naively boasted of the order he had imposed on the bureaucracy. Now he was forced to explain why six of the high officials he had personally selected occupied jail cells. Payoff rings were discovered in the Parking Violations Bureau, the Housing Authority, the Department of Environmental Protection, the General Services Administration, the Board of Education, and the Taxi Commission;

almost 250 lower-level bureaucrats were sentenced before the slow process of criminal justice ended. A biting exposé entitled *City for Sale* appeared in 1988, detailing the corruption and demonstrating that Koch at best had been lax in his administrative responsibilities. The parade of investigations found payoff systems in almost all city agencies, and in time, half of all sewer and electrical inspectors and a quarter of all housing inspectors were arrested for graft. Koch later implied that a small stroke he suffered in August 1987 was partially caused by the scandals. Beyond the corruption, the mayor's embarrassment was compounded when Bess Meyerson, who walked with him during the 1977 campaign and served as his commissioner of cultural affairs, was forced to resign in an unrelated, but extremely messy, marital/criminal scandal. The proud and loquacious mayor silently endured the "death of a thousand cuts" as each trial was played out and his reputation diminished.

As the incessant public scandals sapped his authority, a weakened Koch still faced daily a host of municipal problems that were seemingly immune to mayoral solutions. A new, deadly drug plague identified with "crack" cocaine settled over some neighborhoods, and certain city streets were soon battlefields where dealers murdered their way to territorial domination. As the crime rate soared, thousands of middle-class people of every color decided to flee the devastation. Poverty rates moved beyond 25 percent, and homeless people walked the avenues even as the financial pages were dominated by news of Wall Street mergers and leveraged buyouts. The gap between classes in New York seemed wider than ever before. And the once minor threat of AIDS escalated into a full plague. Koch had been accused as late as 1985 of not paying enough attention to the disease, but as it inexorably spread beyond the gay community, it became a public preoccupation. More than a quarter of all American cases were located in the city, and Koch struggled to obtain new federal funding for AIDS patients. Although the problems faced by New York were essentially national in nature, "Hizzoner" nevertheless had to combat the perception that the job he loved was overwhelming him.

In May 1987, Koch presented his "best budget," a $22.7 billion extravagance under which municipal employment surpassed the levels of 1975. Koch justified the expansion both as affordable—the city had gained 350,000 other jobs during his tenure—and necessary. He won his battle, only to have the revived optimism of his city dissolve in a single day. On October 16, 1987, the New York Stock Exchange lost 508 points, or 22.6 percent of its total value. Even though paper losses were restored after some additional months of trading, the shock of the minicrash lingered. In fiscal terms, 1987 was a year of economic triumph for the city with huge employment (3.61 million), the lowest unemployment in seventeen years, and a large rise in taxable properties. Yet because nine thousand jobs vanished from Wall Street, the engine of city revenues, within four months all other positive statistics were forgotten. Koch's budget proposal in February 1988 called for reduced services, higher taxes, and a freeze on city hiring.

Beset on all fronts, New York's 105th mayor fought to regain his equilibrium as his third term came to an end. Strangely, a not uncritical report entitled *New York Ascendant*, prepared by a Koch-appointed commission, provided some impetus for his political revival. Building on the regional plans of 1929 and 1969, the new document strictly avoided any hint of excessive optimism but offered a blueprint for future growth. Koch's investigators acknowledged that rising poverty levels were threatening the social harmony of the city and that New York had to reverse declining performance levels in education, public safety, and service delivery. Koch was not spared by an analysis that termed his administration's failure to plan for future city needs "shortsighted." Moreover, by supporting so many commercial projects, development had been "too fast, too large, too dense," and the city now faced a glut of office space. The report concluded that since a quarter of the city, including 40 percent of all children, was statistically poor, New York faced a bleak future. Only if the mayor acknowledged these long-term trends could he could hope to reverse them.

As an able politician, Koch selected specific elements of the report and used them to fashion a platform to run on in 1989. He announced a program to rebuild the city's infrastructure, a substantial effort that would create construction jobs and make business more comfortable with city conditions. Even without federal money, Koch launched a major housing initiative to build or rehabilitate more than 252,000 units by 1996. Unlike most such announced programs, this one worked. The public school system, decentralized since 1969 and considered disastrous by everyone but the bureaucrats of Livingston Street, was entrusted to an "outsider" pledged to reinvent the process of education. Chancellor Richard Green began his tenure in unprecedented fashion when, at his initial press conference, he told Koch to "sit down" while his appointee fielded reporters' questions. To widen his constituency, the mayor expanded his schedule of "town meetings" with local communities, sessions in which he discussed pending cuts or new initiatives. The program brought him into personal contact with small groups, including minorities disenchanted with his regime.

During the 1988 presidential campaign, Koch's criticism of Jesse Jackson had alienated him from black voters, and his community meetings allowed him to experience personally the anger of a quarter of New York's voting population. Koch sincerely believed that his programs were helping all minorities, so when challenged by black spokespersons, his combativeness hardly eased the relationship. His reelection hopes were increasingly hostage to the loyalty of a shrinking middle class, developers of real estate, politicians he had good reason to mistrust, and a restive electorate.

On March 22, 1989, the Supreme Court of the United States added another complexity to a mayoral race that was already problematic. Deciding *Board of Estimate v. Morris* for a unanimous Court, Justice Byron White ruled that part of the existing government of the city of New York was unconstitutional—it was in violation of the principle of one person/one vote. The case began in 1981 when Kings County residents went to court claiming that the Board of Estimate, which gave equal representation of one vote each to the boroughs of Brooklyn and Staten Island, could not be legal, since the former held six times the population of the latter. The Supreme Court ultimately agreed. The venerable Board of Estimate, part of city government since 1864 and constituted in its present form since the Lindsay administration, was invalid. New York was ordered to present a new governmental structure to the voters in November. The gigantic task of creating a new charter was finished in sixty days and resulted in the election of a much enlarged and more ethnically diverse City Council. Nevertheless, the process of building a new government under court mandate added even more tension to the upcoming election. (In a parenthetical note, the residents of Staten Island considered their reduced influence so demeaning that they endorsed a movement for secession from the greater city. A state-approved referendum on that proposal contributed to the election of a Fusion candidate to City Hall four years later.)

Continued scandal trials and economic distress had made Koch vulnerable, and eight Democratic candidates announced for mayor by the time the primary season began in June 1989. Within the varied field, the greatest challenge to the incumbent was mounted by David Dinkins (1927–), the black borough president of Manhattan, who believed Koch was unresponsive to minority concerns. Although no race riots had erupted during the mayor's three terms, several highly publicized incidents of police misconduct toward blacks had further undermined Koch's tenuous standing in the black community. The candidate of competence had become a divisive figure, and many white liberals shared the perception that racial misunderstanding had substantially widened since 1977. Dinkins represented himself as a healing leader who could ease black anxiety while serving all citizens of the city.

During the 1980s, middle-class flight from the city to the suburbs had continued, and whites remaining in the outer boroughs appeared increasingly angry with demagogic black "leaders." The view from Queens, Brooklyn, and Staten Island was that no group deserved political power as an "entitlement." Koch's equally quick dismissal of such racial spokesmen as bigots in reverse inflamed raw emotions and weakened his meager black support. Dinkins, appearing calm and statesmanlike, was a black politician who did not repel white voters. Indeed, he often seemed to share Koch's assessment of such raucous leaders. His appeal was dual: First, Koch had grown tired and petty in office, and second, New York's traditional transfer of power to new elements of the voting population had been delayed too long by an inflexible establishment. Whoever won the Democratic primary would probably become the mayor, but the atmosphere was far more racially charged than anyone had expected.

Despite all his difficulties, Koch campaigned as a proven winner. He managed to even the race with Dinkins and move well ahead of his other Democratic opponents with only weeks remaining in the primary season. Then on August 23, in Bensonhurst, Brooklyn, a young black man named Yusuf Hawkins was murdered by Italian Americans who erroneously believed he was meeting a white girl. Funeral services became a spectacle dominated by black speakers charging that white racists condoned murder. Citing previous cases of bigotry, they inflamed racial animosity in an atmosphere dominated by protest marches, tension, and hate. Dinkins won substantial editorial praise for his serene demeanor and appeals for toleration, although he did make clear his belief that if racists were intent on murder, "any nigger would do."

Offering himself as a healer in troubled times, Dinkins won support from many white liberals who believed that Koch, his suburban-dominated police force, and white ethnics generally were unwilling to accept the reality of a multicultural city. Although the *Times* described Dinkins's record as "careful to the point of timidity," on September 12, Democratic voters ended the Koch era. Conceding defeat with unexpected grace, Koch pledged and delivered his total support during the party campaign against Republican nominee Rudolph Giuliani (1943–). Democratic New York was about to elect its first African American mayor.

During the Koch years, the political situation of New York had become far more defined by race consciousness than by ideology. The 1989 mayoral contest between Dinkins and Giuliani solidified this unhappy tendency and brought a further collapse of party discipline. New York, the bastion of Democratic power for many decades, had slowly been transformed into a cauldron of free-floating racial competition, with both sides resorting to the use of racial code words for the duration of the campaign. In his first electoral campaign, Giuliani's public image was defined by his aggressive career as a U.S. attorney. Giuliani had convicted racketeers from Wall Street to Mulberry Street; he had even prosecuted some of the Koch scandals. Cold and precise, he had little of the platform ease demonstrated by his Democratic opponent.

Dinkins won in November by building an electoral coalition that included 90 percent of the black vote, 73 percent of Hispanics, and only 27 percent of whites (including a third of the large Jewish vote). In a city where more than 80 percent of the voters were Democrats, Dinkins proved unable to appeal effectively to the white ethnic population of the outer boroughs. Racial sensibilities were vital to the contest; Republicans attracted whites; and Dinkins managed to win by only 47,000 votes over an untested, awkward candidate. The Democratic victory margin was the smallest in eighty years, but Dinkins and his party retained command of City Hall.

As he left elective office to dabble in law, broadcasting, academia, and publishing, Ed Koch professed happiness that voters had "liberated" him from the mayoralty, a position he often implied was his by right. In a valedictory address largely framed as advice to his successor, Koch told Dinkins he must never be afraid to lead the city, for only that quality would win him the voters' respect. "History will judge me and my administration. I tried to do my best and so will you." But he warned Dinkins to remember that voters want strength from their elected officials. "Give as good as you get" was Koch's parting advice, and no listener could doubt that Koch himself had followed that creed. Nationally, Dinkins's inauguration in a city only a quarter black was hailed as proof that tolerance and ability remained outstanding New York characteristics. Within the city, most citizens hoped that Dinkins would overcome the bitterness of the campaign and encourage cooperation among diverse ethnic groups.

During the three Koch terms, the city had undergone an enormous economic turnaround. With its fiscal integrity established and unrestricted capitalism the ruling spirit of the 1980s, the city led a regional boom: New York's tax revenues, job creation, and income all had increased faster than the national figures. Seven of the ten leading American banks were still located in the Big Apple, as were six of the top financial institutions and four of the six largest insurance corporations. Seventy-five percent of all Americans employed by the securities industry worked in New York, many in the 57 million square feet of office space constructed during a decade of expansion. Some economists argued that overbuilding was responsible for the 1989 drop in real estate prices, but the long-range spending of Koch's massive infrastructure replacement kept construction firms occupied. Wall Street, however, had removed thousands of jobs from Manhattan to outer borough "back offices" or to New Jersey. Although some flagship companies (Mobil, J. C. Penney, Exxon) deserted Manhattan during the 1980s, more than 350 new foreign or domestic financial firms had recently moved to the city. New York still boasted twenty-five of the tallest buildings in the world; its port remained the most active in the nation; and 20 million visitors spent more than $10 billion in the city in 1989.

Beyond its economic clout, the city of New York entered the 1990s faithful to its image as the United States' most ethnically diverse city. Since Congress's reform of the national quota system in 1965, renewed waves of migrants had arrived in New York, a stream enhanced by passage of the Simpson-Rodino Act in 1986. Immigration figures showed that 800,000 newcomers entered in the 1970s, and an additional 854,000 followed in the 1980s. The arrivals thus more than made up for the 1 million whites who left the city in those years. The national census of 1990 contained a shock for supporters of Chicago, which lost its standing as America's second largest city to Los Angeles. But the final figures only strengthened New York's statistical supremacy; its population of 7,322,564 on April 1, 1990, marked an increase of more than a quarter million persons since 1980. But urban demographers found that for the first time, its population was less than 50 percent white, and the proportion of foreign-born residents had soared beyond 28 percent. In contrast to earlier arrivals, the newest New Yorkers came largely from the Caribbean, the Middle East, and East Asia. The city with more Irish than Dublin and more Jews than Jerusalem now could say that it housed more Asians than Hawaii. The borough of Queens had 110 national groups, and Brooklyn had more Bajans than did Barbados itself.

During his successful campaign, Dinkins emphasized that New York was a "glorious mosaic" of all the cultures and languages of the earth. But even as he spoke, the neighborhood structures of the city were undergoing dynamic ethnic change. Dominicans, now the primary immigrant group, dominated the formerly Jewish area of Washington Heights where refugees from Germany had once congregated. Russian émigrés transformed Brooklyn's

Brighton Beach into a "Little Odessa." Colombians colonized both Jackson Heights and Corona in Queens. The large influx of Asian immigrants, mainly Koreans and Chinese, tended to settle in Queens. Mideasterners clustered along Atlantic Avenue in Brooklyn, and Haitians, too, largely settled in Brooklyn. Immigration was again altering the metropolis in unexpected ways.

Religious leaders of the Muslim community claimed that 700,000 followers of Islam worshiped in seventy mosques across New York. Whether or not this number was inflated, city politicians were quick to grant Muslims the privilege of ignoring alternate street parking during religious worship. Koreans became predominant in the green-grocery business; and Indians, working for the Kapoor brothers, appeared to sell half the newspapers in the city. The surge in the Asian population of Queens led wags to label the number 7 Flushing train the "Orient Express." As this diversity mushroomed, New York's mix of cultures and peoples demanded a leader with a healing touch who could overcome inevitable ethnic frictions. The 1990s would test the toleration that New Yorkers continually touted.

Certainly the problems facing David Dinkins's city magnified as its population diversified. Yearly drug arrests were approaching 100,000; municipal spending on a homeless army of at least ten thousand persons surpassed $225 million; and six thousand AIDS cases crowded the hospital system as he took his inaugural oath. Pledging to be mayor for all the people of the city, Dinkins told his audience that the welfare of their children was his greatest priority. Aware that his critics believed he would favor blacks, Dinkins asserted all groups would receive equal treatment at his hands. But like every mayor of the modern era, Dinkins immediately learned that financial matters were always a mayoral priority.

During the interregnum, Dinkins's experts discovered that the current budget was running a deficit. On January 3, after less than seventy-two hours in office, the mayor was forced to delay the hiring of eighteen hundred police officers, order spending cuts, and float the idea of a property tax increase. The city's money problems never eased over the next four years, and Dinkins never appeared to gain control of the monetary process. He had enjoyed great success in the more restricted sphere of borough leadership, but the obligations of a mayor were different.

In Dinkins's first year, fiscal stringency revisited New York. In fact, 1990 marked the worst performance by the urban economy since 1982, during the Reagan recession and just before the "great bull market." Retail sales were severely declining within the city limits and reduced sales tax revenue. Altman's, long a distinguished department store, closed its doors in January, and famous stores such as Gimbel's, Korvette's, and Alexander's also fell victim to the growing preference for shopping in suburban malls. Even before the nation drifted into recession, the New York metropolitan region was mired in ominous statistics. The gross city product fell in each quarter of 1990; job losses exceeded 34,000 in the third quarter alone; and construction lagged. New York was home to a population of 70,000 lawyers, a profession long thought recession-proof, but in 1990, major firms began to lay off associates for the first time in memory. Business conditions became so bad that bankruptcy proceedings became a growing legal specialty. During Dinkins's single term, the city lost 400,000 jobs, an economic disaster that wiped out all the cumulative gains of the Koch era. Although the mayor put up a brave front, claiming that the business of the city was proceeding normally, the city's lenders thought otherwise. In October 1990, Standard and Poor's raters placed the city on a "credit watch."

Bankers were not the only New Yorkers unimpressed with the mayor's performance. Dinkins's initial appeal to many voters was his pledge to heal racial tensions. Having long lived in Harlem, the mayor appeared to understand the frustrations and empathize with the ambitions of poor but ambitious people. But when an ongoing dispute between a Korean grocer in Brooklyn and his black customers escalated into a bitter, radical-led boycott, the mayor refused to intervene. His tentative handling of this small dispute in time alienated virtually everyone involved and caused the wider citizenry to question his commitment to equal racial justice. More lethally, the first summer of his term saw a series of drug-related, drive-by shootings that resulted in the deaths of several children. Again, the mayor appeared slow to react, enabling the *Post* to publish a classic banner headline that encapsulated the times—"Dave Do Something!" The city media, sensing either weakness or hypocrisy, often implied that Dinkins was more concerned with his daily tennis game and the ceremonies of office than in running municipal affairs. Before the end of his first year in office, a credibility gap had opened, one the mayor was never able to close.

In January 1991, the annual budget dance began anew. The prognosis was not encouraging. The city's expenditures had doubled in the past decade while the cost of living rose only 50 percent. The homeless were more visible than ever. In 1990, the value of taxable real estate fell by 7 percent, its first loss in a decade, and the revenue-producing area of southern Manhattan was particularly affected. Notwithstanding the shrinkage in the city's tax base, Dinkins negotiated a series of very costly union contracts, obtaining labor peace without productivity concessions. Critics of the mayor were particularly incensed by the large—they said unaffordable—pay raises granted to public schoolteachers, whose union had strongly backed the Democratic ticket.

So serious was the situation that another state takeover of city finances was rumored. Only the usual combination of new taxes combined with reductions in service ended that possibility. Yet even after this "doomsday" budget was adopted, the recessionary downward spiral continued, job losses escalated, and little additional state or federal aid materialized. Jibes at the mayor's crowded social calendar increased accordingly. In a vain effort to prove that he shared the city's austerity, Dinkins reluctantly canceled a scheduled trip to South Africa in September. But when the African National Congress agreed to finance his visit in November, the criticism became more pointed. The mayor might have a foreign policy, but he appeared indifferent to the plight of his city. MAC Chairman Felix Rohatyn, a hero of the 1975/ 76 crisis, chastised the administration for permitting the city to "degrade itself." One prominent scholar wrote that the condition of New York was a "self-imposed catastrophe" caused by a willful disregard for fiscal realities.

Dinkins was not so much willful as philosophically committed to the "unique welfare state" that New York had provided for its citizens over the past two generations; he steadfastly believed in the entitlements that allowed America to perceive his city as the home of deadbeats and slackers. By law, New York participated in federal programs such as Medicaid, AFDC, and income support, but it also provided massive additional benefits for homeless individuals and families, protected foster children, and cared for AIDS patients. As the largest landlord in the city, New York spent almost half a billion yearly to maintain 48,000 apartment units in foreclosed properties, and it remodeled an additional fifteen thousand structures annually. Only New York City maintained an eleven-thousand-bed, sixteen-unit municipal hospital system that served as the primary care facility for the poor, but it cost $800 million annually. City University of New York had nineteen academic campuses, educated 190,000 students, and offered one of the best educational bargains in the country, but it too was expensive.

Frills in other cities were considered essential to life in New York, and Dinkins, a liberal whose career was constructed on such assumptions, accepted all these functions as necessities. In fact, the city actually spent less per capita on education and parks than did other major urban centers, and its costs for police, fire, and sanitation services were only slightly more expensive. It was massive numbers, compounded by bureaucratic inefficiency, that made city expenditures so immense. Now, pressured by the continuing impact of Reaganomics and foreshadowing the politics of the 1990s, New York had to contemplate a reduction of big government. Perhaps it was futile to expect this mayor—who deeply believed in the city's obligation to help all its citizens—to abandon his lifelong commitments.

Beyond the social dilemmas stemming from the financial situation, Dinkins's narrow margin of political support eroded because he appeared to favor his black constituents above other groups. Observers considered his staff inept, and he was more justifiably accused of cronyism in appointments. As vocal black spokesmen loudly proclaimed that it finally was "our turn" to lead the city, Dinkins's thunderous silence seemed to endorse their reasoning. A single tragic accident in Crown Heights, Brooklyn, on August 19, 1991, seemed to fix this conclusion in the minds of many New Yorkers. A seven-year-old Guyanese boy was killed by a car carrying the Lubavitcher rebbe, the leader of a Hassidic sect. Erroneous reports implied that the child's death occurred because a Jewish ambulance service refused to take him to a hospital. Angry black crowds took to the streets, and suddenly cries of "Kill the Jews" filled the summer air. Three hours after the incident, someone did stab a Jewish man to death. Four nights of disturbances ensued, and the tepid official response was attributed to a mayor and commissioner reluctant to oppose black rioters. Only after the mayor's entourage was stoned did the police move in to clear the streets. In October, a jury, citing police mishandling of evidence, freed the accused murderer, but few believed that justice had been served. Dinkins's failure to respond as compassionately to the murder of a Jew as he had in the Hawkins case cost him dearly in the world's largest Jewish city. Even the most liberal Jews believed the mayor had not acted evenhandedly. Not even Dinkins's stellar performance in maintaining urban peace in New York during the 1992 Los Angeles riots restored his lost credibility as a healer. Newspaper columnists increasingly referred to him as a transition mayor.

It was the unhappy fate of David Dinkins to preside over the city of New York as the prosperity of the 1980s entered a brief trough. As the Bush administration in Washington struggled to contain a national recession, the city's revenues fell sharply. But welfare and poverty costs rose to twenty-year highs. Facing a reelection campaign in 1993, Dinkins found it psychologically impossible to reduce the services to which citizens had become accustomed. Both unemployment benefits and welfare rolls expanded as less money was available. Basic to the city dilemma was both a structural imbalance that magnified the impact of bad times and a mind-set that made saving impossible when things improved. Even the "austere" budget Dinkins proposed for fiscal year 1993, one that cut funds to cultural institutions by almost 30 percent, compounded the uncertainties. By 1992, the city—in advance of the nation—was already starting to rebound, and its real estate revenues unexpectedly rose. But Dinkins's inability to anticipate economic trends or demonstrate familiarity with the arcane details of city finance alienated ambivalent voters all too ready to interpret his job performance as inferior. More thoughtful critics, assessing his weak appointees and fiscal unsteadiness, simply found him inept.

In the end, his race had at least as much to do with Dinkins's failure to be reelected as it had with his victory four years earlier. Instead of leading the city toward greater racial understanding and color-blind policies, virtually all the actions of the Dinkins administration were judged for their ethnic impact. Blacks and Hispanics, vital elements of the mayoral coalition, had long believed they suffered systematic police brutality and demanded increased city action. To ease their anxieties, Dinkins agreed to establish a Civilian Review Board to hear complaints against the police, even though he knew the idea had been divisive in past years. Once more the proposal led to confrontation. The result on this occasion was a "police riot" on September 16, 1992, in City Hall Plaza. The scorn that some demonstrating police officers displayed against their mayor was openly racist. More significant for the upcoming election, however, was the active participation of Rudy Giuliani, the once and future Republican candidate for mayor, in the chaos. The former U.S. attorney solidified support from the police union while alienating liberal opinion. Despite all the controversy, the performance of the Civilian Review Board was dismal, as it found it impossible to make cases against police brutality.

In the 1990s, the drug culture became an obsessive concern of many New Yorkers. The ravages of the "crack" epidemic spread like wildfire, but the police had little success against a plague that largely afflicted blacks and Hispanics. Washington Heights became notorious for open trafficking in a wide variety of drugs, and after the police killed a drug dealer, a "riot" instigated by dealers disturbed the urban peace. The bogus "riot" coincided with a flare-up of Dinkins's continuing troubles with the Lubavitchers of Crown Heights, which confirmed their opposition to the incumbent.

Nothing the mayor tried expanded his basic coalition. The city did play host in 1992 to the Democratic National Convention that named a victorious candidate, but Bill Clinton's coattails did not help Dinkins in 1993. Washington did recruit Dinkins's black police commissioner for the incoming administration, but although the mayor selected an Irish-American police officer as his successor, the appointment failed to win him police support. During 1993, adopting the conservative spirit of the new politics, Dinkins promised to "get the government off the back" of small business enterprise, but no one appeared to take that pledge seriously. Instead, a growing coterie of liberal critics denounced the mayor for cuts he authorized in child welfare programs. Mayor Dinkins took additional criticism from educators for personnel cuts ordered by School Chancellor Joseph Fernandez. The Welfare Department mismanaged the city shelter system and was declared to be in contempt of court orders. Contracts signed with nineteen municipal unions, giving them 8.25 percent raises over three years, were interpreted by the media not as cheaply obtained labor peace but as another mayoral failure to win productivity gains. Critics said the mayor was attempting to buy reelection with labor votes, and the Financial Control Board considered canceling the generous contracts. Welfare cases again passed the million-client mark while AIDS and TB care mandated soaring health costs. Finally, during the unhappy springtime of 1993, terrorist bombers devastated the World Trade Center. City voters increasingly longed for strong, effective leadership.

The mayoral race of 1993 offered voters a choice between the contending visions of government held by David Dinkins and Rudolph Giuliani. Race was always an unmentioned, but potent, force in their political calculations. Early in the year, nearly every commentator predicted a close race, and the heightened racial animosity made for a poisonous atmosphere; "values" often became a code word for less exalted feelings. The strange permutations of the conservative-liberal debate even caused turmoil in the school system when the contract of Chancellor Joseph Fernandez, hailed as the most innovative of educators when he came to New York in 1989, was terminated by the Board of Education. The conservative majority of the board believed that social issues rather than educational achievement dominated the chancellor's agenda. Opponents called Fernandez "King Condom" for emphasizing sex education in the schools, and his advocacy of a "rainbow curriculum" discussing alternative lifestyles was condemned. Fernandez was never a mayoral intimate; he often feuded with Dinkins; but his liberalism became yet one more burden for the Democrats in 1993. Inept school administration resurfaced as an issue in September, when the newly installed chancellor was forced to close down the system for eleven days to remove the asbestos in many school buildings.

As the campaign progressed, it deteriorated into one in which voters cast ballots based on their fears, not their hopes. Sadly, racial concerns defined much of the voting expectations, and it was the Dinkins forces who bore primary responsibility for introducing the issue. A columnist for *El Diario* asserted that "people with racist tendencies sympathize with Giuliani," and the mayor was silent. When Dinkins's campaign manager said that Giuliani reminded him of a prominent southern racist, the mayor responded only that such "was not my characterization." When Baptist ministers endorsed Dinkins while labeling Giuliani a fascist and when his supporters attacked a Puerto Rican member of the Republican slate for marrying a Jew, the mayor did not object. Tacit appeals to race gave an unpleasant tinge to the Democratic campaign, and they culminated in a series of "attack ads" showing Guiliani's performance during the "police riot" of 1992. While there was ample evidence of racial innuendo by some Republicans, none was personally identified with Giuliani. In a far more polished campaign that erased the bad memories of 1989, Giuliani adopted a "positive" approach that merely attacked Dinkins's competency. He charged the incumbent with failing to understand city people and their problems.

On November 2, 1993, David Dinkins became the first black mayor of a major American city to lose in a first attempt at reelection. Defeat came because he had failed to expand his existing coalition and instead had permitted it to erode around the perimeter. Relying almost exclusively on the power of bloc ethnic voting, Dinkins lost support among Jews, white college graduates, and Hispanics. He was deserted by liberals who believed he had shamelessly played the race card. Even his strategy of ethnic mobilization was flawed. Democratic voter registration drives were so ineffective that Dinkins actually received fewer black votes than he had in the previous election. Running in an overwhelmingly Democratic city, Dinkins won only 21 percent of white votes, whereas Giuliani garnered seven of ten. The drag at the top of the party ticket was so great that the other two Democratic nominees for city office also failed to carry a majority of white votes, though each did well enough to win. Despite Dinkins's rejection, all major offices outside City Hall remained under Democratic control.

Some analysts suggest that the contest not did not repudiate a black mayor so much as reject New York's version of the welfare state. Others find that race and bigotry were decisive. The slim Republican margin of victory, only 53,000 votes, can be attributed to many factors—among them voter weariness, racism, incompetence, or simply four years of economic turmoil. The healer of 1989 had failed to achieve a sense of order, and most of his policy initiatives had been ineffective. Moreover, in the context of twentieth-century metropolitan history, New York's election of a Republican mayor with liberal-reform support was not unprecedented; it seems to occur every thirty years. Perhaps the city merely anticipated the national repudiation of Democratic domination that delivered Congress to the Republicans only a year later. But in the matter of race, one point must be made. New York is never color blind, but it is tolerant. It respects talent and punishes political ineptitude. It thus appears scurrilous, even dangerous, to assert that race was solely responsible for Dinkins's defeat.

Rudolph Giuliani, elected the 107th mayor of New York, ran as a Fusionist candidate because he hoped to benefit from echoes the word evoked from New York's political past. He was a conservative, yet statistics demonstrated that his margin of victory was won by votes cast for him on the Liberal Party line of the ballot. Giuliani conducted a well-run campaign, emphasized law and order and government efficiency, and refused to participate in any racial competition. Still, in Italian and Irish areas, Giuliani earned vote percentages comparable to those won by Dinkins in black precincts. Since the election was so close, any advantage could have been decisive, and the new mayor clearly obtained Democratic defectors. Most important, ex-Mayor Koch publicly endorsed Giuliani in August and joined his campaign. Koch had come to believe that his successor was incompetent and that the city was "deteriorating in every way." Moreover, Felix Rohatyn had resigned as chairman of MAC after his eighteen years of exemplary service ended with several public clashes with Dinkins over finance. Finally, Robert Wagner III, one of the most respected if underpublicized Democrats in Manhattan, announced that a vote for Giuliani would be "best for the city." The defection of these Democrats made it possible for those with similar beliefs to cast ballots for a Republican.

Like LaGuardia and Lindsay before him, Giuliani became New York's mayor in the wake of a national victory by a Democratic president. But unlike his predecessors, he stood apart from the progressive ideology that dominated Washington. Giuliani, new to elective office, chose to present himself as an advocate of law and order, an ordinary man whose main goal was to protect citizens from the plague of crime. Despite statistical gains in crime fighting, Dinkins never convinced voters that he was tough enough to deal with street violence. Giuliani, by contrast, pledged not only to be tough with felons but also to move vigorously against "quality of life" offenses that made life in the city so tense. No mayor in the history of the modern city identified himself so closely with the NYPD. Peddlers, aggressive beggars, "squeegee men" who insisted on wiping the already-clean windshields of cars stopped at lights, fare beaters on the subway, and even "token suckers" now became targets of police action. A tough Irish cop from Boston, William Bratton, who led the transit police before becoming police commissioner, promised to initiate community-oriented policing that would never "define deviancy down." Together, these two strong personalities restored safety to the city's streets, although their success was never fully endorsed by representatives of minority communities. In time, the relationship between Giuliani and his police chief became troubled, and Bratton left after only twenty-seven months in office.

Immediately after delivering his inaugural address, Giuliani learned the lesson of each new incumbent—that the city's fiscal situation was worse than expected. Budgetary projections constantly fluctuated, but their import —as interpreted by Giuliani—was that Dinkins had foolishly continued liberal redistributive politics while ignoring their impact on future budgets. A hiring freeze, worker attrition, and productivity concessions by the unions would be needed immediately. A chastened but initially cooperative Democratic City Council did succeed in paring the 1995 budget by almost $1 billion, but Giuliani only responded with more demands. His conclusions were announced in the brusque, no-nonsense style that soon became his hallmark. The new mayor was a leader who appeared to prefer public confrontation to quiet negotiation.

The element of intimidation in Giuliani's posture was demonstrated in his bloody but inconclusive fight to control the vast expenditures of the school system. Chancellor Raymond Cortines had replaced Fernandez only the previous September, but he already was earning kudos as a classroom innovator. Recognition of the central role that education must play in training underskilled youths was becoming more widespread. In addition, Cortines claimed to be making inroads against the entrenched educational bureaucrats at Livingston Street, a school headquarters so inefficient that it could not produce up-to-date figures for teachers in the system. Ignoring these accomplishments, Giuliani publicly demanded that the chancellor pare $332 million more from 1994 fiscal year school spending. Although such a request was impossible to implement, the mayor did impose a fiscal monitor on the Board of Education.

When Giuliani broadly hinted at his desire to dismantle the entire school system, Cortines announced his resignation. Although intervention by Governor Mario Cuomo reversed that hasty decision, bitter feelings remained. The mayor continued to publicly hector the chancellor and in private referred to him as a "whiner" who chose to be a "little victim" rather than an educational leader. A supportive Board of Education offered Cortines a new contract, but his public battles with the mayor continued until the chancellor left in disgust in October 1995. At issue between these men was not educational policy but the power to channel monies to the 1 million students, 65,000 teachers, and one thousand buildings of the school system. Before it succeeded in naming Rudy Crew as its seventh chancellor in eleven years, the board endured further rancorous battles with the opinionated mayor.

During Giuliani's first summer, the periodic New York scandal of corruption in the Police Department resurfaced. The Mollen Commission discovered "willful blindness" toward lower-level corruption by high police commanders. The "blue ribbon" panel charged that former Commissioner Ben Ward had knowingly refused to investigate the rumors to avert bad publicity and that internal investigations and the police union together ignored evidence of "rogue cops." As so often happened in the past, the commission stated that only an independent investigatory body named by the mayor could change a police mentality that tolerated, and perhaps even justified, some graft. Even as trials were held and cops were punished or transferred, Giuliani deftly used the continuing scandal to advocate a merger of all three police forces in the city—regular, transit, housing—into a single unit under his final authority. Policemen and their unions believed that the mayor was on their side and did not oppose the plan with past vehemence. The mayor won his fight in 1995, achieved the long-sought union, and proclaimed a major victory for administrative efficiency.

The greatest evidence of Giuliani's maverick, isolated status was his willingness to alienate both present and potential political allies. In March 1994 when President Bill Clinton came to Brooklyn College for a town meeting on the crime issue, the mayor simply refused to juggle his schedule and appear. For a city dependent on federal aid, this hardly seemed a wise course of action. Later that same year, when state Republicans selected a candidate for governor strongly identified with Senator Alfonse D'Amato, an old foe of the mayor, Giuliani bolted his party. Disregarding advice from Ed Koch that he at least provide "a fig leaf of an endorsement" to his party nominee, the mayor endorsed the incumbent Democrat Mario Cuomo. Furthermore, he labeled candidate George Pataki a "puppet" of D'Amato, who would "trash" ethical standards. That November, when Pataki upset Cuomo as part of a national Republican tidal wave, Giuliani's status as a Republican began to be questioned.

Giuliani was a maverick mayor whose personal hero was La Guardia, so he had no qualms about standing in lonely defiance. He utilized his many press conferences as publicity vehicles in which he set down absolute principles, mocking all those who disagreed with his gospel. Early in 1995, instead of standing firm with a Republican Congress seeking to enact a vaguely worded "Contract with America," Giuliani publicly decried the conservative tendency to blame America's problems on immigrants. His own administration supported newcomers and even provided assistance to illegal immigrants. On September 19, 1995, when he became the first mayor since O'Dwyer to address the United Nations, Giuliani used the podium to praise the tolerance and diversity of his city, a metropolis that welcomed powerful delegates as warmly as it did poor, "storm-tossed" immigrants. Purposefully contrasting New York with the anti-foreign vitriol of Congress, the mayor declared, "you can't be a New Yorker—you can't be part of this city—and deny the contribution of immigrants. . . . Our own nation owes its existence to the hard work, determination, and vision of immigrants." New York City is often accused of conducting an independent foreign policy, and residents of the Big Apple enjoyed having their mayor articulate the spirit of their city.

But people appreciated even more the restored sense of public safety achieved under Giuliani. "Quality of life" policing proved remarkably effective: from 1994 to 1996 the index of all major crimes declined 16 percent, 14 percent, and 7 percent, while murders fell by half. Although the city had never been as crime-ridden as its critics charged, aggressive media reports of lurid outrages made it seem far more dangerous than other places in the nation. Giuliani's New York deployed more police, armed them with better weapons, improved their computer technology, and took back the streets from petty criminals and felons. Even though the funding had been initiated by Dinkins, and a previous commissioner had fostered neighborhood policing techniques, the results became visible under Mayor Giuliani. He and Police Commissioner Bratton received kudos for the obvious improvement, but when Bratton appeared to claim excessive credit he was forced to resign in March 1996. Amazed city residents did not care to apportion responsibility nor to ponder the impact of national prosperity on crime rates. Their lives seemed more secure, and while Giuliani was mayor, an impossible dream became solid reality.

Giuliani's abrasive style made scores of enemies. He feuded with Republicans in Albany and Washington and was openly scornful of the Democratic majority on the City Council. He often seemed at odds with the liberal traditions of the city, calling for belt tightening, privatization of hospitals, the sale of the city's radio and TV stations, and less spending on libraries. Council demands for additional social expenditures were ridiculed, and he paid no heed to fiscal critics who said that small tax reductions were foolish while a long-term budgetary imbalance existed. He even broke with Ed Koch, who had deserted his party to support Giuliani's election. In December 1995, the combative mayor disregarded the recommendations of a Koch-instituted judicial screening system for his own appointees. Outraged that his "proudest" achievement had been slighted, Koch immediately accused Giuliani of "megalomania" and used his newspaper column to blast the mayor; the attacks were later collected into *Giuliani, Nasty Man*. Until 1996, the word "liberal" was used as an epithet by Giuliani, and his policies showed far more concern with cuts than compassion.

But as criticism grew and reelection neared, Giuliani wisely moderated his program. The Wall Street boom of the mid-90s created enormous new streams of revenue and, at least temporarily, made budgetary rigor unnecessary. The mayor's decision to eliminate the hotel occupancy tax in 1996 fostered five years of tremendous growth in tourism. 1996 saw a record-breaking 31.2 million visitors to New York; this number increased each year, peaking at 39.4 million in 2000. Public concern over inadequate city response in abuse cases was alleviated by the creation of an independent agency administering Children's Services in 1996. And the mayor, having ousted a school chancellor he deemed ineffective, comfortably worked in tandem with Chancellor Rudy Crew to attack a complacent educational bureaucracy. In 1996, "the two Rudy's" won legislative approval for a law taking appointive power from ineffective school boards and restoring it to district supervisors, the chancellor, and ultimately the mayor. Giuliani never was able to achieve his long-range goal of mayoral control over the Board of Education, but during this period of cooperation with an obliging chancellor, additional programs were funded and some testing showed improved student performance. Finally, national welfare reform in 1996 allowed Giuliani to create and continually brag about the largest "workfare" program in the nation, a "tough love" approach to relief that reduced the number of welfare recipients from 1.1 million under Dinkins to under 700,000 in 1997. Critics claimed that few real jobs were offered and no skills were being fostered, but the mere size of the program made it significant. By the end of 2001, welfare rolls in the city would fall below 480,000.

As the mayor faced reelection in 1997, the one irrefutable fact arguing for his return was the continued drop in crime. People believed they were safer; since 1990 the number of homicides had fallen a staggering 63 percent. Gains were somewhat tainted by a vile incident of torture in a Brooklyn precinct in August of 1997; the policemen who committed the atrocity allegedly bragged it was "Giuliani time." In truth, the policemen had not said anything of this nature. Giuliani denounced the attack on Abner Louima, and although his relationship with the black community suffered, his support was never dependent on that voting bloc. Moreover, he faced a Democratic opponent, Ruth Messinger, who had been weakened by a divisive primary race. The mayor denounced her as a typical West Side, big-spending liberal out of touch with the reality of city life. The race was never really close. Giuliani was comfortably elected as his outer-borough coalition was buttressed by additional support from women and Jews. Race was not decisive in the election, but whites were four times more likely to vote for Giuliani than blacks, while blacks favored Messinger by an even larger margin.

Rudy Giuliani is a political original, a leader with strong convictions who believes he is always right. His many foes call him a bully and a control freak, while his supporters see a man with the strength to tame a wild metropolis. Voters had approved a Charter revision in 1993 mandating that his second term would be his last, but few observers expected the former prosecutor to spend so much of it in legal disputes. He began by suing *New York* magazine for advertising itself as "the only good thing . . . Giuliani hasn't taken credit for"; naturally he lost. More significant was his continued vendetta against the Legal Aid Society and a series of First Amendment decisions by judges denying his efforts to keep city documents secret. The mayor also attempted to obtain political goals by suggesting changes in the City Charter. Continued losses in court made Giuliani appear childish and petty. Mayoral tilting against "decadent" art shows in 1999 and 2001 led him to deny funding to the Brooklyn Museum, which subsequently led to another embarrassing legal rebuff. A forlorn attempt to create a "decency commission" was either the stuff of hubris or farce, depending on one's point of view. He did manage to dump Chancellor Crew, but failed to impose his chosen successor on the Board of Education. Meanwhile, the administrative austerity of his first term vanished, and spending, which had been reduced by 2 percent from 1994 to 1997, rose by 11 percent during his second term; the number of city employees soared beyond 250,000. The mayor appeared both bored and contentious. He had put the city through four years of "obedience training" and now seemed anxious to leave.

Some believed Giuliani's indifference stemmed from ambition for higher office, but he hardly seemed to be smoothing his pathway to Albany or Washington. He was constantly at odds with Republican Governor George Pataki, and his running feud with the Port Authority kept that animosity at a high pitch. The mayor's always tentative relations with city minorities hit rock-bottom after two innocent black men died as a result of aggressive police action. The cases of Amadou Diallo (February, 1999) and Patrick Dorismond (March, 2000) were not the only instances of excessive force, but while federal officials declared the NYPD treatment of brutality cases to be severely flawed, the mayor automatically defended his cops. His inability to express real regret at the excesses caused his job ratings to drop to 32 percent in the summer of 2000.

Yet despite all the furor, Giuliani remained the preferred candidate for the Republican senatorial nomination in ∴000. Giuliani seemed poised to prove an exception to the adage that mayors of New York never go on to higher office. Yet, instead of a coronation, Giuliani's endured an "anno horribilus." His troubled marriage disintegrated, and his public appearances with a new companion hardly burnished his image as a moral arbiter. Most significantly, the mayor was diagnosed with prostate cancer and withdrew his name from Senate consideration. His recovery, which followed arduous treatment, was a triumph of both will and medicine and drew universal respect. In December of 2000 he told the city that the last year of his term was "given to me" and that he would work hard to serve New York productively.

What Giuliani's governmental legacy would have been is difficult to assess. While cutting taxes by $3 billion he vastly increased city debt and left a structurally unbalanced budget. His "workfare" program reduced welfare rolls by more than half, but few persons were trained for permanent jobs. His pledges of more housing and better relations with minorities were never achieved. He spent much of 2001 on the construction of two minor league baseball stadiums and negotiating major league facilities for the Yankees, Mets, and Jets. Reading the balance sheet on his term, one finds that the rich got richer (Wall Street, with 4 percent of the city's total jobs, receives a quarter of city wages) and the poor got safer (crime fell yet another 12 percent in 2001); one dismal fact was that the city had 50 percent more soup kitchens at the end of his eight years, and that homelessness and poverty had increased.

Then came September 11. While the president was virtually incommunicado on the day of the terrorist attack, Rudy Giuliani stepped forward, epitomizing the spirit of New York and the determination of the nation. The mayor went to the scene and survived falling buildings. His every word and action were correct, his presence embodied both courage and compassion. The pettiness that had threatened to undermine the accomplishments of seven years and eight months was totally eclipsed by a personal heroism that represented the finest ideals of city and nation. *Time* would name him Person of the Year; the president of France would call him "Rudy the Rock;" and Queen Elizabeth II would confer knighthood on the leader who had become "mayor of the world." Terrorism changed Giuliani from an insensitive lame duck to a virtual saint.

But the transformation could not totally repress the old, "bad" Rudy. Lavish praise led to a belief in his own indispensability, and he endorsed Charter amendments which would have permitted him to serve another term. Although that plan failed, the Democratic candidate for mayor agreed that a three month extension might be wise. Strangely enough, the Republican candidate, business legend Michael Bloomberg, rejected the suggestion. The previous December, Bloomberg had come to City Hall requesting Giuliani's support for what was seen as a quixotic candidacy, but he was forced to wait until late in October to receive the endorsement he craved. Giuliani, in fact, withheld the announcement of his support until even he recognized that he would have to leave office.

The election of 2001 was one of the strangest in New York history. Since the Democratic Party enjoys an almost fivefold margin among registered voters, its nomination for City Hall normally settles any race. But the attack of 9/11 forced cancellation of the scheduled primary and the postponed balloting failed to select a majority candidate among four choices. Not until a third run-off on October 11 was Mark Green nominated. Green, the city's Public Advocate, had long been Giuliani's least favorite Democrat. His victory was difficult, and he had been accused of permitting, perhaps even encouraging, racist canards against his Hispanic opponent. Green had less than a month to unify his party and would fail in the attempt; large numbers of Hispanic and black voters "sat-out" the November election. Because of the Democratic rupture, it became possible for a Republican to win.

Michael Bloomberg, a lifelong Democrat who changed his party affiliation in order to make a vanity run at City Hall, shocked everyone in April 2001 by saying he would willingly spend $30 million on the race. By October he had already done so, and the reality of Democratic infighting suddenly made his victory possible. Because the money he spent was his own there were no limits on campaign expenditures, and he immediately contracted for every available advertising slot. Buttressed by endorsements from both Giuliani and Koch, the billionaire's campaign suddenly caught fire as New Yorkers became convinced that a business-like approach to governing would benefit the city. Green later said his campaign was the victim of a "perfect storm," one in which every element worked to intensify the gale that blew him away. In the end, Bloomberg spent $72.23 million to win the most expensive non-presidential campaign in American history. Each vote cost him $96.99 in advertising costs, but he was inaugurated as the 108th Mayor of the City of New York on January 1, 2002.

No one, perhaps not even Bloomberg, expected his triumph. In time-honored fashion, the new mayor discovered that the city cupboard was bare, and that the budget deficit projected for his first fiscal year would be $4.76 billion. To help him plan the needed cuts, Bloomberg selected four deputy mayors and a corporation counsel who were registered Democrats, and pledged to work closely with the newly elected Democratic Council, public advocate, and comptroller. The new administration was a liberal Democratic one in all but name, but whether it could close the yawning deficit and impose across the board cuts was uncertain. Most important, Bloomberg immediately established that he was not "Giuliani lite." Raymond Kelly returned as Police Commissioner, and the mayor invited black, Hispanic, and union leaders to sessions at City Hall, a courtesy his predecessor had consistently refused. He insisted that the federal government fulfill its promise of $20 billion in reconstruction aid, opined that a suitable memorial for lost New Yorkers at "Ground Zero" need not fill the entire site, and artfully tabled Giuliani's plans for new stadiums. He hosted a fund-raiser for President George Bush, traveled to Albany to receive the blessings of Governor Pataki, and even granted Giuliani the privilege of organizing his papers by private contractor. A neophyte without political training, Bloomberg quickly orchestrated a broader based mayoralty than Giuliani. In businesslike fashion he prepared for the fiscal storms certain to hit New York.

New York is the city that best embodies the American spirit. The census of 2000 showed that it surpassed eight million people for the first time; almost 40 percent of them were foreign born. Reflecting global reality, its population is "majority minority" and includes persons from every nation on earth. The city acculturates them so successfully that 300 take the oath of American citizenship each day. Even after the tragedy of 9/11, the metropolis remains the preeminent business arena on earth and its most vital intellectual and artistic center. Although devastated by the loss of the twin towers, New York still has more than 50 percent of all the fifty-story skyscrapers in the world, and fully intends to build more. It is, of course, a city in perpetual crisis. Its schools are a disaster, its port has moved to another state, its transit system challenges the citizenry each day. But somehow New York works. New Yorkers are not born, they are made. As survivors of a cruel winnowing process, they are arrogantly certain that "no other place is good enough" for them. With all of its contradictions and woes, it would be very foolish to think that the challenges of a new millennium will defeat this amazing city.

Appendix 1
Mayors of New York City

Thomas Willett 1665

Thomas Delavall 1666

Thomas Willett 1667

Cornelius Van Steenwyck 1668–1670

Thomas Delavall 1671

Matthias Nicolls 1672

John Lawrence 1673–1674

William Dervall 1675

Nicholas De Meyer 1676

Stephanus Van Cortlandt 1677

Thomas Delavall 1678

Francis Rombouts 1679

William Dyre 1680–1681

Cornelius Van Steenwyck 1682–1683

Gabriel Minvielle 1684

Nicolas Bayard 1685

Stephanus Van Cortlandt 1686–1688

Peter Delanoy 1689–1690

John Lawrence 1691

Abraham De Peyster 1692–1694

Charles Lodwik 1694–1695

William Merrett 1695–1698

Johannes De Peyster 1698–1699

David Provost 1699–1700

Issac De Reimer 1700–1701

Thomas Noell 1701–1702

Philip French 1702–1703

William Peartree 1703–1707

Ebenezer Wilson 1707–1710

Jacobus Van Cortlandt 1710–1711

Caleb Heathcote 1711–1714

John Johnson 1714–1719

Jacobus Van Cortlandt 1719–1720

Robert Walters 1720–1725

Johannes Jansen 1725–1726

Robert Lurting 1726–1735

Paul Richard 1735–1739

John Cruger 1739–1744

Stephen Bayard 1744–1747

Edward Holland 1747–1757

John Cruger Jr. 1757–1766

Whitehead Hicks 1766–1776

David Matthews 1776–1784

James Duane 1784–1789

Richard Varick 1789–1801

Edward Livingston 1801–1803

De Witt Clinton 1803–1807

Marinus Willett 1807–1808

De Witt Clinton 1808–1810

Jacob Radcliff 1810–1811

De Witt Clinton 1811–1815

John Ferguson 1815

Jacob Radcliff 1815–1818

Cadwaller D. Colden 1818–1821

Stephen Allen 1821–1824

William Paulding 1825–1826

Philip Hone 1826–1827

William Paulding 1827–1829

Walter Bowne 1829–1833

Gideon Lee 1833–1834

Cornelius W. Lawrence 1834–1837

Aaron Clark 1837–1839

Isaac L. Varian 1839–1841

Robert H. Morris 1841–1844

James Harper 1844–1845

William F. Havemeyer 1845–1846

Andrew F. Mickle 1846–1847

William V. Brady 1847–1848

William F. Havemeyer 1848–1849

Caleb S. Woodhull 1849–1851

Ambrose C. Kingsland 1851–1853

Jacob A. Westervelt 1853–1855

Fernando Wood 1855–1858

Daniel F. Tiemann 1858–1860

Fernando Wood 1860–1862

George Opdyke 1862–1864

C. Godfrey Gunther 1864–1866

John T. Hoffman 1866–1868

T. Coman 1868 (acting)

A. Oakley Hall 1869–1872

William F. Havemeyer 1873–1874

S. B. H. Vance 1874 (acting)

William H. Wickham 1875–1876

Smith Ely 1877–1878

Edward Cooper 1879–1880

William R. Grace 1881–1882

Franklin Edson 1883–1884

William R. Grace 1885–1886

Abram S. Hewitt 1887–1888

Hugh J. Grant 1889–1892

Thomas F. Gilroy 1893–1894

William L. Strong 1895–1897

Robert A. Van Wyck 1898–1901

Seth Low 1902–1903

George B. McClellan 1904–1909

William J. Gaynor 1910–1913

Ardolph L. Kline 1913 (acting)

John Purroy Mitchel 1914–1917

John F. Hylan 1918–1925

James J. Walker 1926–1932

Joseph V. McKee 1932 (acting)

John P. O'Brien 1933

Fiorello H. La Guardia 1934–1945

William O'Dwyer 1946–1950

Vincent R. Impellitteri 1950–1953

Robert F. Wagner 1954–1965

John V. Lindsay 1966–1973

Abraham D. Beame 1974–1977

Edward I. Koch 1978–1989

David N. Dinkins 1990–1993

Rudolph W. Giuliani 1994–2001

Michael Bloomberg 2002–

SOURCE: The Green Book

Appendix 2

Population of Boroughs of New York City (as defined by consolidation of 1898), 1790–1990

	Manhattan	Bronx	Brooklyn	Queens	Staten Island	Total
1790	33,131	1,781	4,495	6,159	3,835	49,401
1800	60,515	1,755	5,740	6,642	4,564	79,216
1810	96,373	2,267	8,303	7,444	5,347	119,734
1820	123,706	2,782	11,187	8,246	6,135	152,056
1830	202,589	3,023	20,535	9,049	7,082	242,278
1840	312,710	5,346	47,613	14,480	10,965	391,114
1850	515,547	8,032	138,882	18,593	15,061	696,115
1860	813,669	23,593	279,122	32,903	25,492	1,174,779
1870	942,292	37,393	419,921	45,468	33,029	1,478,103
1880	1,164,673	51,980	599,495	56,559	38,991	1,911,698
1890	1,441,216	88,908	838,547	87,050	51,693	2,507,414
1900	1,850,093	200,507	1,166,582	152,999	67,021	3,437,202
1910	2,331,542	430,980	1,634,351	284,041	85,969	4,766,883
1920	2,284,103	732,016	2,018,356	469,042	116,531	5,620,048
1930	1,867,312	1,265,258	2,560,401	1,079,129	158,346	6,930,446
1940	1,889,924	1,394,711	2,698,285	1,297,634	174,441	7,454,995
1950	1,960,101	1,451,277	2,738,175	1,550,849	191,555	7,891,957
1960	1,698,281	1,424,815	2,627,319	1,809,578	221,991	7,781,984
1970	1,539,233	1,471,701	2,602,012	1,986,473	295,443	7,894,862
1980	1,428,285	1,168,972	2,230,936	1,891,325	352,121	7,071,639
1990	1,487,536	1,203,789	2,300,664	1,951,598	378,977	7,322,564

From 1874 to 1895 New York City consisted of Manhattan and part of the Bronx. The total population of the city was 1,206,299 in 1880 and 1,515,301 in 1890.

SOURCES: U.S. Department of Commerce, Bureau of the Census, *Census of Population 1960* (vol. 1, part A, table 28), 1970, 1980, 1990.

Bibliography

GENERAL WORKS

In the study of urban history in general and that of New York City in particular, the secondary literature alone is voluminous. What follows is an idiosyncratic sampling of the great variety of materials, old and new, that deal with the history and development of the Empire City. It is hoped that the selection will encourage readers to study more deeply the history of the great American metropolis.

Albion, Robert G. *The Rise of New York Port, 1815–1860*. New York, 1939.

Allen, Robert S., ed. *Our Fair City*. New York, 1947.

Anderson, Jervis. *This Was Harlem: A Cultural Portrait 1900–1950*. New York, 1981.

Archdeacon, Thomas. *New York City, 1664–1710: Conquest and Change*. Ithaca, N.Y., 1976.

Asbury, Herbert. *The Gangs of New York*. New York, 1927.

Atkins, George. *Health, Housing and Poverty in New York City, 1865–1898*. New York, 1947.

Auletta, Ken. *The Streets Were Paved with Gold*. New York, 1975.

Barck, Oscar T. *New York City during the War for Independence*. New York, 1931.

Bayor, Ronald H. and Timothy J. Meagher. eds. *The New York Irish*. Baltimore, 1996.

Beggs, Donald, ed. *New York: The City That Belongs to the World*. New York, 1956.

Bender, Thomas. *New York Intellect*. Baltimore, 1987.

Bercovici, Konrad. *Around the World in New York*. New York, 1924.

Berger, Meyer. *The Eight Million*. New York, 1942.

Bernstein, Iver. *The New York City Draft Riots*. New York, 1990.

Berrol, Selma C. *Getting down to Business. Baruch College in the City of New York, 1847–1987*. New York, 1989.

———. *The Empire City: New York and Its People, 1624–1994*. New York. Praeger, 1995.

Blackmar, Elizabeth, and Roy Rosenzweig. *The Park and the People: A History of Central Park*. Ithaca, N.Y., 1992.

Blake, Nelson. *Water for the Cities*. Syracuse, N.Y., 1956.

Bonomi, Patricia U. *A Factious People: Politics and Society in Colonial New York*. New York, 1971.

Booth, Mary L. *History of the City of New York*. 2 vols. New York, 1867.

Brace, Charles L. *The Dangerous Classes of New York*. New York, 1872.

Brown, Henry C. *From Alley Pond to Rockefeller Center*. New York, 1936.

Callow, Alexander B. *The Tweed Ring*. New York, 1966.

Caro, Robert A. *The Power Broker: Robert Moses and the Fall of New York*. New York, 1974.

Chauncey, George. *Gay New York: Gender, Urban Culture and the Makings of the Gay Male World, 1890–1940*. New York, 1994.

Churchill, Allen, *The Upper Crust: An Informal History of New York's Highest Society*. Englewood Cliffs, N.J., 1970.

Condon, Thomas. *New York Beginnings: The Commercial Origins of New Netherlands*. New York, 1968.

Connable, Alfred, and Edward Silverfarb. *Tigers of Tammany*. New York, 1967.

Conrad, Peter. *The Art of the City: Views and Versions of New York*. New York, 1984.

Costello, Augustine. *Our Firemen; A History of the New York Fire Department*. New York, 1887.

Costikyan, Edward N. *Behind Closed Doors: Politics in the Public Interest*. New York, 1966.

Diamond, Edwin. *Behind the Times: Inside the New New York Times*. New York, 1994.

Dolan, Jay. *The Immigrant Church: New York, Irish and German Catholics, 1815–1865*. Baltimore, 1975.

Douglas, Ann. *Terrible Honesty: Mongrel Manhattan in the 1920s*. New York, 1995.

Drennan, Matthew, et al. *The Corporate Headquarters Complex in New York City*. New York, 1977.

Duffy, John. *A History of Public Health in New York City, 1625–1866*. New York, 1968.

Ellis, David M., et al. *A Short History of New York State*. New York, 1957.

Ellis, Edward Robb. *The Epic of New York City*. New York, 1966.

Ernst, Robert. *Immigrant Life in New York City, 1825–1863*. New York, 1949.

Ewen, David. *The Life and Death of Tin Pan Alley*. New York, 1967.

Federal Writers' Project of the Works Progress Administration. *New York City Guide*. New York, 1939.

Flick, Alexander, ed. *History of New York State*. 10 vols. New York, 1933–1937.

Freeman, Joshua B. *In Transit: The Transit Worker's Union in New York City, 1933–1966*. New York, 1989.

Gilje, Paul A. *The Road to Mobocracy: Popular Disorder in New York City, 1763–1834*. Chapel Hill, N.C., 1987.

Goldberger, Paul. *The City Observed: New York*. New York, 1979.

Grinstein, Hyman B. *The Rise of the Jewish Community in New York, 1654–1860*. New York, 1945.

Griscom, John H. *Sanitary Condition of the Laboring Population of New York.* New York, 1845.

Hammack, David C. *Power and Society: Greater New York at the Turn of the Century.* New York, 1982.

Hawkins, Stuart. *New York, New York.* New York, 1957.

Headly, Joel. *The Great Riots of New York, 1712–1873.* New York, 1873.

Hershkowitz, Leo. *Tweed's New York: Another Look.* Garden City, N.Y., 1977.

Historic Houses in New York City Parks. New York, 1989.

Howe, Irving. *World of Our Fathers.* New York, 1976.

Jackson, Kenneth T., ed. *The Encyclopedia of New York City.* New Haven, Conn., 1995.

———. *Crabgrass Frontier: The Suburbanization of the United States.* New York, 1985.

Janvier, Thomas A. *In Old New York.* New York, 1894.

Kaestle, Carl F. *The Evolution of an Urban School System: New York, 1750–1850.* Cambridge, Mass., 1973.

Kammen, Michael. *Colonial New York: A History.* New York, 1975.

Kasson, John F. *Amusing the Million: Coney Island at the Turn of the Century,* New York, 1978.

Kessner, Thomas. *Fiorello H. La Guardia and the Making of Modern New York.* New York, 1989.

Klein, Alexander. *The Empire City: A Treasury of New York.* New York, 1955.

Klein, Milton M. ed. *New York: The Centennial Years, 1676–1976.* Port Washington, New York, 1976.

Kluger, Richard. *The Paper: The Life and Death of the New York Herald Tribune.* New York, 1986.

Koch, Edward I. *Mayor.* New York, 1984.

Kouwenhoven, John. *Columbia Portrait of New York City.* New York, 1951.

Lately, Thomas. *The Mayor Who Mastered New York: The Life and Opinions of William J. Gaynor.* New York, 1969.

Lamb, Martha. *History of New York City.* 2 vols. New York, 1880.

Leonard, John W. *The History of New York City.* New York, 1910.

Lieberman, Richard K. *Steinway & Sons.* New Haven, Conn., 1995.

Limpus, Lowell. *History of the New York Fire Department.* New York, 1940.

Lossing, Benson J. *History of New York City.* New York, 1884.

Lowi, Theodore J. *At the Pleasure of the Mayor.* New York, 1964.

Mackay, Donald. *The Building of Manhattan.* New York, 1987.

Mandlebaum, Seymour. *Boss Tweed's New York.* New York, 1975.

Maurice, A. B. *New York in Fiction.* New York, 1899.

McCullough, David. *The Great Bridge.* New York, 1972.

McNickle, Chris. *To Be Mayor of New York: Ethnic Politics in the City.* New York, 1993.

Mohl, Raymond. *Poverty in New York, 1783–1825.* New York, 1971.

Morris, Charles R. *The Cost of Good Intentions: New York City and the Liberal Experiment.* New York, 1980.

Morris, Lloyd. *Incredible New York.* New York, 1951.

Mushkat, Jerome. *Tammany: The Evolution of a Political Machine, 1789–1865.* Syracuse, N.Y., 1971.

Myers, Andrew B., ed. *The Knickerbocker Tradition: Washington Irving's New York.* New York, 1974.

Nevins, Allan, ed. *The Diary of Philip Hone.* 2 vols. New York, 1927.

Newfeld, Jack, and Paul Du Brul. *The Abuse of Power: The Permanent Government and the Fall of New York.* New York, 1977.

O'Callaghan, E. B. *History of New Netherlands.* 2 vols. New York, 1846–1848.

Osofsky, Gilbert. *Harlem: The Making of a Ghetto.* New York, 1966.

Ovington, Mary. *Half a Man; the Status of the Negro in New York.* New York, 1911.

Pleasants, Samuel A. *Fernando Wood of New York.* New York, 1948.

Pomerantz, Sidney I. *New York, an American City. 1783–1803.* New York, 1938.

Ravich, Diane. *The Great School Wars: New York City, 1805–1973.* New York, 1977.

Reich, J. R. *Leisler's Rebellion: A Study of Democracy in New York.* New York, 1953.

Reimers, David M. and Frederick M. Binder. *All the Nations Under Heaven: An Ethnic and Racial History of New York City.* New York, 1995.

Richardson, James F. *The New York Police: Colonial Times to 1901.* New York, 1970.

Richmond, J. F. *New York and Its Institutions.* New York, 1873.

Riis, Jacob. *How the Other Half Lives.* New York, 1890.

———. *The Making of an American.* New York, 1901.

Rischin, Moses. *The Promised City: New York's Jews, 1870–1914.* New York, 1970.

Rodgers, Cleveland, and Rebecca Rankin. *New York: The World's Capital City.* New York, 1948.

Rosenwaiker, Ira. *Population History of New York City.* Syracuse, N.Y., 1971.

Rothery, Agnes E. *New York Today.* New York, 1951.

Sante, Luc. *Low Life: Lures and Snares of Old New York.* New York, 1990.

Sayre, Wallace S., and Herbert Kaufman. *Governing New York City: Politics in the Metropolis.* New York, 1956.

Silver, Nathan. *Lost New York.* New York, 1967.

Simon, Kate. *New York: Places and Pleasures.* New York, 1959.

Smith, Al. *Up from the City Streets.* New York, 1927.

Sobel, Lester A. ed. *New York and the Urban Dilemma.* New York, 1976.

Spann, Edward. *The New Metropolis: New York City, 1840–1957.* New York, 1981.

Stern, Robert A. M., et al. *New York 1900: Metropolitan Architecture and Urbanism, 1800–1915.* New York, 1983.

Sternlieb, George, and James W. Hughes. *Housing a People in New York.* New York, 1973.

Stiles, Henry M., ed. *The History of the County of Kings and the City of Brooklyn, New York, from 1683–1884.* 2 vols. New York, 1884.

Still, Bayrd. *Mirror for Gotham: New York as Seen by Contemporaries from Dutch Days to the Present.* New York, 1956.

Stoddard, Lothrop. *Master of Manhattan: The Life of Richard Croker.* New York, 1931.

Stokes, l. N. Phelps. *The Iconography of Manhattan Island, 1498–1909.* 6 vols. New York, 1915–1928.

Syrett, Harold. *The City of Brooklyn.* New York, 1944.

Taylor, William R. *In Pursuit of Gotham: Culture and Commerce in New York.* New York, 1992.

Tunnard, Christopher, and Henry H. Reed. *American Skyline.* New York, 1953.

Ultan, Lloyd. *The Beautiful Bronx, 1920–1950.* New York, 1987.

Van der Zee, Henri, and Barbara Van der Zee. *A Sweet and Alien Land: The Story of Dutch New York.* New York, 1978.

Van Pelt, Daniel. *Leslie's History of the Greater New York.* 2 vols. New York, 1899.

Wakefield, Dan. *Island in the City: Puerto Ricans in New York.* New York, 1960.

Ware, Carolyn F. *Greenwich Village, 1920–1930.* Boston, 1935.

Werner, Morris R. *It Happened in New York.* New York, 1957.

White, E. B. *Here Is New York.* New York, 1949.

White, Norval. *New York; A Physical History.* New York, 1987.

Wilentz, Sean. *Chants Democratic: New York City and the Rise of the American Working Class, 1788–1850.* New York, 1984.

Willensky, Elliot. *When Brooklyn was the World, 1920–1957.* New York, 1986.

Wilson, James G., ed. *The Memorial History of the City of New York.* 4 vols. New York, 1892–1893.

Yeadon, David. *New York's Nooks and Crannies.* New York, 1979.

BIBLIOGRAPHIES OF NEW YORK CITY

Brooklyn Public Library. *List of Books on Greater New York in the Brooklyn Public Library.* 3rd rev. ed. Brooklyn, 1909.

Dunn, James T. "Masters' Theses and Doctoral Dissertations in New York History (1897–1951)." *New York History* 33, 1952.

Elberson, Harold, and Sidney Ditzion. "Sources for the Study of the New York Area: A Bibliographic Essay." *New York Area Research Council.* New York, 1957.

Institute of Public Administration. *Selected Recent References on Materials Relating to the Operation of the Government of the City of New York.* New York, 1959.

Municipal Reference Library. *Notes.* 1914– (indexed).

New-York Historical Society. "Books about New York City, Primarily History, Published from 1898–1947." New York, 1948.

New York Public Library. "Selected List of Works Relating to City Planning and Allied Subjects." *New York Public Library Bulletin* 17, 1913.

Port of New York Authority. *A Selected Bibliography of the Port of New York Authority, 1921–1956.* New York, 1957.

Reynolds, James B., ed. *Civic Bibliography for Greater New York.* New York, 1911.

Selected Bibliography on Revision of the New York City Charter. Princeton, N.J., 1933.

Shaw, Thomas S. *Index to Profile Sketches in the New Yorker Magazine.* Boston, 1946.

Spielvogel, Samuel. *A Selected Bibliography on City and Regional Planning.* Washington, D.C., 1951.

United States Works Progress Administration, Division of Professional and Service Projects. *Guide to Manuscript Depositories in New York City.* New York, 1941.

Vormalker, Rose L. *Special Library Resources.* New York, 1941.

Index

About the Author

Before his retirement in 1996, George J. Lankevich was a Professor of History at Bronx Community College, The City University of New York. Author of numerous books, he most recently contributed over thirty articles to *The Encyclopedia of New York City*.